W9-AMU-241

A MANAGER WITH A MISSION
DAVEY JOHNSON—1985 REFLECTIONS:

I remember in 1969, when I played for the Orioles, we were beaten by the Mets. Everyone on our team at the time made a silent vow: Hey, okay, so we got beat. Let's come back next year and go all the way wire-to-wire. And that's what happened. We won the division, beating Minnesota in the playoffs 3-0, and then in the World Series we beat Cincinnati four out of five games.

And that's what I want to see happen to the Mets in 1986.

I told the players the day before the 1985 season ended, "I want you to make up your minds we're going to win it next year."

After the meeting, I went back to my office to be alone for a while. I swore to myself: *Next year, by God, nothing is going to stop us.*

And in 1986, nothing did stop the
Amazing Miracle Mets.

ABOUT THE AUTHORS

DAVEY JOHNSON, a thirteen-year major league veteran, has been the manager of the New York Mets since 1984. Taking over a year after they finished last, he led the Mets to a second-place finish. In 1973, he hit 42 home runs while playing second base, tying Rogers Hornsby's record for the most home runs hit by a second baseman in a single season.

PETER GOLENBOCK has written and cowritten a decade's worth of bestsellers, including *Dynasty*, *The Bronx Zoo*, *Number 1*, *Balls*, *Bums*, and *Pete Rose on Hitting*. He lives in Wilton, Connecticut.

BATS

**DAVEY
JOHNSON
and
PETER
GOLENBOCK**

BANTAM BOOKS
TORONTO • NEW YORK • LONDON • SYDNEY • AUCKLAND

This book is dedicated to Mary Nan, Florence, Frank Cashen, and to my coaches and every one of my players on the New York Mets.

D. J.

To Rhonda, who is better than Eleanor Roosevelt; Ma, who always let me know that anything I did was okay; Viv Sohn, who made it possible for me to get started; and to Phyllis Grann, who is to editing what Michelangelo is to ceiling painting.

P. G.

*This low-priced Bantam Book
has been completely reset in a typeface
designed for easy reading, and was printed
from new plates. It contains the complete
text of the original hardcover edition.*
NOT ONE WORD HAS BEEN OMITTED.

BATS
*A Bantam Book / published by arrangement with
G. P. Putnam's Sons*

PRINTING HISTORY
*G. P. Putnam's Sons edition published April 1986
Bantam edition / May 1987*

*All rights reserved.
Copyright © 1986 by Dynasty, Inc., and Dave Johnson.
Cover photograph copyright © 1987 by
Ronald C. Modra / Sports Illustrated.
Library of Congress Catalog Card Number: 85-32055.
This book may not be reproduced in whole or in part, by
mimeograph or any other means, without permission.
For information address: G. P. Putnam's Sons,
200 Madison Ave., New York, NY 10016.*

ISBN 0-553-26460-5

Published simultaneously in the United States and Canada

*Bantam Books are published by Bantam Books, Inc. Its
trademark, consisting of the words "Bantam Books" and the
portrayal of a rooster, is Registered in U.S. Patent and Trademark
Office and in other countries. Marca Registrada. Bantam Books,
Inc., 666 Fifth Avenue, New York, New York 10103.*

PRINTED IN THE UNITED STATES OF AMERICA

O   0 9 8 7 6 5 4 3 2 1

FOREWORD

AFTER WORKING with Davey since early in spring training, by October I had learned that there is little glamour to managing a major league ballclub. Every move you make is scrutinized and analyzed, and even if you make nine successful moves in a row, if you screw up the tenth, the wolves begin to howl.

By the October St. Louis series the pressure on Davey was itense. He had to patch together a makeshift pitching staff, he was three games back, and he was facing a barrage of second-guessing from fans and press alike. He wasn't sleeping well, but he never let on how he was feeling. Davey would not let them see him sweat.

Before the finale, I made a trip to Woolworth's in downtown St. Louis and bought a whisk broom and a mug that read NUMBER 1 PILOT. I fantasized about presenting the whisk broom to a poor-sport St. Louis writer who had hassled me because I had openly rooted for the Mets in the press box. I had dared clap for Darryl Strawberry as he circled the bases with the winning run of the series opener. The next day the reporter had me barred from the press box.

All reporters are rooters, but this guy took it harder than most. The broom, my revenge, was to signify the sweep of the Mets over the Cardinals. He was lucky it didn't have a handle.

The mug was for Davey, whom I had grown to know, understand, and admire greatly.

In his hotel suite late in the afternoon before the finale Davey presented me with a bottle of champagne, which we agreed to share in the clubhouse after the game if the Mets won. I envisioned pouring the bubbly into the NUMBER 1 PILOT mug, handing it to Davey, and basking in the joy he and his players would be feeling. It would have been a fitting celebration of a long and rewarding season for both of us.

Despite a season filled with an inordinate number of injuries and late-inning disasters, Davey had led the Mets to within one game of tying for the division title.

All season long Davey had struggled with personal problems and with his own emotions, fighting to put on a brave face when things were going badly and maintaining his equilibrium when the temptation might have been to blow his cork. All he needed was one more win, and the brass ring would be his.

Before that game, I returned to my seat behind Bob Murphy in the back of the radio booth and watched as the Mets were defeated by one crummy run. Afterward, cursing the fates as I took the elevator down to the clubhouse, I learned the difference between being a player and being a fan when I went inside. With the loss still a fresh wound, Davey and the Mets players politely stood and answered the questions of the newspaper, radio, and TV reporters. It was a loss that meant the end of their pennant hopes, but neither Davey nor the players acted glum or morose. Certainly not as glum or morose as I felt.

I left the clubhouse, my briefcase in hand, and walked the underground corridor past the room set aside for the cheerful wives and laughing kids of the Cardinal players, up the stairs, past the smiling security guard, and out onto the street, where swarms of St. Louis fans were celebrating their good fortune. Car horns tooted in the warm October night and periodically a whoop from a raucous fan could be heard.

On the sidewalk not far from our bus was a metal trash container. I went over to it, opened my briefcase and took out the whisk broom and the mug, both of which I dropped into the bowels of the trash can. I closed my briefcase, and with glistening eyes, I walked onto the bus and sat, alone, in the dark, waiting for the players and coaches to climb aboard.

When they arrived, they were subdued, but not grim-faced. They listened to their Walkmans, as always, or they talked quietly as we drove to the airport. For Davey and the players, losing was part of the game. It was something to be taken in stride. They had played their best, and they didn't feel there was anything to be sad about. They were professionals, and minutes after suffering a pennant-crushing defeat, they could accept the loss and look ahead. The players, as it turns out, are the only people connected with the game who are not fans or do not act like fans.

There are a number of people I wish to thank, including Nelson Doubleday, the owner of the Mets, who gave Davey permission to do this book with me; Jay Horwitz and Arthur Richman, who made me feel so at home while I was on the road; Jay's assistant, Dennis D'Agostino; equipment manager Charlie Samuels; general manager Frank Cashen; coaches Vern Hoscheit and Bill Robinson; and players Ron Gardenhire, Clint Hurdle, Howard Johnson, and Rusty Staub for their friendship and insight. Thanks, too, goes to my literary coaching staff—Sterling Lord, and Phyllis Grann of G. P. Putnam's Sons.

This was an experience to be cherished. I suspect when you finish *Bats*, you will respect those who play the game even more.

Peter Golenbock
Wilton, Connecticut

1

OCTOBER
1985

AN HOUR AND A HALF after the game, I went into the trainer's room to get a respite from the press and also to check on the wounded. Gary Carter was sitting on a bench with ice on his knee. It's become a nightly ritual for Gary. Next to him was Wally Backman icing his ankle and his knee.

Steve Garland, the trainer, walked over looking solemn. He said to me, "Dave, I think we ought to have Wally x-rayed. His ankle might be broken." During the game Wally, our second baseman, smashed himself up in a head-on collision with Rafael Santana, our shortstop.

"Forget it," I snapped. "Just forget any X ray. We have four games left, and we have to win tomorrow if we're going to have a Chinaman's chance for the pennant. If Wally can run on it, he can run on it. If he can't, he can't, and then we'll worry about treatment."

I was vehement. "You don't worry about injuries this time of year. We're in a pennant race. We're one game back of St. Louis, and we have to beat them tomorrow." I looked at Wally. "If you can walk, you can play."

Wally nodded.

It was past midnight when I walked the block from deserted Busch Stadium to the Marriott, where the team is staying. I downed a couple of beers in the bar, which was filled with rabid Mets fans wishing us well. I'm amazed at how many of them have flown out to St. Louis to root us on. Their enthusiasm is gratifying. We have played one long, exhilarating but frustrating season, creeping back from the dead, despite injuries, despite everything. One game, tomorrow's game, will tell the story.

I tried to sleep, but all through the night kept waking. I didn't think about the game we have just won. That is history. My thoughts are always on the next game, and they're troubled. My pitching is short. I'm forced to start Rick Aguilera. It's asking a lot from a rookie, but I have no alternatives. My hands are tied.

I tried to go back to sleep, and after an hour or so, or maybe it was two hours or maybe twenty minutes, I was awake again. I asked myself, If Aguilera gets knocked out early, who am I going to bring in? Who the hell's going to be my long-relief guy? It would have been Doug Sisk, but Sisk has bone chips in his elbow and will soon undergo surgery. I settled on Eddie Lynch, if he's healthy. But I was arguing with myself: Eddie hasn't showed he's healthy the last month. Why should he be healthy? And yet, I'm still not sure whether Eddie's hurting or not. He won't tell me. I asked myself, Who do I go to if Lynch isn't ready? Do I dare use Wes Gardner, a rookie just up from Tidewater? I told myself, Wes hasn't pitched badly the few times I've used him. I argued back, But he has no experience. My mind wouldn't stop working. Can I use one of the other kids from Tidewater, maybe? No. But if it isn't Lynch, then who? I decided I have no choice but to go with Tommy Gorman, who hasn't been effective at all recently. Still, during the season he's been the one who's handled long-relief situations. I asked myself, The way Tommy's been pitching, how can I go to him early in the game? I countered, But what about the seven shutout innings he threw against the Pirates early in the year? I countered back, But what about the home run he gave up to Rick Camp in the bottom of the eighteenth against Atlanta? Camp is a pitcher who had never hit a home run in his entire career, for heaven sake! But who else do I have? Without Sisk, it has to be Eddie, and if it isn't Eddie, it has to be Tommy Gorman. How can I pitch rookies with no experience in the most important game of the year? I asked myself. I can't. My best hope is for Aguilera to go at least seven. But he's only going on four days' rest, I told myself.

I slept, woke, and dozed until the phone rang. Outside my hotel window I could see the sun reflecting off the Gateway Arch. Morning had finally arrived, and Frank Cashen, the Mets general manager, was calling. He wanted to meet with me in the coffee shop to talk about Eddie Lynch's health and our roster for the playoffs. I dragged myself out of bed and got ready for the day.

Frank was also concerned about Lynch, enough to want to send him back to New York this afternoon for tests. The trainer suspects he has sciatica, a pinching of nerves that causes pain to run down his leg. I told Frank, "I want Lynch to stay here in case I need him tonight." Frank nodded. Lynch will be examined first thing after we get back to New York. He'll be in uniform, but I still have no idea whether he is in any shape to pitch if I need him.

When I finally caught up to Eddie, he admitted that he doesn't know either. I told Eddie, "I need you tonight, but only if you're healthy. I don't want heroism. I want you to let me know exactly what your condition is, understand? No romancing."

Eddie said, "I'm feeling better, but the only way I'll really know is to warm up and throw a little bit before the game." I assured him we'd do that. Eddie said, "Don't worry, Skip. I'll be honest with you. I don't want to risk the pennant for us."

I let Eddie go and turned my attention to the schedule of games for the championship. We still have to get by St. Louis, but as manager you have to plan for all eventualities. Los Angeles clinched the Western Division title last night, and if we win the National League East, the schedule calls for us to open in LA on Wednesday. We play Wednesday and Thursday, are off Friday, a travel date, then play three days at Shea, have an off day, and then go back to LA. I thought to myself, If we can just get by the Cardinals tonight, I know we can beat the Dodgers.

2
MANAGING
101

I USED TO GET MAD at my father, rest his soul. He was a very low-handicap golfer, and we would often go out together for a round or two. I'd face a twenty-foot putt, and I'd bend over and tap it, and the ball would stop short of the hole. I'd ask him, "What did I do wrong?" He'd say, "You didn't hit it hard enough." I thought to myself, No fooling. I could see that. Any idiot could see that. But the question was, Why didn't I hit it hard enough? I damn sure was trying to hit it hard enough. What I wanted to say was, Dave, you were hitting in an uphill lie, or, The shot was against the grain of the green. Or even, You quit on it. But he would not, or could not, ever give me a reason.

I have always been cognizant of why something happens, why a marble sticks in the ring, why in golf you have to keep your arm straight to hit the ball straight, why you have to keep your eyes on the ball. I once asked my brother Fred why a ball curves, and he told me and showed me how to do it. Perhaps just as important, I also wanted to know why something didn't happen when I wanted it to. Once you know why things don't happen, you can avoid them not happening again.

I've been this way my whole life. When I was a player, I would often ask my manager, "Why did you hit-and-run in this situation?" "Why did you bunt?" "Why did you play the infield in?" Sometimes they would feel that I was second-guessing them, but it wasn't that. I wanted to know *why*.

And if the manager wanted to know why I as a player did something, I could tell him. When I was playing for Baltimore, Earl Weaver and I would argue about this. Once when I was playing second base, there were runners on first and third, and the runner on first was picked off. We were throwing the ball back and forth, and I was holding the ball when the runner on third broke for home. I saw him out of the corner of my eye, and when he started for home, I turned and threw, not realizing that the runner between first and second had just started sliding. All I had to do was reach down and tag him before I threw, and we would have had a double play. The only problem was, I was looking homeward, and I didn't see him. That is *why* I didn't tag him. When I told Earl, he said, "That's an excuse, not a reason."

But I learned from asking why. I learned about myself and I learned about the game. I was able to study how managers treated people and made decisions. Equally important, I learned what not to do, how not to act from managers whose actions didn't make much sense to me.

It's as though I've been going to a school for managers since I was seven years old.

I began my major league career with the Baltimore Orioles in 1965. I was twenty-two years old. In eight years with the Orioles, we won four American League pennants, including three in a row between 1969 and 1971. We lost the World Championship in 1969 to the Mets but came back to defeat the Reds the next year.

In 1972 I was suffering from an arm injury, and that winter was traded to the Atlanta Braves. The Braves cured the injury, and the next year I hit 43 home runs, breaking Rogers Hornsby's record for most home runs hit by a second baseman in a season.

After another injury, I was out of favor in Atlanta, and so I went to Japan for two years. My second year I helped the Tokyo Giants rebound from a last-place finish to win the pennant and get us into the Japan Series.

After two years in Japan I returned to the majors and helped the Phils win their division in 1977. The next year I finished my career as a player pinch-hitting and playing part-time for the Cubs. I hit .300 and they released me the last day of the season.

As long as you can play the game of baseball, you always want to continue to play. The year before the Pirates had expressed interest in me, and so during the winter meetings after the '78 season I approached Pete Peterson, the general manager of the Pirates. I said, "I'll sign for nothing, and you can pay me what I'm worth." I figured Pete would say, "Sure, Dave, no problem, I'll sign you right now." But he didn't do that. What he said was, "I'll get back to you." I was disappointed, but I wasn't really upset. I had hurt my back that year, and in my own mind I really wasn't sure if I could play another year. If he had wanted me, I would have made a serious effort to get well and come to spring training. But he hesitated, and as fate would have it, his hesitation started me off on my managerial career. The winter meetings were being held at the Hilton Hotel in Orlando, and after I finished my conversation with Peterson, I took the elevator to the second floor, where I was asked by Ron Fine, the owner of a new Triple A team, the Miami Amigos, and his general manager, Joe Ryan, whether I was interested in being player-manager for his team.

My first question, naturally, was, "What's it pay?" He said, "About twenty thousand." I said, "Make it twenty-five and I'll take it." He said, "Fine."

The next morning Pete Peterson called back to say he wanted to sign me. I said, "It's too late. I've signed with another club."

I sometimes wonder if Peterson had said yes instead of "I'll get back to you," I might not have ended up as manager of the New York Mets. Fate is funny that way.

The Interamerican League, which was a renegade Triple A league, played most of its games in the Caribbean. It was known as a renegade league because none of the teams were affiliated with major league teams. In addition to my team, the Miami Amigos, there were teams in San Juan, Puerto Rico; Panama City, Panama; Santo Domingo, Dominican Republic; plus two Venezuelan teams, Caracas and Maracaibo.

Trying to play all over the Caribbean wasn't always easy. Sometimes I lost players on game day because of their nationalities. If they had Cuban passports, sometimes we couldn't get them through customs, and we'd have to leave them behind until we finished playing the games, or we'd have to send them back to Miami.

Our games were always colorful. Wendy's was one of our sponsors, and they sponsored our ballgirls, who were called the Hot and Juicies. They were professional models with big boobs and skimpy outfits, and they ran out onto the field a couple times a game and distracted everybody. We were renegade, all right. Everything about the league was renegade.

Most of the players had been dropped by major league teams or farm teams and were playing as a last resort. We had a talented but unstable outfielder from the Milwaukee Brewers by the name of Danny (Sundown) Thomas. We had the Tyrone brothers, Wayne and Jim, who had been released by the American Association. One of our pitchers, Oscar Zamora, had a shoe business in Miami, and he would sell shoes during the week and pitch weekends. We had all kinds of screwy arrangements.

The Interamerican League was a good concept, and it created all sorts of goodwill between our country and the other Caribbean countries, but the league had financial problems and folded before the season ended.

My year at Miami was a tremendous learning experience. Because my players were all veterans, I had to make sure I used them properly and fairly; otherwise they would have packed up and gone home. I gave everyone a chance to play. I treated them like men, with no Mickey Mouse rules. I'm sorry the league folded when it did. Even though we were fifteen games in front, we had only begun to jell.

Toward the end of the season Joe Ryan got sick, and I became general manager. I signed George Mitterwald, and we traded him to the Oakland A's and got two players, Woody Woodward, a centerfielder-shortstop, and a guy named Stein who never showed up. I had a guy named Porfirio Altamirano from Nicaragua and sold him to the Phillies for $20,000. At the end I was selling players left and right. I sold one of the Tyrones to Japan and made some money. I did some pretty damn good business.

The next year the team owners bought a franchise in Shelby,

Montana, and they wanted me to run it. They offered me $20,000 plus half the money for any players I developed and sold. I was also going to be the manager. It could have been a good deal, but I needed to make some real money, and so for a year I left baseball for real estate.

I managed an apartment complex I owned in Orlando with my uncle. It was a test for me because it was a low-income apartment, and the tenants didn't like to pay their rent. They had grease fires, all kinds of fires. I had one drowning in the pool. I had a rent strike. Whenever they tried to think of things to keep from paying the rent, I had to find ways to get them to pay it. I even joined the judge's softball team. It didn't help.

During the year I was away, I was considering the possibility of volunteering as the baseball coach at the University of Central Florida. But the Mets' Joe McIlvaine, who used to be my neighbor in Goldenrod, Florida, when he was an area scout, called me from out of the blue and said, "How would you like to manage for us?" The Mets general manager, Frank Cashen, apparently had taken notice of the job I did with the Amigos.

I said to McIlvaine, "Manage where?" He said, "In the Texas League." That sounded interesting. I said to myself, My mother lives in San Antonio. I went to school at Texas A&M and Trinity. Jeez, I'll get to see my beloved state of Texas. That sounds great. I said to Joe, "Where in Texas?" He said, "In Jackson, Mississippi."

That threw me a little, but I recovered. I said, "How much you going to pay me?" He said, "Seventeen thousand." I said, "You got to be kidding me? There's no way. That doesn't even pay the rent." He said, "That's all I can pay you." I almost had to hold out to get him up to $18,000. In the one year I had managed and owned that apartment complex, I sold it for a $435,000 profit, half of it mine. I had worked at that for six months. Why should I work for the Mets for a crummy $18,000?

Because I missed baseball. I said to myself, You would have worked at the university for nothing. Take the job at Jackson. I figured it had to be more fun than fighting a rent strike.

3

CLIMBING THE LADDER

BEFORE THE SEASON BEGAN, everybody predicted that my Jackson team would be the worst club in the Texas League. We were expected to finish dead last. In the spring exhibitions we won exactly one game, and that against a team from the lowly rookie league. We lost about a dozen. Management was all upset and worried.

I wasn't. I could see that most of our players were young, untried kids who were out to prove something. I liked the makeup of the ballclub, liked the chemistry. Toward the end of the spring we made a trade and got a talented young outfielder, Marvell Wynne, who is now with the Pirates, and soon after we got him, I wrote on the clubhouse wall, "Jackson is going to win the Texas League Championships. Signed, Davey Johnson."

We came out of the chute and won eight in a row. We were in first place the whole way and won the first half. I then had to send most of my team up to Tidewater, and as a result we didn't win the second half. We did, however, win the playoffs for the overall league championship.

At the end of that season, Mets minor league executive Lou

Gorman called and said, "Congratulations on your fine job." I was pleased. I said, "Thank you very much." He said, "We want you to go back to Jackson." I said, "You what? You've got to be kidding me. I'm not going to ride those buses again for no pay." He said, "We'll give you a five-hundred-dollar raise." Emphatically I said, "No. Get somebody else."

The Mets must have liked my work, because Gorman said he had an alternate job for me. "Okay," I bit, "what is that?" He said, "Roving instructor. You'd work with all the prospects in our organization." It sounded like a perfect job for me. "For how much?" I asked. "Seventeen five," he said.

I had won the Texas League championship, and they were cutting me back five hundred dollars!

My first year at Miami I had gotten $25,000 to be player-manager, and I won the championship. The next year I got $18,000 and won a championship. Now I'm in my third year of minor league baseball, and I'm making $17,500, going in the wrong direction. I said, "If I'm in this five more years, I'm going to be paying them." I took the job. I knew the education would be invaluable. The money would come.

As special assignment instructor, I worked with all the teams in the Mets organization, from the rookie leagues on up. I didn't have defined duties. They said, "Work with whomever you want." I had freedom and autonomy. I worked with the kids, and I got to know intimately the talent in the entire farm system. I also got to see from the inside what goes on in the minor leagues, including a number of practices that I felt were detrimental to the advancement of the players. One of the worst was the tendency for managers to audition players. Managers stick a player out there, and if the player doesn't do well immediately, the manager will call the front office and say, "Get me someone else."

A player cannot perform at his best if he feels that what he does today is going to affect his role tomorrow. If a manager selects a starting pitcher, the pitcher shouldn't lose his job based on one or two or even three bad outings. A manager has to be patient with his players and use them consistently. A manager cannot be too quick to judge; otherwise he ends up putting too much pressure on the player.

Another thing minor league managers do that hurts their players is rant and rave at them. If you send a young kid out to the

19

mound and he walks four or five batters, the worst thing a manager can do is sit in the dugout screaming and hollering, throwing his cap, swearing at the guy to throw strikes. The pitcher knows he's supposed to throw strikes. When the kid goes out the next time, not only does he worry about walking the batter, he's also worried that his manager is going to be screaming at him. You don't scream at a player. It's destructive. I know how impressionable young players are, because I was one myself.

In watching the various teams in the minor leagues, I noticed that one thing minor league managers ought to do—but don't—is establish a player's position on the team, particularly a pitcher's. To do a good job, a pitcher must know his role, whether he starts or pitches in long or short relief. A pitcher won't be effective if a manager uses him one day in short relief and the next day uses him as a spot starter. This was a lesson I learned years ago from Earl Weaver. Each pitcher had a role, and Earl consistently used him in that role.

If a manager uses a young pitcher inconsistently, he can't prepare himself to pitch, and he cannot be successful. The manager will then have the nerve to run down the guy's talent after having made it impossible for the poor guy to do well.

In the minors the best prospects, the best arms, should be starters. These kids started in high school, and they need to start. Age is a factor, too. I hate to see any seventeen-year-old kid in the bullpen. He needs to start, because he can improve most quickly that way. A manager can also find out how much elasticity his arm has. Does he burn out in five innings? You only find out by letting the kid start every five days over the course of a season.

Minor league managers make these mistakes, and yet I can understand why. How many top-quality people are willing to work eighteen-hour days for $20,000? It's the same problem that plagues public education. The pyramid is upside-down. The most important teachers in the minor league system end up earning the least money. It's nuts.

I loved my job as roving instructor. If a player had a problem, I always tried my darnedest to explain to him the *why*. In a positive, constructive way I tried to make the player understand what he was doing wrong and learn to overcome it. I enjoyed teaching all the facets of the game. I dealt with pitchers, infielders, outfielders, the whole nine yards. It was really enjoyable.

When I first joined a team, the players were a little wary, especially around the batting cage. Most hitting instructors try to change the position of the hands or the stance. By the time a player gets through with a hitting instructor, his mind is so muddled, he has no chance to hit.

My clinics were simple. I just looked to see if the player had a flaw in his swing, and if the player had, say, an uppercut or a lunge, I would show him how to correct it. Otherwise, my philosophy is K.I.S.S. Keep it simple, stupid.

It was gratifying that almost every minor league manager welcomed me. They even encouraged me to put on a team uniform so I could talk to the players during the game. Only one manager, Jack Aker, didn't want me around. Aker, who managed the Mets' Triple A Tidewater team, saw me as an adversary. And in retrospect, he wasn't being paranoid. I ended up taking his job.

The Mets knew I wanted to be the Tidewater manager, because in the discussion that led to my being named roving instructor, I had told them straight out, "I want the Triple A job." They had said, "We've already signed Aker." I had said, "That's the job I want." One year later it was still the job I wanted.

4
HOLDING OUT

IN 1983 I was offered the Tidewater job, and as badly as I had wanted it, I almost didn't take it. Steve Schryver had just been hired by the Mets as director of their minor league operations, and in one of his first contract negotiations he decided to play hardball with me.

I told him, "Steve, I want twenty-five thousand dollars, otherwise I'm not going to take the job." He was offering me $22,000. I kept saying, "I have to have twenty-five thousand. I just have to have it." He kept saying no. He was trying to sign the second most important manager in the farm system, and he was haggling over a crummy $3000.

About that time, A. Ray Smith, the owner of the Louisville Cardinals, the St. Louis Triple A club, called me up and asked me if I was interested in managing his ballclub. I said, "A. Ray, thank you for the consideration, I just might be interested." He said, "I'll pay you thirty thousand dollars and give you some fringe benefits." Here was a guy big-leaguing me! Here was a first-class operation!

Schryver and I met again, and during the meeting I ripped up the contract right in front of him. I said, "Maybe I'll go to another organization." "Like Louisville?" he said. His intelligence was pretty good. "Like Louisville," I said. He said, "I hope you enjoy it there."

I was ready to jump ship. I had one foot on a banana peel and the other out the door. But logic was keeping me from committing myself. I had invested two years in the Mets organization, I had friends in the Mets organization, and I knew the kids. If I had left after spending the year as roving instructor, it would have been wasted. I waited a little longer. But I vowed the Mets were going to pay my price.

Finally, they came around. Lou Gorman interceded. He overruled Schryver and gave me the money, and so I signed. But for a long while it still left a bad taste in my mouth.

5

THE TIDES TURN

THE TIDEWATER TEAM was a melting pot of deflated egos at the start of the 1983 season. We had returnees from the championship Tidewater club of the year before, players like Marvell Wynne, Kelvin Chapman, and Rusty Tillman who had had good years, but who still weren't deemed ready for the majors and who were disappointed and even disgusted to find themselves shipped back to Tidewater again.

We also had players who had been on the Mets roster and who had been shipped back down, players like Gary Rajsich, Wally Backman, Ron Gardenhire, and Clint Hurdle. For these players it was an upsetting situation.

Clint was the prototypical Tides player. When he first came up to the majors, he was a Kansas City Royals prodigy once featured on the cover of *Sports Illustrated* magazine. He had been a stand-out in the 1980 World Series, but the next year he suffered from back problems, and it was downhill from there. When he came to me at Tidewater, his career was hanging by a thread. He had been cut by a terrible Cincinnati Reds team in '82, only to resurface with the equally terrible Seattle Mariners team in the spring of

'83. Clint had been promised a spot on the Mariners by the general manager, Danny O'Brien, and the day before the season was to start, manager Rene Lachemann told him he had indeed made the club.

But the next day the Mariners released Clint.

O'Brien called him into his office and told him he had vetoed Lachemann's decision. O'Brien was ignoring his own promise to Clint, making Lachemann look like an idiot, and breaking Clint's heart. O'Brien said, "I've changed my mind, Clint. I decided to go with younger kids." It was a hell of a time to tell him.

It was too late for Clint to hook on with another major league team, but he phoned the Mets, and on the first day of our season, Clint was sent to play for me at Tidewater. I wasn't thrilled at the time, because I had just handpicked my team, made all the tough decisions, and here they were sticking me with another player. Besides, I never like surprises.

Nevertheless, from the beginning Clint showed character. It's what I've always loved about him. I didn't have a position for him, and so Clint started out as our designated hitter.

He had just been cut by two of the worst teams in baseball, and here he was DHing for a minor league team from the National League, which doesn't use the DH.

Clint was upset, but he didn't bitch about it. He came to me like a man, and he said, "I'll DH. I'll do whatever you need for me to do, but if a situation should arise where I can get some work in the field, think of me." I told him, "I understand how you're feeling, but right now there isn't much I can do about it."

That's another of my tenets: A manager must be honest with his players. It's the least a manager can do.

Clint's chance came when our third baseman, Mike Bishop, was called up to the Mets. Even though Clint had never played third base before, I wanted him to take the position. I felt Clint would help our team if he could make it at third.

I told him, "Look, you can play the outfield and you can play first, but there are a lot of guys who can do that. Here's a chance to learn a new position." I said, "It'll make you that much more attractive, not only to the Mets but to everybody else."

I've always felt that another of a manager's important tasks is to make a player view his career realistically. The hardest thing for a player to do, especially a player who has been successful all his life, is to accept the fact that someone else might be better than he: "What do you mean, I can't play every day? This guy's better? Who says so?" The manager has to do a difficult juggling act to keep his players happy. But you can do it if you let every player know exactly where he stands. You have to present the picture and ask him to be a man about it. "Get your emotions out of the way. Here it is in black and white."

I told Clint, "Gary Rajsich is my first baseman, and the three kids I have in the outfield, Strawberry, Winningham, and Marvell Wynne, are ahead of you." But I let him know that I thought he could make it at third. Clint didn't think he could, but I did. When he agreed to give it a try, I threw him right in the game, that night.

The first night he made two errors. He was very nervous. But I knew what he was going through. I could remember what it was like subbing for Brooks Robinson in Baltimore and Nagashima in Tokyo. Third takes a lot of getting used to. I told him I was going to leave him out there and that he shouldn't worry. This was not an audition.

Clint stuck it out, finally began to relax, and prospered. He desperately wanted to get back to the big leagues, and he was willing to work hard to do that. And he had faith in me, which was nice, since you have to remember, he didn't know me from Adam. He had no guarantees that I wasn't just using him or bullshitting him, time-honored baseball traditions.

By the end of the season he was an adequate major league third baseman. He made up his mind to have a good attitude, to bust his butt, and he helped bolster some of the other Mets rejects, like Ron Gardenhire and Wally Backman.

When Gardenhire and Backman came to me, they were in no mood to play in the minors. These guys could have been a lot of trouble. But as soon as they arrived, I made it clear to them that I thought the Mets had made the wrong decision, and explained exactly what they needed to do to get back to Shea. I said, "If you want to do it, fine. If you don't, that's fine too. But I want to win." They assured me they did too.

My goal was to give them back their confidence, and there is really only one way to do that: Every day I wrote their names onto the lineup card, and I let them play. Sure, I showed them a few things, like the right way to make the double play, but the best thing you can do for players who have been sent down is to pat them on the back and send them out.

Over and over I told them, "The way you get back to the big leagues is by working your ass off here." But it was Clint who really brought the message home. As bad as Wally and Gardy felt, they had to look at Clint, twenty-six years old, a former big league player who had once had his picture on the cover of *Sports Illustrated*, and think, If he can do it, I can too. They would say to Clint, "How do you stay strong? How do you continue to go on like you do?" Clint would tell them, "I got nothing else I want to do." Gardy and Wally felt the same way.

It took a little longer to reach Gary Rajsich. During the whole first half of the year his attitude seemed to be, "I don't care."

We had many talks on the bus or over a beer in the bar before he admitted the truth: To punish the Mets, Gary wasn't playing as hard as he could. He said, "I don't want to play good for the Mets. I hate them."

When he said that, I felt like a psychiatrist who had just made a breakthrough. Oh, so that's it! I thought. To Gary I said, "You know who you're really hurting—yourself." When he finally was able to admit how he felt, he was a lot happier, and he went on a tear the rest of the year, hitting 28 home runs and ending up the Most Valuable Player in the Triple A World Series.

We were all committed to winning. There were no petty jealousies on the team—racial, ethnic, or monetary—and when guys are totally committed to one another, each player gives the team an unbelievable amount of strength.

I remember one game we played against Columbus, the Yankee farm team. It was in the Triple A World Series, and we were beating up on them real bad, winning something like 11–1 after four innings. There was a runner on and Ron Gardenhire was up. Johnny Oates, the Columbus manager, wasn't holding the runner on at first, so I had the runner steal second.

Oates, infuriated that I ordered a steal with such a big lead, had his pitcher throw at my next batter, who happened to be Ron Gardenhire. The pitch hit Gardy square in the head, knocking him ga-ga out. A brawl broke out. My scrappy little infielder, Kelvin Chapman, took out their pitcher—just nailed him—and the umps threw Kelvin out of the game.

I had two infielders left. One was Wally Backman, who had been sitting on the bench with his swollen left hand wrapped in bandages because he had gotten hit by a pitched ball the night before. The other, Gardenhire, was lying sprawled on home plate.

When the umpire threw Kelvin out, I saw red. I said, "That SOB Oates has his SOB pitcher hit my guy in the head, and you throw my second baseman out of the game?" The umpire pushed me away, and who came rushing over but Wally, screaming, "I'll kick your ass if you touch my manager." So I ended up having to do everything I could to keep Wally from getting thrown out.

Everyone calmed down, and I had to find myself an infield. I whispered to Gardy, "You have to play." He said woozily, "I'm all right, I'm all right," as he was shaking out the cobwebs.

Wally knew he had to play. He was already unraveling the bandages from his hand, saying, "Give me a glove, damn it. I can play."

Do you think for a minute I was going to lose with players like that?

In addition to spirit, competitiveness, and character, the other thing that made us winners was our pitching. We had kids like Ronnie Darling, Tom Gorman, Walt Terrell, Tim Leary, and Terry Leach—an outstanding staff.

Like every other team, it took them a while to learn how to win. Early in the season I lost a lot of games giving these guys their baptism. A pitcher would get in trouble, and I would deliberately leave him out there, make him battle, make him fight, in order for him to get the experience of pitching with less than his best stuff. He'd be behind by three runs, struggling and looking into the dugout, pleading, "Get me out of here." I would turn away. I'd say to myself, He got into it, he gets out of it.

After all, this was Tidewater, the minor leagues, and it is in the minor leagues that pitchers are supposed to learn their craft.

What I tried to do with Ron Darling was typical.

When Ronnie originally signed with the Texas Rangers, he had been a three-quarter motion pitcher at Yale. He threw a fastball and a slider and maybe a few curves. His slider was exceptional. He had pitched eleven innings of no-hit ball against St. John's and Frank Viola that stands as one of the greatest college games ever pitched.

When the Rangers got him, they immediately tried to make him throw straight overhand. Their intention was to help him to develop a curveball. It's hard to believe anyone would mess with someone with that much talent, but they did! And when we got him, pitching coach Al Jackson and I immediately changed him back to his natural three-quarter style. In his one year at Tidewater he doubled his strikeouts.

Ron had other problems. A pitcher has to have tempo and rhythm. That spring Mets manager George Bamberger had told him, "Slow down your body motion so you can get your arm through." George had wanted Ron to bring his arms up over his head more slowly, to bring up his leg slower, to bring his arm through slower. Ron, however, has a tendency to take things to extremes, and he was pitching in slow motion. Then at the end of his delivery, he would try to release the ball quickly to get some speed on it. It didn't work.

Ron sped up his delivery for the first time in the All-Star game for the International League against the Cleveland Indians. He struck out three batters in two innings and looked overpowering. I knew then that he was on his way to becoming an outstanding pitcher.

In his first start for me after the All-Star game, Ron pitched four outstanding innings. I was so overjoyed with his performance that I took him out, saying, "You think about what you just did and hold it in your mind. Don't worry about who gets the win." After the game Ron told the press, "I think the manager's handling me with kid gloves." I chuckled. He was right.

The next time out he pitched five innings, and again I took him out, but by then I knew he was ready for the big leagues. The Mets called him up, and he pitched a couple of real good games for them at the end of the year.

Although the first half of the season we lost a lot of battles, the Governor's Cup Championship trophy will attest to the fact that we certainly did win the war.

During the first half we had a stretch in which we lost something like thirteen games in a row. I wasn't worried. To prove how much confidence I had in my players, one day during the streak I picked a lineup out of a hat. I put in all the names, and the players drew for spots in the batting order. It didn't work, but it was my way of saying, "Don't worry about it, guys. We're still going to win."

Halfway through the season, when we were still far from first place I said, "We will not only win the playoffs, we will also win the Triple A World Series."

I'm sure the players thought I was crazy. But I had said the same thing at Jackson when we were in last place, and we had won.

Things jelled for us in September. We didn't really play great baseball until the last two weeks of the season. We were in fifth place. You had to finish in the top four to get into the playoffs. We really turned it on and ended up fourth. Then we got to the playoffs and blew everybody out of the water.

The players by then knew exactly what they had to do and how to get it done. It was as if the players were saying to themselves, "Take this, last-place Mets. Watch us. We can play. We're winners."

That whole season I was putting together a nucleus of players I knew would help the Mets become a better team: young pitchers, extra men for the bench, part-time players. Wally and Gardy were certainly better players than anybody the Mets were using. I was preparing for when I would be managing the Mets in '84.

I hadn't been offered the job, and I didn't really know if it would be offered to me, but since I had decided that if it wasn't I would no longer stay in the organization, I went ahead and planned as if the job would be mine.

6
THE NOT-SO-AMAZING METS

THE NEW YORK METS were in absolute shambles when I took over as their manager in October 1983, right after the World Series. The Mets had finished dead last, more than twenty games out, and what made it worse, they hadn't even been interesting or fun to watch, like the Mets were under Casey Stengel. The team drew barely a million fans.

The team expected to lose. The manager, George Bamberger, the Orioles pitching coach when I was playing there, had been a great pitching coach. He inspired his pitchers. As manager of an entire team, he lacked that inspiration. During spring training he told his players, "Boys, if we can play .500 ball, I'll be happy." No wonder losing never seemed to affect anyone. For a decade the Mets would win sixty games. And lose a hundred. They had been losing for so many years that they took it for granted. They'd play, shrug their shoulders, and take a shower. It was just a paycheck.

Bamberger was, and is, a good guy. The players, especially the pitchers, liked him immensely. Nothing seemed to bother George. He always seemed relaxed. When George quit mid-season, he was replaced by Frank Howard, the gentle giant, who did little to change the players' attitude.

George and Frank, like plenty of managers, liked to go with veterans. They were comfortable with pitchers like Craig Swan and Mike Torrez, and players like catcher John Stearns, even though these veterans were hurt or at the end of their careers. When you play a veteran, you know beforehand what kind of performance to expect. There are few surprises. They usually run true to form.

When the Mets traded for a young catcher, Junior Ortiz, they didn't play him even though they were in last place. He sat on the bench and watched Ron Hodges, who had been a backup his whole career. To me it seemed a little late in his career for anyone to be thinking about his becoming a number one catcher. Meanwhile Ortiz never got a chance to show his stuff.

At the start of the season Bambi did choose two youngsters, Jose Oquendo, a shortstop, and Brian Giles, a second baseman, but he picked them over two other, more talented youngsters, Gardenhire and Backman. Bambi never really gave Gardenhire a chance, telling the press, "The job is only Gardenhire's until Jose Oquendo is ready." Oquendo managed to hit a sparkling .200.

And even when Bambi decided to go with Oquendo and Giles, he really didn't commit himself to them, because instead of letting them play every day, saying, "You guys are my shortstop and second baseman," he played another veteran utility infielder, Bobby Bailor, almost every game, either at short or second, and let one of the other two play alongside him. Even if Bambi had stayed on, he still would have to wonder for 1984, Can I count on my kids, or do I have to get someone else?

To me, it was a shortsighted approach. If you don't answer that question, you're always going to remain stagnant. A baseball team is like a vampire. You always have to feed it new blood.

Fortunately for me, at the end of 1983 general manager Frank Cashen decided to make a change. Frank had been hiring paternal, older managers. Every player's dad. Cashen decided to go to a younger manager. He decided he wanted someone decisive and outspoken, someone who wasn't afraid to make a decision, who wasn't afraid to gamble. I knew in my own mind that I was the man for the job. I had won as a player with the Orioles and in Japan. I had managed three years in the minors and had won all three years. I still didn't know whether Cashen would give me the chance, but I was sure that if anybody could turn the Mets around, I could.

7

MOLDING MY
TEAM

AFTER MY TIDEWATER SEASON ended in mid-September, Mets general manager Frank Cashen and I met. Frank made it clear he wasn't going to rehire Frank Howard, and during our conversation, he showed me a list of ten skills he felt a big league manager had to have. I looked at it. The usual things: communication, knowing the game, et cetera. I said to him, "I've got those ten. What else are you looking for?"

To this day I don't know whether Frank was considering anyone else. There was talk about Rene Lachemann, and Gene Mauch's name also was floating around.

Though Tidewater's season was over, the Mets still had about three more weeks to play, and during our meeting I was thinking to myself, I'm in your farm system. I know the talent. I've managed your Triple A club to a championship. Hire me now so I can come up and watch the team play for the rest of the season. Because if I was going to be the Mets manager in '84, bringing me up would have allowed me to see for myself what the problems were, and it would have given me a head start on next year.

But Frank didn't call, and I figured, They're not considering me. I guess they're looking in some other direction. And in my mind I began mulling which organization I would work for next.

A couple days after the Mets' season ended, I got the call. Frank Cashen flew me to New York and asked me if I wanted the job. I had known Frank when we were both in the Baltimore Orioles organization. I respected him tremendously. At the same time I wanted him to know that as a manager I was going to be my own man.

I said, "I want the job. But I want you to understand that I'm opinionated as hell and stubborn in that I believe my view is better than your view unless proven otherwise. I want to make my own decisions. I want to pick my players and use them the way I see fit. I'm reasonable, but I have to have the authority to make decisions. I'm not going to put up with a lot of interference."

Frank nodded. We shook hands.

Frank officially announced my appointment at the World Series in Philadelphia. The Mets made a big deal out of it. I saw more writers than I had seen in ten years. The question I was asked most often was: What are you going to do differently next year?

What I really wanted to say was, "I should have been up here seeing this ballclub so I could have a little better feel for it, because I haven't seen these guys play on the major league level." What I did say was, "I know the talent on the minor league level, some that I already sent up to the Mets. The lineup needs to be changed, and I need to get more young arms on the pitching staff."

Dave Kingman of the Mets sent me a telegram as soon as he heard: "Congratulations and good luck." One of the things I really meant to do was write him a thank-you note, because it meant a lot to me, but I just didn't take the time to do it.

I had been a teammate of Dave's with the Cubs, and I understood Dave and liked him. People said he was moody, but once I got to know him, I didn't find him that way. He played hard, awfully hard. He alienated reporters and got bad press, but the players always liked him.

In his years with the Mets, Dave had some good seasons. For a while he was the Mets only long-ball threat, but with the newly acquired Keith Hernandez playing first, Dave would have had to play the outfield, and with George Foster, Mookie Wilson, and Darryl Strawberry in the lineup, he wouldn't have gotten very much playing time.

Also, from what I understand, Bamberger and Dave hadn't gotten along. Bambi had asked him to pinch-hit, and Dave refused.

Shortly after I was hired, Frank Cashen released Kingman. I didn't have a say in it. I suspected Frank was going to get rid of him, but I didn't think he would let him go before the winter meetings in December.

When Kingman was released, I was upset because Dave probably thought I was responsible, and I felt bad about that, especially after he was thoughtful enough to send that telegram. As it turned out, it was probably for the best. Dave would never had gotten the playing time with the Mets that he got DHing in the American League.

I went with Frank Cashen to the December meetings in Memphis. I learned that a lot of hot air emanates from those winter meetings. Club officials talk trades more than actually make them. Everybody, it seems, wants to dump his headaches and at the same time steal your best prospects. I remember Pat Gillick of the Toronto Blue Jays having a meeting with us. We had expressed some interest in a couple of their players, including Jimmy Key, whom I had seen pitch, but when we started to list whom we were willing to give up for him, Gillick didn't seem to be listening. Finally, he said, "You have a guy who we might consider trading Key for." We said, "What's his name?" Gillick said, "Gooding, something like that." I said, "Yeah, you would be, wouldn't you?" But he wasn't about to get Gooden. I wouldn't have traded Dwight Gooden for the entire Blue Jay team.

I ran into Dick Howser, who asked me if I thought he should take a chance on Steve Balboni, whom the Yankees were shuttling back and forth to Columbus and had never given a real chance. The Yankees always boast a stockpile of excellent prospects to trade because George Steinbrenner has no patience to let them develop. Balboni had played against us at Tidewater, and I liked his power. I told Dick, "Get him, but he's going to have to play every day." Dick made that trade a couple days later.

Frank only made one major deal. He traded two guys I could have used, relief pitcher Carlos Diaz and Bob Bailor, for a pitcher, Sid Fernandez, who wasn't ready to play regularly in the spring. In the end it turned out for the best, but in the short run, it handicapped me. My roster was weakened right from the start, but Frank figured correctly that sooner or later this hard-throwing left-hander, Fernandez, would be extremely valuable.

Frank did make one mistake in judgment that winter. At the start of the '83 season he had reacquired Hall of Fame pitcher Tom Seaver from the Cincinnati Reds. Seaver unquestionably was the greatest player in the history of the Mets franchise, and though he only finished 9–14 in '83, he was still a legend and a crowd-pleaser and a hell of a pitcher. During the off-season Seaver was celebrating his thirty-ninth birthday, and the decision Frank faced was whether or not to protect him on the forty-man roster. If he had protected him, he would have stood to lose one of the young minor leaguers. If he didn't protect him, he stood to lose Seaver. The real question was whether another team would take a chance on a thirty-nine-year-old pitcher with a million-dollar contract.

In retrospect there were a couple of kids who had no chance of making it to the majors. But Frank was higher on them than I was, and he opted to keep the kids on the roster rather than Seaver. He figured no one would take Seaver. Frank was wrong. The White Sox grabbed him. Bye-bye to Tom Seaver from New York.

What bothered me was that I was not privy to Frank's list. We all could have used Seaver in '84.

By the spring I had more questions than I had answers. My outfield of George Foster, Mookie Wilson, and Darryl Strawberry seemed set, and I had Hubie Brooks and Keith Hernandez on the corners. The rest was in the stars.

My first priority was to make sure Frank Cashen would allow me to keep a nineteen-year-old minor league pitcher by the name of Dwight Gooden. In my mind Dwight (Doc) Gooden was ready for the big time.

I had worked with Doc for about three weeks when he first

broke in at Kingsport in the Appalachian League in 1982. He had been the Mets, number one pick in the amateur draft. I remember him throwing on the sidelines. As I stood next to him as he worked out, I asked him how he gripped his fastball.

He said, "Cross-seams if I want it to go straight or ride up, and with the seams if I want lateral movement." I was thinking, Jeez, he has some poise. He was firing bullets, his curve broke three feet, and every pitch was a strike or close to it. What control he had. I said admiringly to myself, This kid is seventeen years old, and the catcher isn't jumping all over the place for the ball. Wow!

Doc was always a really good athlete, and he learned quickly. We put Doc through drills, taught him the correct pickoff motion, drilled him on fielding bunts, and we had him practice covering first on balls hit to the first baseman.

One day pitching coach Al Jackson noticed that Doc would stand flat-footed and just use his arm to throw to second for a double play. Al said, "No, you catch the ball and take a step toward second, and then throw. Put something on it."

The next time the ball was hit back at Doc, he took a step to second and threw so hard he just about knocked the shortstop down. He sent a pea down there chest high! It was as though the shortstop had run into a cannonball! I kept my mouth shut, but I felt like saying, "I like it better flat-footed, Doc."

I saw Doc pitch his first game in the minor leagues, and he was very impressive. Doc wasn't a thrower, like most youngsters. He was a pitcher. The first time he got two strikes on a hitter, you could see the killer in him, because he added about a yard on his fastball, moving it in on the hitter. Whenever the batter seemed to come close to hitting his fastball, Doc would mix up his pitches and throw him a curveball. He did this all at seventeen.

And yet, as great as his talent was, what I remember best about Doc was his poise and even temperament. He had a terrible team behind him, but he never complained once. They'd allow three or four errors, and sometimes he'd have to get five outs in an inning, but it never fazed him. That was his first year. I'll never forget it.

The next year Doc pitched at Lynchburg in Double A, where he won nineteen games, and at the end of the year he came to me at Tidewater. He pitched three games for me, winning a playoff game and a Championship Series game. He was overpowering. I knew he was ready for the Mets, my Mets. Dwight was to be my stopper in the rotation. I had to have him. Doc was a luxury Bamberger didn't have. You didn't have to be a genius to see that this kid was going to star in the big leagues. I had to have him.

I started working on Frank for Dwight. I would say to him, "Let's have an open mind going into the spring." Every time I brought it up, he'd pick up his beer and say, "Here's to the ladies," trying to change the subject. Frank said, "More ballplayers are hurt by bringing them up too quickly than for any other reason. You have to allow youngsters to mature sufficiently in the minor leagues." And he would bring up the case of twenty-one-year-old Darryl Strawberry, who had been brought up in '83 against Frank's better judgment.

Darryl had been hitting .333 at Tidewater, and the media was calling for Frank to bring him up, and so was Bamberger, and eventually Frank caved in to the pressure. Darryl came up and struggled. Frank says he will go to his grave feeling that Strawberry would be a better player today if they had let him have a full year in Triple A.

Doc, I was convinced, was different. It became a ritual. I would bring Gooden's name up and Frank would try to change the subject. But I was persistent enough so that I knew when we went into the spring, Frank would have an open mind. Frank also was aware that it is easier for a pitcher to make the transition to the big leagues than it is for an everyday player.

In the spring Doc had back spasms and a torn fingernail on his pitching hand, but he still was very, very impressive. About a week before the team broke north, I said, "Frank, well, how's your open mind?" He said, "I'll let you have him."

I had also wanted Frank to let me start another young minor leaguer, John Gibbons, at catcher. He had hit a couple points short of .300 at Jackson, he had a gun for an arm, and I liked his spirit. I thought he was a better hitter and better defensively than his competition, Ron Hodges, Junior Ortiz, and another rookie, Mike Fitzgerald.

I knew I wasn't going to be playing Hodges, who was the regular from the year before. I liked Ronnie, but once a week against a tough right-hander. He had never been an everyday catcher. He had played all his career behind John Stearns.

Gibby beat out the competition, and Frank again let me have my way. I named Gibby to start the season at catcher, but some players are plagued by bad fortune, and Gibby was one of them. The last week of spring training, Joe Lefevbre of the Padres rounded third and tried to score. John went up the line to tag him, and Lefevbre smashed him in the cheekbone with his elbow and put him on the disabled list. By the time Gibby healed, he was too far behind to cut it. I had to send him back to Tidewater.

When Gibbons went down, the next catcher I tried was Ortiz. As I said, Bambi hadn't played him enough for anyone really to judge him. I decided to find out. He played for a couple of months, and as it turned out, he wasn't a good enough hitter.

The next catcher I tried was Mike Fitzgerald. Fitzie was the best offensive catcher in the organization. The only drawback was his arm. He wasn't a really good thrower.

When I finally put Fitzie in a ballgame, he got a big base hit and drove in a run, and when I let him play again the next day he did the same thing for me. He did it about three days in a row—played very well, caught very well—and I left him in there.

Around this time in early May I faced my most difficult task. I had to release some veteran pitchers.

When I started the season, the Mets had significant contractual obligations to Mike Torrez, Craig Swan, and Dick Tidrow. Swannie was making somewhere around $600,000, Torrez $500,000, and Tidrow $350,000. Even before spring training, I had said to Frank Cashen, "I'm going to go with these guys and try to get some production out of them, but if they can't help me early, I'm going to my kids at Tidewater." He agreed.

The three veterans pitched well in spring training. But in my mind, if they didn't start the season strong, I wasn't going to keep them long. They had had poor years in '83, and if they started off poorly, they were gone.

One of the reasons I was inflexible on this count was a vow I'd made after a conversation with Paul Richards, who had always been an idol of mine. Paul had managed for a dozen years with the White Sox and then the Orioles. At Baltimore, Paul had structured the famed Kiddy Korps pitching staff, and he had made Baltimore a pennant contender because he handled pitchers so well. He was an exceptional analyst and judge of talent.

One day when I was playing for Atlanta I ran into him in a coffee shop. He and some of his buddies were talking about the Atlanta ballclub. He said to me, "Dave, if I had a one-year contract, I would play you and Mike Lum," meaning two veterans. "But if I had a two-year contract, I'd play Marty Perez and Frank Tepedino," two younger players. I swore to myself at the time, If I'm ever a manager I'll never let the length of my contract make any difference as to whom I play.

When you play veterans, you may lose more games with them than if you had played talented young kids coming up, but your chances of getting rehired improves drastically because you can never be second-guessed by the front office or blamed by the press. If you take what appears to be a gamble—and going with young kids is always a gamble—and you're wrong, you're gone. Especially if you're on a contender. You also forfeit your chance of developing any talent.

You prostitute your baseball beliefs when you start making decisions based on the length of your contract. There can be only one answer to the question of who should play. When Richards tied whom he would play to his contractual status, it confirmed something I had suspected all along: For a lot of baseball people, protecting themselves is top priority, more so even than winning.

Once the season began, Tidrow and Swan were getting hit pretty hard, giving up some long home runs, and I decided they and Mike Torrez had to go.

I went to Frank, and I said, "I have to go with the younger arms down at Tidewater 'cause I'm getting shelled with these guys." He let me do it.

I had to call them in and close the door and tell them. It was a painful experience. My only consolation was that I wasn't springing it on them. I had told them in the spring where they stood, and so when the end finally came, they weren't shocked.

Swan took it like a man. He said he understood, but, of course, he didn't. No player really understands. Craig felt he could still pitch, and he hooked on with California. He had his arm operated on out there. He had a blood clot that was impinging on his circulation. He felt he would be back, but I don't think he ever will.

When I released Tidrow, Dick didn't try to come back. He hung it up. I think he was happy I released him. On some level he knew he had reached the end of the line.

The toughest one by far was Mike Torrez. I cut him loose in June. Mike had just been through a divorce and had financial difficulties. He was an intense competitor, a battler, and a great guy. But I knew our future was in front of us. We couldn't be respectable with a so-so thirty-eight-year-old starting pitcher. It was tough on him. He took it hard. He wanted to go somewhere else to pitch, but he never did.

I called up Brent Gaff and Tommy Gorman from Tidewater, and we traded for hard-throwing Bruce Berenyi. Then I moved Eddie Lynch from the pen into the starting rotation.

If I did nothing else in '84, I am most proud of having established the young arms in the pitching rotation. It was certainly a gamble, but an educated gamble. If they had failed, I would have failed. But in truth I never really was worried. I've always said, "You can't be afraid to play the kids." Now it was time to practice what I preached, and when I put them out there, they responded. Gooden won seventeen as a rookie, Darling won twelve and demonstrated that he had the potential to be a twenty-game winner, and Walt Terrell won eleven games. Lynch and Berenyi each won nine for me in partial seasons. Gorman was 6–0, and Gaff pitched strongly in relief.

My plan at the start of the season was for four of the five pitchers in my rotation to be young, with the expectation that three of the four would develop. Then the next spring I would bring two more young kids up, and maybe one of them would make it, until I had five, young, strong starters.

As I did in Tidewater, I handled the kids with kid gloves. I fought myself to be patient with them, trying to give them positive outings, coaxing them along. By the end of the year I had a very strong pitching staff. I had Gooden, Darling, and Terrell; I was breaking in Sid Fernandez; and I had Bruce Berenyi for the second half. When Frank acquired Berenyi from Cincinnati, we gave up Jay Tibbs, one of our best minor league pitchers, and another top draft pick, Eddie Williams, but Bruce was worth it.

Berenyi throws over ninety miles an hour and he has one of the best sliders in all of baseball.

When Frank told me he was available, I asked Keith Hernandez on the QT, "What kind of stuff does he have?" Keith said, "Get him." And we did. And he won nine games for us the second half of the season.

At first base Hernandez was a rock, brilliant in the field, a professional at bat. Keith was a constant. Every day I sent him out to play, and he shined.

One factor in the Mets' return to prominence was Frank's acquisition of Hernandez at the trading deadline, June 15, 1983. Keith was unhappy when he came, because he went from the first-place Cardinals to the last-place Mets, and from what I understand he threatened not to sign with the Mets in '84 if he didn't see some improvement in the team by year's end. Apparently Frank convinced him to stay, because at the end of the year he signed through the 1989 season, thank heaven.

There are few players who compete with the intensity of Keith Hernandez. He brings an enthusiasm and a killer will to win. Out in the field, Keith keeps the players on their toes. He never stops talking, reminding the infielders how many outs there are, constantly telling the young pitchers what a particular batter likes to hit, going to the mound when a pitcher needs a boost or a kick in the butt. It's like having a coach out on the field.

Through the tail end of the '83 season Keith wasn't really happy, but he made the best of it, played hard, and it didn't take the fans long to fall in love with him. In '84 I fell in love with him as well.

I realized I had to strengthen my second and short combination, and I knew just what to do: I sent Giles and Oquendo to the minors and inserted Wally Backman at second and Ron Gardenhire at short. I also brought up infielder Kelvin Chapman. All three had been given up for dead. But they were my kind of players.

Unfortunately, Gardy was injury-prone. In the spring he won the job from Oquendo, and for a month he was hitting in the .320s when he pulled a hamstring.

When he got hurt I called up Rafael Santana from Tidewater. For much of his career Raffy had been buried behind the Cardinals' Ozzie Smith in the St. Louis chain. At Tidewater I had seen Raffy play for the Cards' Louisville team, and when he became a free agent after sitting behind Ozzie, we grabbed him.

When I put Raffy in at short, he played like an MVP for about three weeks, and then he got hurt. He slid into second base and caught his finger on the fielder's spikes and was out.

My shortstops were going down like dominoes, and now I was stuck. Fortunately for me, over the winter Frank Cashen had traded for Ray Knight from the Houston Astros. Ray had always been a quality third baseman and a fine hitter, and I was glad to have him. Ray's acquisition allowed me to move Hubie Brooks from third base to shortstop.

Changing a player's position can be a tricky thing to do without hurting the player's career. Why managers shuffle their players around is beyond me. I see them do it time and time again, and it astounds me. Sometimes it does make sense. Moving Babe Ruth from pitcher to outfielder made sense. Shifting Stan Musial from pitcher to outfielder made sense. Moving Mickey Mantle from shortstop to the outfield made sense. Several years ago the Yankees paid a million dollars for outfielder Dave Collins and shifted him to first base. Collins is 5'9". The third baseman could barely see him across the diamond.

At Atlanta Clyde King almost ruined my career by trying to make me a first baseman. Although I had been a second baseman on the National League All-Star team, Clyde decided to move me to first base to let Marty Perez, a good fielder but a weak hitter, play second. With one move he weakened two positions. I never got the hang of first. One time I had my foot in the middle of the bag and got it stomped on, injuring some ligaments. I played hurt the last half of the season. At the end of the year Clyde promised that I'd get my old position back the next year, but when I arrived at spring training camp, the first words out of Clyde's mouth were, "Get a first baseman's mitt." If I ever wanted to kill a man, it would have been right there. I don't know what stopped me.

I never forgot. So I thought very hard before making the decision to move Hubie Brooks from third to short and play Ray Knight at third.

I had always thought Hubert seemed uncomfortable at third. He didn't know whether to play in or to guard the line, and at short he had more area to roam, and Hubert can run. So I moved him over there, and because he played shortstop so well, and especially well against Montreal, Hubert became the key bait in the Gary Carter deal. The Expos were looking for a shortstop, and Hubert was the one they wanted.

During spring training I told reporters, "If we can stay close to .500 by June 1, by then my young pitchers will have gained enough experience to get over their inconsistency, and after that, look out, we're going to be a force to be reckoned with."

And that's exactly what happened. From opening day through the spring, we would either win a close ballgame or we'd get blown out. Gooden, Darling, and Terrell usually pitched well. We didn't score many runs, but the pitching usually kept us competitive.

Our weakness was middle relief. In games when I had to hook the starter early, Tidrow or one of the other middle relievers would inevitably give up three or four more runs, and rather than bring in one of my top men, Doug Sisk or Jesse Orosco, to finish, I would save them for another day even if it meant that we got a sound drubbing.

We were right at .500 on June 1. We then won twenty out of twenty-six, catapulting us into first place. We held it through August, even though we were still having trouble scratching out runs. We weren't dominant, but as Doug Sisk emerged as a force in the bullpen, we were tough to beat. Doug would take it from the sixth inning and close it right out. Or he could come in for one inning and put out the fire. Frequently he'd walk a batter, giving me cardiac arrest, then get a double play, but one way or another, he'd get us out of it. And when Doug needed a rest, Jesse would come in and blow them away. The two of them were unbeatable.

What hurt us most the last half was losing Sisk. When he went down with a bad arm, there was no one to take his place. He got hurt in August against the Chicago Cubs, our pennant competition. We had beaten the Cubs at Shea in the first game, and in the second game Ron Darling had a 5–2 lead. I brought Doug in, and he finished the game with a sore arm.

With Doug out, we lost six in a row as the Cubs went on a tear and passed us. We then went to Wrigley Field for a three-game series, and they beat the stuffing out of us.

We ended up winning ninety games, and we finished second, six and a half games behind the Cubs, who were one game from winning their first pennant since 1945, but who choked and blew the pennant to the San Diego Padres.

I couldn't wait for the next season to begin. I knew damn well that the Cubs, who had career years from a number of their players, would only get worse. And I also knew we would only get better.

8

THE MAN WITH THE BOW TIE

NELSON DOUBLEDAY and Fred Wilpon bought the Mets in January 1980 from relatives of Mrs. Joan Payson, the team's founder. The Mets had fallen on hard times, and the new owners desperately needed an experienced baseball man to run the franchise, and they selected Frank Cashen, who had helped Harry Dalton build the Oriole dynasty when I was playing there. When Frank took over the Mets in 1980, he said the Mets would be contenders in five years. It took the Mets exactly five years. Frank had always been an astute judge of talent, and his reputation has only been enhanced by the success of our farm system and by his wheeling and dealing.

The first of his outstanding trades was for George Foster. The Reds were dumping their high salaries, and their general manager, Dick Wagner, coveted one of our catchers, Alex Trevino. Frank was able to trade Trevino, who had only so-so talent, and a couple of pitchers who never made it for Foster. None of those guys ever helped the Reds much, and of course Foster continues to be a premier power hitter.

The deal that really turned the Mets around, though, was

Frank's trade of outfielder Lee Mazzilli to the Texas Rangers for pitchers Walt Terrell and Ron Darling. When Frank asked me my opinion, I told him, "Man, get the Rangers on the phone right now."

I had seen those kids in the Texas League when I was at Jackson. Ronnie had starred at Yale, and everybody who had seen him pitch there said he was going to be a great one. I also knew how badly the Rangers were screwing him up.

Looking back, Frank picked the Rangers' pocket. He got two excellent starting pitchers for a journeyman outfielder. But at the time the trade infuriated Mets fans. Mazzilli was known as the Italian Stallion. He was the Mets matinee idol, and when Frank gave him up for two guys who had never played in the major leagues, New Yorkers were angry. New York, you have to understand, is different from any other town. It's a "now" town—"What are you going to do for me *today*?" New Yorkers want stars, and Mazzilli shone. But Frank knew what he was getting, and he had the courage of his convictions. Without Darling and Terrell, we would have continued to be mediocre in '84.

Frank's other major coup was acquiring Keith Hernandez from the Cardinals in June 1983, for pitcher Neil Allen. Frank will be the first one to tell you that Hernandez fell into his lap. Joe McDonald, who used to work for Frank, was at St. Louis, and he called Frank one day out of the blue and said, "If you'll talk about trading Neil Allen, we'll talk about trading Keith Hernandez." Frank previously had offered Allen in a trade to the Cards for Bull Durham, but the Cards had turned him down. Frank took a deep breath and said to McDonald, "Okay, I'll talk about it." Hernandez was, and is, one of the quality ballplayers in the National League. Frank had heard that Keith and Whitey Herzog weren't getting along. He knew that Whitey was the kind of guy who would dump a player quickly and go on. There was even some drug talk. Frank checked around, and his sources indicated that though Keith might have been into drugs, it wasn't so prevalent that it was affecting his play. He did not have a drug dependency.

McDonald said, "Allen won't be enough. We need something else." He asked for one of two minor league prospects, Rick Ownbey or Jeff Bittiger. He gave Frank the choice. Frank sent him Ownbey. The whole discussion took ten minutes. Keith's arrival improved the whole attitude of the New York Mets.

Frank wasn't finished. In December, he made two trades. In the first, he traded Walt Terrell, whom I hated to lose, for Detroit third baseman Howard Johnson. I wasn't privy to this deal. I liked Terrell, liked him a lot, but Frank knew he would be giving up Hubie Brooks in another deal, a blockbuster deal, and he didn't feel he had a choice.

He was reluctant to leave third base solely to Ray Knight, because Ray had undergone an operation over the winter, and Frank wasn't sure he could cut it anymore. Neither was I.

Frank had been talking with the Tigers for a couple of years about Howard Johnson. Our scouts had liked Howard. They thought he was going to be an outstanding third baseman. There was talk that manager Sparky Anderson wasn't as high on Johnson as we were and was willing to give him up. The Tigers had played in the World Series against San Diego, and though Howard had played all year long, Anderson didn't use him in the playoffs or World Series. I guess he gave up on him, and so Howard became expendable. The Tigers needed pitching, and though Frank really didn't want to give up Terrell, the Tigers insisted, and he finally gave in.

Frank completed the big score three days later. During the winter Frank and I did a lot of talking about the type of player we should be pursuing, and I suggested that we should be looking at right-handed power hitters like Jack Clark of San Francisco, or either Jimmy Rice or Dwight Evans of Boston, players who are run producers. In 1984 the Cubs had averaged 4.7 runs a game, the Phils 4.4, and we only averaged 4 runs a game. We agreed that unless our 1985 pitching staff is head-and-shoulders above everyone else, we're going to have trouble competing.

It isn't easy to acquire a power hitter of the caliber of Clark or Rice. The trick is to convert what one team sees to be a liability into an asset for your own team. Frank Cashen, I feel, did exactly that. Frank acquired Gary Carter from the Montreal Expos.

Frank initiated the talks two years ago. He told John McHale, the Expos general manager, "If you ever decide to give up your catcher, I'd be very interested in talking to you about it." The Expo catcher, of course, was Carter.

We were playing Montreal at Shea the last series of the '84 season, and Frank and McHale said, "Frank, we're going to make changes with our ballclub. We're going to break it up. We've had the same group of players together for years and every year we're picked to win, and we never do. McHale didn't mention Carter specifically in the conversation, but Frank was hopeful.

His break came in late November. McHale called Frank. He said, "That player who we talked about"—meaning Carter—"we're thinking about trading him." They talked about other things, and McHale told Frank he was going to get away from the day-to-day operation of the general managership. Murray Cook, he said, would be in charge. "Talk to Murray," McHale said, and so Frank began discussions with Cook.

"Would you trade him?" asked Frank.

"Yeah," said Cook, "if I can get what I want for him."

Naturally, Frank said, "What do you want for him?"

Cook said, "An infielder who can hit, and a few other people." Frank and Cook started writing names down. It became clear that the one player Cook would insist upon was Hubie Brooks. Frank countered by insisting on a shortstop in return, and Frank asked for Argenis Salazar, a young prospect in the Montreal farm system. Initially, Cook agreed. Cook then said he wanted a center fielder, and Frank gave him the choice of Mookie Wilson or Herm Winningham, and Cook took Winningham because he was younger, which surprised Frank, because Mookie is a star. Cook wanted a catcher back, which was no big deal, because Carter was certain to play almost every day, making the rest of the catchers pretty well expendable, and so we gave up Mike Fitzgerald. The final stumbling block was that they also wanted a young pitcher. Cook asked for Roger McDowell. Frank turned him down. Cook then asked for Calvin Schiraldi, another of our young pitchers. Frank said no to him too. His third choice was Floyd Youmans, who used to be a high school teammate of Dwight Gooden's. Frank finally agreed.

In the middle of negotiations, Frank called to tell me about the pending deal. "I'm holding my breath," I said. The deal seemed done when Frank called me again. "The Expos insist on withdrawing Salazar from the trade," he said. "How do you feel about that?"

I said, "I don't care. We'll throw in another player if they want another one in order to get Carter. He's the kind of guy we need."

Frank agreed to drop Salazar from the package, and the deal was completed. But before it could be announced, the Expos had to get Carter to agree to come to New York.

I said to Frank, "I know Gary. If you need me to call him, I'll be glad to." I wanted so badly to phone Gary and say, "Come on, man, we're going to have fun. We have all these young pitchers and you can be the catalyst to make them win. You can be the ingredient to bring it all together, and New York is the place you should be, not Montreal. You'll own the town." But I didn't. Frank said it wasn't necessary, and he was right. Gary agreed to come to the Mets a day or two later.

I did get to talk to Gary afterward. He said, "Anything you want me to do, I'll do. I'll play first, third, outfield, anything, whatever you want."

I said, "Gary, don't change a thing. We'll be fine."

When the trade was finally announced, a lot of people took pot shots at Gary. They said, "He plays too much for himself, he's selfish, he's blah blah blah." That's the biggest crock of malarkey I ever heard in my life. Gary's a professional. He's sensitive. He's caring. He gives you everything he has to give, every minute of the game.

When the media began spreading stories about how self-centered Gary is, I said, "Great. I like selfish players, because they strive for perfection." In fact, I tell my guys, "Take care of number one. Get your rest at night. Play as good as you can. Work as hard as you can. Worry about yourself and I'll worry about everyone else. Let me worry about fitting all the pieces together."

Of course, I also know the dimension Gary adds to our ballclub. A lot of people don't understand how valuable he's going to be: Here's a number four, cleanup hitter who was tied for the league lead in rbi's in the National League last year. He's also a very selective hitter. I'm talking about a hitter who doesn't fish for a lot of bad pitches, doesn't strike out much, and the majority of the time hits the ball hard, puts it in play, and has a good on-base percentage for a big guy.

Last year I only had one selective hitter, Keith Hernandez. Now I have lefty and righty selective hitters up in front of a couple of free swingers, Darryl Strawberry and George Foster, and I know it's going to make them better hitters just by example. And in talking about Gary, I haven't even mentioned his defensive skills. Gary calls an outstanding game. What an acquisition. What a trade! Let spring training begin!

9

IMPRESSIONS

FINDING A MIX OF players I am comfortable with, an ultimate team, is a process that begins in spring training. I start with an initial combination of players, evaluate what I see, and substitute players who I feel would fit better for players I don't think fit the mix. I look at that mix, reevaluate, winnow out another player or two, and either bring up a player from the minors or buy or trade for one from another team, trying different combinations in search of one I'm comfortable with, until the roster is finally set in my mind.

We are going to spring training this year in much better shape than last. In '84 things were so unsettled I had trouble picking a team at the end of spring training. It wasn't until the very last day that I finally settled on the twenty-five players to take north. This year, even as early as February, I pretty much know who the twenty-five are going to be, give or take a couple.

Despite the fact that we traded Hubie Brooks, I'm starting the season with a shortstop I'm satisfied with, Ron Gardenhire. I'm comfortable with my second base situation, platooning Wally Backman and Kelvin Chapman. Keith Hernandez is a quality player at first, and I feel good platooning my new kid, Howard Johnson, and veteran Ray Knight at third, even though Howard is a switch hitter and Ray is going to have to sit out more than he would like. Ray will hit against left-handers, and Howard against right-handers, and since more pitchers are right-handed, Howard will get to play more.

The outfield again will be George Foster, Mookie Wilson, and Darryl Strawberry, quality players, and Gary Carter is an All-Star catcher. Last year my pitching staff was all mixed up. This year I have the youngest and potentially the strongest staff in baseball, even without Walt Terrell. As a result, I'm already a lot smarter going into 1985.

My greatest concern during the off-season was the possibility that Dwight Gooden might hold out and miss some of spring training. After Fernando Valenzuela's outstanding rookie season for the Dodgers, he held out, missed critical practice time and didn't play as well as he should have the rest of the year. I didn't want that happening to Dwight. I didn't want it to happen to me.

During the winter at a banquet in New York I talked to Dwight about it. "Doc, listen, between you and the gatepost, let me give you some good words of wisdom. You had a great year, and you should get lots of money, a big raise. Hold out until the last minute, but sign, regardless. Don't hold out into the spring. Please. Tell them you're not going to sign, but give in on the last day." He promised me he would.

I was sure he had the sense not to screw himself up by reporting late, but I still sweated through his negotiations.

Two days before spring training began, he signed.

On the day the entire squad was scheduled to report I addressed the players. It was a far cry from my address of the year before. Last year I called a meeting to inform the players that the country-club atmosphere from the former era was over. I told them, "During the game I don't want to see the reserves sitting in the clubhouse playing cards." That's how lax discipline was. I said, "Your job is out on the baseball field. Even if you're not playing, you can learn something while you're on the bench."

I told them, "I want everyone pulling as one, rather than three guys pulling for us and the rest of the players pulling in the other direction." Last year I had to get the players into good habits, winning habits. This year I don't have to repeat myself.

I stuck to my basic speech. I went over my rules. I told them, "Don't ever embarrass the ballclub." That's the big one. I said, "I don't believe in setting a time for grown men to be in bed or off the streets, but you better not drink and drive, and you better make sure to tip the maids. Another rule: No dogs and children in the clubhouse, not necessarily in that order."

I told them I didn't believe in a dress code during spring training. "After all," I said, "this is Florida. Just don't go overboard. Don't come in barefoot or without a shirt on. Another rule: No signing autographs during workouts. If you're going to be late, and you have a reason and if you call me ahead of time, I have no problem. If you're late for practice and you don't call, the first time you get a warning, the second time it's going to cost you a hundred or two hundred, depending on how late you are. You have to be out of the training room fifteen minutes before the start of practice. Those are the rules. I don't like to restrict you. All of you should know how to act."

Most of spring training involves getting in shape, exercising, reviewing basics with repetitive drills, hitting in the batting cage. Spring training is also a series of impressions—events and conversations and thoughts that stick in my mind:

I thought it important that Gary Carter know that I intend to lean on his judgment when it comes to handling our pitching staff. I told him, "I want your input because I know you keep a book on all the pitchers." Gary said, "I sure do. I keep it daily, and I update it all the time on every hitter in the league." I said, "I know you have a pretty good reading on some of my young pitchers, and I'm sure you can help every one of them."

We analyzed each of our pitchers. I said, "Sid Fernandez and Bruce Berenyi tend to allow the umpires to affect the rest of the ballgame." Gary said, "Let me handle that. I'll go out to the mound and say, 'Let me handle the ump. I'll let him know he took a pitch away from you, so don't worry, just concentrate on the next one.'"

I then discussed my philosophy on handling our young pitchers. "First and foremost, I tell them, 'Let's go out there and be aggressive about throwing in the strike zone.' We won't have in-depth meetings where we say, 'This guy is a fastball hitter, but he can't handle the up-and-in fastball. This other guy can't hit the breaking ball down-and-away.' All that does is cloud a young pitcher's mind. Paralysis by analysis. No, all I say is, 'Come with your strength. Come right at them.' I want those kids to be aggressive in the strike zone early in the count. That's the key. That's why we don't spend a lot of time going over hitters."

I want Gary to know exactly what goes on in my mind. Every time I see Gary running around out on the field, I'm more and more happy he's there.

Vern Hoscheit, who coaches the catchers, has Gary working his butt off. Vern, whom all the players call "Dad," is the greatest coach of catchers I have ever known. We've been friends since I was in the Baltimore organization, where he trained Andy Etchebarren, Larry Haney, and Curt Blefary. He gave Curt an extra three or four years in the big leagues. When he was hired by the Oakland A's, he made Adrian Garrett into a catcher for manager Dick Williams, and then his big coup was transforming outfielder Gene Tenace into a major league catcher. He has tutored Clint Hurdle, and now it was his job to improve All-Star Gary Carter.

Vern jarred Gary. He told him, "Gary, in my opinion, you're not the best defensive catcher in the world. You could be a lot better." Gary was offended but his curiosity was piqued. He said, "What do you mean?" Vern said, "Your footwork could be better when you throw, your blocking could be better. You sometimes hold your mitt the wrong way. If you scoop snow, you don't turn the shovel upside down. It's the same when you go to block the ball. You hold the mitt up, so that if the ball hits the web, it'll come in. If it hits the web upside down, it goes through." Gary said, "I guess I did make a lot of trips back to the backstop last year."

Vern organized a catching drill. First he set up a pitching machine on the mound. He then had the equipment manager bring out a pile of forearm pads, like in football, and some boxing gloves.

Gary, who was standing with the other catchers, didn't have the slightest idea what Vern was up to. He looked at the pile of equipment and said, "What in the world is that for?" Vern said,

"You guys are going to wear it." Gary said, "Vern, I can't do that. The public is watching. I'll be embarrassed." Vern said, "Gary, tell you what. You be last. Let the young fellows do it first."

Gary was insistent. "I'm not going to use that stuff."

Again Vern said, "You don't have to. I wouldn't make you do anything you didn't want to do."

Vern began the drill with Ronn Reynolds behind the plate. Reynolds was wearing the forearm protector and the boxing glove on his right hand. The first pitch the machine threw bounced the ball in front and to the left of the plate and Reynolds shifted over and caught a ninety-mile-an-hour bullet off the forearm pad. Vern had the machine bounce ten balls to Reynolds's right, ten to his left, and ten straight at him. That machine would have beaten Ronnie black and blue if he hadn't been wearing the pads and boxing glove for protection. Hurdle went next, then Gibbons, then two of our other kids. Finally it was Gary's turn. On went the forearm pads. On went the boxing glove. Gary didn't care anymore what he looked like. He told Vern, "You ain't getting me, buddy."

Another thing we wanted to do was strengthen Gary's arm. We made him throw every day, whether his arm hurt or not. This was a philosophy Bamberger had stressed when he coached for Earl Weaver. Bambi stressed that all players must throw for twenty minutes a day before they did anything else.

It was a concept I had learned even earlier from Luis Aparicio, our shortstop, who had taken me down to Venezuela to play with him during the winter of 1964.

He said, "Dave, the only way to have a strong arm is to throw for twenty minutes a day." Louie would drag me out and throw with me even if my arm was killing me. Before, I figured that if my arm hurt, I should rest it. Louie taught me differently. After about six weeks, I discovered that I could throw the ball through a wall! And I never again had that tingling sensation going down my arm from a hard throw.

I wanted Gary to learn the same lesson. Vern would work with him every day and Gary certainly tried, but at the end of the third week he said, "Vern, I can't throw today. My arm is dead."

Vern said, "You're throwing today, Gary."

Gary was beginning to hate ol' Vern. But at the end of six weeks, Gary had a cannon. Gary put his arm around Vern and said, "Thanks, Dad, I'm throwing much better. Everything is easier for me."

Not that Gary didn't teach the kids a thing or two.

One day Gary was standing next to John Gibbons, from whom he took away the starting catching job. When he saw John catch a low pitch, he said to him, "Listen, roll the hand around from the inside, and that will help you catch the low pitch, and the umpire might still call it a strike." Gibby did it a couple of times, looked at Gary, and in his Texas drawl said, "'Preciate it."

◆ It was clear that Gary was going to be our starting catcher. Ronn Reynolds, a young catcher, came ambling over to talk to me. He said, "I just want you to know that I'm not going to give you any problems. I just want to know where I stand."

I said, "Ronnie, I can't tell you too much. I may only go north with two catchers, and if I do, I probably won't take you. But let me tell you, I know the situation you've been in the last three years. I know you came out of Double A and went to the big leagues and didn't play three years ago. Then when you came back down, I couldn't play you because Fitzgerald was hitting .320. And last year it was Gibbons and Hurdle playing ahead of you at Tidewater, but you managed to get enough at bats to hit over .260.

"You progressed through all that adversity. If I have to send you down, it'll be through a numbers game and not because you can't catch up here. I have already suggested Frank trade you to another major league club or put you in a better situation."

"I believe you," he said.

He didn't two years ago. When we were together at Tidewater, he was complaining a lot about not playing, and I had to call him on the carpet. I said, "I'm the manager of this ballclub, and when I take you out for a pinch hitter or don't play you, you're sulking over there like a ten-year-old kid. I can't please everybody. Even though I like you and I'd like to accommodate you, I can't without doing something worse to somebody else. So grow up." And he did.

Ronn, like most young players, is looking for security, and I can't say that I blame him. I would like nothing better than to see such a dedicated young player get the opportunity to play. I promised him I would do my darnedest to get him to a situation where he could play every day. He was a lot happier after that. They all are, when they get an understanding that at least I understand.

◆ It was ten in the morning, and Rusty Staub showed up and asked me if he could hit. The man's my age, and he could get up out of bed without taking BP all winter and he'd still hit. I don't know what he's worried about. I told him, "Rusty, you could hit at midnight in a coal mine."

◆ When Darryl Strawberry reported to camp, he strolled in with his bat over his shoulder and glove on, grinning like the cat who just ate the mouse. Darryl said, "Dave, I'm ready. I'm going to tear them up this year. I'm sleeping, eating, drinking nothing but baseball. You ain't going to worry about me, not once, not one time." I said, "Darryl, I hope so. You're my security blanket. I'm counting on you." Darryl said, "Don't worry about it. You're not going to get my money this year." I said, "Darryl, the boys at the orphanage sure appreciated your money that I gave them last year."

We were smiling. He seemed to have a maturity I hadn't seen in him before. Two years ago he came up to the Mets, a young man with a lot of green potential. He came from Los Angeles, where all his life he had been ballyhooed. Athletics had always been easy for him. He had never suffered adversity, and adversity is what teaches you and makes you tough.

Last year Darryl started out the season on the cover of every national magazine. The media pressure was suffocating. The writers all expected a twenty-two-year-old to win the Triple Crown, and when he proved himself mortal, they criticized him, and Darryl let it affect his play. He felt everyone was looking at him, and he began to slump. He would have black moods when he wouldn't smile, and he put far too much pressure on himself. There was a period when he couldn't do anything at bat. Instead of wiping the slate clean and coming out smoking, he struggled and pouted and dogged it in the field. He kept making mental mistakes, missing the cutoff man and throwing to the wrong base. He fought himself. He fought me, and I kept having to fine him. The money went to an orphanage on Long Island.

I'd tell him, "Listen, you're in a little slump, and you feel you're letting yourself down, the team down, letting me down. Forget it. Shake it off. You aren't letting anyone down. You're still going to have a great year." And he'd come away feeling great, but before long that black mood would return.

One time I told him, "One month I hit thirteen home runs. You can do that. You can finish with thirty home runs and a hundred rbi's." By August I was getting through to him, and in September, he hit ten home runs.

By the end of the year he was back on track. Despite his problems, he still finished with 26 home runs and 97 runs batted in. This year he has a wife and a baby and a new attitude. He should really be something.

♦ Keith Hernandez is hurting inside, but he still goes out and hits line drive after line drive. Wake him up at midnight, and he'll hit you a line drive. Keith has been undergoing the trauma of an ugly divorce, and he has finally managed to get custody of his two kids for one week each month. I gave Keith the day off. He said, "Thanks, now I can spend the whole day with the kids."

♦ Ron Gardenhire was in the batting cage. He said to me, "Dave, I'm getting into shape. I only weigh 180 pounds." I said, "That looks fine." He said, "That won't make any difference to you, because I'm going to be at Tidewater, won't I?" I said, "Ron, don't talk like that." Gardy's going to be my shortstop. He's beaten out Rafael Santana and Jose Oquendo for the job.

Oquendo came into spring training thinking I wouldn't give him a fair shot. And maybe he was right. It hurts me, because I know that Jose Oquendo thinks that I haven't done what was best for him. Two years ago we didn't give him the chance to play a full year, and we didn't again last year. Now this year Ron Gardenhire and Rafael Santana are going to be my shortstops.

I had a meeting with Oquendo and told him, "Jose, the best thing for you is to go down to Tidewater and play every day." He said, "I want to play every day, but I want to play in the big leagues." I said, "Would you rather sit behind a player in the big leagues or play every day in Triple A?" He said, "I'd rather sit behind a player in the big leagues." I don't understand that. When you're twenty-two years old, you've got to want to play every day to get better.

I promised Jose that we would try to trade him if we saw he would have to go back to the minor leagues. Before the end of spring training we traded him to the Cardinals. Now he's behind Ozzie Smith, the best shortstop in baseball. He would have been better off playing at Tidewater.

◆ I have one young pitcher, Roger McDowell, twenty-four years old, who has a natural, nasty sinker, great control, and he does everything you want a pitcher to do. He's great at covering bases and good at fielding. In intersquad games our hitters kept saying, "Who is this guy?"

With Brent Gaff hurt, it looks like McDowell is going to win his spot. I know I'm going to get some resistance from the front office about keeping Roger. He had some bone spurs removed from his elbow a year and a half ago and he missed most of last season. He pitched all of seven innings for Jackson in Double A. But he does everything as well as anybody in camp.

You always try to do what's best for the player. In Roger's case, the best is probably for him to go down to Tidewater and start every fifth day, get regular work, and make sure his arm is going to be sound. But we're supposed to be contending for a pennant, and when you're a contender, you have to take the guys who you feel are ready to help you. Right now, I'm leaning toward Roger.

I spoke to Frank Cashen about him. I said, "I will protect his young arm and not abuse it. I'll take care of him, and in turn, he'll take care of me." There was another argument for keeping McDowell. I said, "Doug Sisk is having trouble throwing strikes. My guess is he still has shoulder problems like he had last year. He walks a lot of batters, and it scares you half to death when he's not throwing the ball over the plate. What I would suggest is using Roger to set up Jesse in games when I can't afford to take a chance on Doug's wildness." Frank agreed, and I was happy. It'll spread the work load of my relievers. And I'll get to keep McDowell.

♦ Of all people, I had to fine Dwight one hundred dollars for missing the seven o'clock bus to West Palm Beach. I knew it was an honest mistake. He overslept, got to the ballpark at seven-fifteen, missed the bus, rented a plane and flew to West Palm. He was very embarrassed when he arrived. It didn't hurt him as much as it hurt me. Doc is usually the first one to the ballpark. He came to my office with a hundred dollar bill, laid it on my desk and said, "It'll never happen again." I said, "You could give me a check." I was thinking, Maybe he would like to deduct it. Doc said, "Nope, cash." I have a sneaky suspicion his Dad had said, "Son, you messed up. You bring the man hard cash."

Despite the fine, which is no big deal, I predict great things from Dwight. He doesn't need an awful lot of coaching. He's one in a million. He is very well adjusted, never nervous. He has fine parents. I can tell he had a very good upbringing. He knows who he is, what he wants to accomplish, and exactly how he's going to do it.

♦ Ron Darling, on the other hand, is a thorn in my side. His control has been terrible. I asked him whether his arm was giving him a problem, and he said it wasn't. I asked him what he thinks about when he's out on the mound.

You have to understand that he's a Yale guy, very intelligent, but for a person that smart he doesn't take the time to analyze his own stuff. I said, "Ron, when you go out there and you see you're missing the plate by a foot, don't you realize your control isn't so hot and that perhaps you would be better off throwing it right down the middle and hoping it will hit the corner, rather than trying to hit the corner and having it end up a foot outside? Why don't you make it simple?"

"You're absolutely right, Dave," he said. "I'm going to keep it simple." Then this dreamy look came over him. "Here's what I'm going to do: I'm going to start the batter out nipping the outside corner, and then I'm going to dive inside with a slider, and I'll throw a hook outside . . ." I was shaking my head, but he didn't stop. "If I cut the fastball away and then throw my biter down and in . . ." Arrrrgh! I want to strangle him by the throat until he's dead. He wants every pitch to be perfect, but he can't see the forest for the trees. His ball moves so much they're not going to hit it! But he's so stubborn. When he puts it all together it's going to be scary, but it looks like it's going to be a slow process with Ronnie.

◆ Sid Fernandez is pitching as if he didn't care. In one game he didn't even back up home on a throw to the plate. He got halfway there and stopped.

After the game I said to my coaches, "I can't live with his lack of effort." And I know he's an intense competitor. That's what I don't understand. Christ, when you're out there, take it to them. To me it seems like Sid's taken a step backward.

After Sid gave up five runs, Mel Stottlemyre, our pitching coach, asked him, "Sidney, what's going on? What's wrong? Get mad. Let's go." He replied, "How do I look?"

Other than the fact that you were taking too much time between pitches, your command was lousy, you were throwing too many balls, and the quality of your pitches wasn't what it should be, other than that, Sidney, you looked great.

You can get by without control in the minors, but not in the big leagues. This raises the distinct possibility he won't make my ballclub.

◆ Another player who's of concern to me is Howard Johnson. Howard has been struggling in the exhibitions, and my third base coach, Bobby Valentine, told me that Howard is troubled by rumors I'm going to send him down to Tidewater. I told Howard, "Vicious rumors do get started, but there is no truth to this one." Howard is struggling because Howard is doing what every young player does when he comes to a new club. He tries to impress everyone with how hard and how far he can hit a ball, and the result is he tries so hard, he screws up.

He was getting into the shower, buck-ass naked, and I yelled at him, "Relax, have some fun, don't try to hit one 590 feet to impress the coaches and me, because you already have. We like your talent. What you should be thinking about is being comfortable with your timing, and hitting the ball hard enough to get a double. We want you ready for opening day."

Howard is very sensitive and quiet, very intense, very much

the competitor. He has an outstanding glove, contrary to what his manager, Sparky Anderson, said about him when he was at Detroit. He's got a good arm, great speed, a nice swing, and his bat potential is very good. He's going to be outstanding. He looked relieved when he left, but I'm sure the only relief in sight will be when he gets a couple of hard base hits.

I was talking about how hard Howard's been pressing with Gary Carter. Gary said, "It's the same way with me. When I came over here, I was nervous. I didn't know what it was going to be like." Then he said, "I really love the way we talk. You communicate with me, and it makes it very easy."

I said, "It can't be any other way."

I don't necessarily want to be known as a "players' manager," but if you treat players the way they would like to be treated, you don't have to go out of your way to make them happy. If they're relaxed and comfortable on the field and in the clubhouse, it's so much easier for them to contribute.

10
CUTDOWN

THE END OF SPRING TRAINING is a tough period for me. I'm in great spirits until I have to start making cuts, sending kids down to the minors. My heart goes out to them, especially the ones with tremendous desire. It makes me moody, and I don't feel good about it because I'm affecting the livelihoods of these players. I feel great pressure because I damn sure better not make a mistake. These decisions weigh heavily. I feel miserable about having to do this. I feel like the grim reaper.

I remember when I was first playing Hank Bauer benched me, which isn't as traumatic as being cut, but I was really down on myself until Sherm Lollar, the longtime catcher, sat me down and told me, "Listen, kid, there are nineteen other teams you can play on. Don't think poorly of yourself if you don't make it here." As a manager, I've tried to pass that philosophy on to players who haven't made the team. There's always another chance.

I was standing with Wes Gardner out in the outfield when I delivered the bad news. Wes is a relief pitcher. I told him, "Right now my relief corps is set. What I'm looking for is a fifth starter.

But that could change. I may realign my pitching staff, move a reliever into the starting rotation, so be ready. You never know." I also told him there were a lot of other clubs he could pitch for. "So keep your chin up and keep going at it." He said, "I will. I knew it was a numbers game, and that I was going to get caught in it."

I cut John Gibbons and Rick Aguilera. Gibbons is the young catcher who would have been my number one last year if he hadn't had his cheek fractured. Gibby needs to go down to Tide-water and play every day. I told him, "You are still the top catching prospect in the organization. You need some at bats. You should think about trying to hit thirty doubles. Don't worry about the homers. Have a great year, and you'll be in the big leagues a long time." Gibby was anxious to go. He wanted to play.

Aguilera, a young pitcher with tremendous talent and poise, also took it well. He said, "Thank you for inviting me." I said, "Thank you for an outstanding performance."

When I told Frank Cashen I wanted to send Sid Fernandez down to Tidewater, he suggested that I keep Sid in long relief and start Eddie Lynch. I said, "We're just postponing the move, and it's not in Sid's best interest." But I told Frank I would ask Sid whether he could pitch long relief while working to get his control back. This is the great relationship Frank and I have. We talk together, make decisions together.

Sid was honest with me. He said, "I can't do anything in the pen." I knew that, but it was refreshing to hear him say it. He said, "I need to work my problem out. Mel can't help me and neither can John Cumberland at Tidewater. I need to solve this for myself, and I need to do it by pitching." Which he will do at Tidewater.

Sid has shown much more maturity this year, and this time I'm sure he will straighten himself out and get it right. Starting at Tidewater will not destroy this kid's competitive spirit. I know he'll be back.

I asked my coaches their opinions on twenty-four-year-old re-lief pitcher Roger McDowell. Everyone was in favor of keeping him, and Frank said I could. Promoting McDowell meant send-ing Calvin Schiraldi and Bill Latham down.

I went into the clubhouse where, coincidentally, McDowell,

Latham, and Schiraldi were playing cards together. I told the three pitchers that one at a time I wanted to talk to them in my office. They all knew what I wanted to see them about. I said, "I'll take you first, Latham."

He came in, and I handed him the bad news. I told him how well he had pitched and how impressive he was. I said, "I'm looking for a fifth starter, and there's a good chance I'll be looking to Tidewater. You had a great spring, and you came close to making it." He was clearly disappointed, but he took it fine. He thanked me and said he enjoyed the spring and the opportunity to pitch.

I came back out and said, "Okay, who's next?" Evidently Schiraldi and McDowell had cut the cards to see who was next. McDowell had won. Schiraldi got up. I said, "Come in, Calvin." He came into my office. I said, "You had better command than some of my starting four pitchers."

He said, "I think so too."

I said, "You had a good spring, and you're getting better all the time, and I'm going to be looking for a fifth starter, and it could come from Tidewater." And I told him I was sending him down. He had figured he was going. He was just waiting to hear me say it.

Then I called in McDowell. He had a scared look on his face. I didn't want to prolong the suspense. As soon as he came through the door, I said, "Congratulations, you've made my club."

McDowell has earned it. He's pitched well all spring. I'm going to have to pamper him, not use him too much, because he was out all last year with a bad arm. It's a gamble, his coming from Double A, but it's an educated gamble. The coaches believe he should be on the ballclub and so do the players, which makes my decision so much easier. On a pennant-contending ballclub the manager should make decisions that the players agree with.

Roger said to me, "It's no April fool, is it?" It was the first of April.

I said, "No, you made the club."

He lit up like a Christmas tree. So did I. It was still a rough, rough day.

11

AGGRAVATION

OF ALL THE THINGS that can turn a manager gray overnight, injuries are at the top of the list. Some injuries happen right in front of you: a collision on the field, a batter getting hit by a pitch. But most injuries, especially to arms, simply appear as if by black magic. I hate surprises. When I plan, I expect everything to go according to my plan.

When a player is hurt, he may have to be shelved for a while, and sometimes you have no way of knowing when he'll return. The longer you have to wait the harder it wears on you. Injuries may be part of the game, but they aren't a very nice part.

During the final days of spring training third baseman Ray Knight was practicing his throws at third when his elbow locked. Ray immediately went to see the team doctor, who said Ray has bone chips. The doctor said Ray could only straighten his elbow 155 degrees, and as a cure he recommended several days rest.

When I heard about the bone chips I was confused and angry. Over the winter Ray had had arthroscopic surgery on his shoulder. Why wasn't his elbow taken care of then? I called Frank

Cashen, saying, "Rather than have this problem all year long, we ought to call Dr. Andrews, who did the surgery on his shoulder, and ask him if he were to operate on his elbow, how long Ray would be out." I told Frank, "Let's call right now, because if it's only going to be two or three weeks, let's operate on it now. We've got a week to go in the spring and a lot of days off early in the season, and I won't have to worry about it for the rest of the year."

When I got back to the clubhouse Ray Knight had already called Dr. Andrews, who said if he were to operate he'd only be out two weeks. I went back to Frank. "Ray's doctor says he'll only be out two weeks. Let's do it now. Let's get it done." Frank agreed, and Ray flew to Atlanta for the operation.

The other aspect of the job that ages managers is the attention and pressure of the media. No one on earth is under greater scrutiny or has to put up with more criticism than a baseball manager. Also, sports doesn't get covered like most news events. There is more opinion on the sports pages than anywhere else in the newspaper. I've never met a sportswriter who didn't have a strong opinion about something. Sports sells newspapers, and especially in New York the sportswriters are always looking for a controversial angle in order to sell papers.

I thought it was funny: All winter long the New York writers had been stressing how great a chance we have to win this year. For months they built their stories around the notion that we were going to be infallible, that we would never lose a game.

We opened our exhibition season against the Phillies and lost. I picked up the paper the next day, and the story began, "From a winter of fantasy to the harsh, grim truth of reality . . ."

A day later we split our squad, and half our team went up against Tom Seaver and the White Sox. We won 2–1. To the New York media it was a big win. In reality, it meant nothing, just as our loss to the Phillies meant nothing. What happens in New York is that too much is made out of nothing, particularly in the spring, when all I really care about is getting my players into shape.

Regardless of what kind of squad I show up with, the New York media write it like it's the whole team, and if we lose, trumpet it as a sign of bad things to come. They'll write, "The

Mets just aren't that good." What they should be writing is, "The game today didn't mean a thing."

What is most dangerous about the media is that the most innocuous thing you say can get you in trouble. Over the winter Frank Cashen and I were discussing what moves to make with respect to our roster. I was in favor of releasing Ron Hodges. He was my third catcher, and I knew Frank Cashen was uncomfortable paying him a $300,000 salary when he was not strong enough offensively or defensively to be the number two.

But in doing that, I also felt we had to keep John Stearns. I knew he was making $400,000 for two years and hadn't played much because of injuries. "I would still like to have a veteran catcher," I said to Frank. "John showed me he was healthy for the last month of the season. Let's give him a twenty-percent cut and keep him."

I knew Johnny would have liked to come back, because he felt we had something going here. He would have been good on the club. He's a competitor. He can play third, first, doesn't strike out, and he can get out in front of a fastball. I would really have liked to keep him.

Frank disagreed. He chose to let Stearns become a free agent, and also against my urging, decided not to protect Rusty Staub, figuring no one else would pick up a forty-year-old pinch hitter.

I told Frank, "There aren't many people who can come off the bench and hit a fastball, pull it, and drive it in the gaps." I felt that if I needed a pinch hitter to make contact, hit the ball hard against the hard-throwing right-handers—and there are a lot of them—the man I wanted was Rusty. And I wanted him badly.

Frank decided instead to let Rusty declare himself a free agent and to protect one of our young players, the same thing he did with Tom Seaver. Frank felt that Rusty would not be claimed, because he was forty and only a pinch hitter, a luxury for most teams. It turned out he was right, and we were able to re-sign him after all. But I didn't know that then.

When the season was over, the reporters asked me what I hoped to see happen. "I'd like to keep Stearns and Staub for next year," I told them, "because they would add to what I'm trying to create."

Later, when Frank announced his decision not to protect Rusty and Stearns, the reporters wrote that there was dissension between Frank and me. Frank, who is very sensitive, was upset. He told me, "I don't want you saying things where you and I are in disagreement. We can disagree in private, but not in public."

I said, "Frank, I'm not disagreeing. You're making the decisions. And once you do, I'll do everything in my power not to create a problem between you and me. Because there aren't any. Besides," I said, "a little controversy sells newspapers." I laughed. He didn't. I didn't need the newspapers making trouble out of nothing.

Late in spring training I found myself in a similar situation, only this time it was much worse. On the day Ray Knight flew down to Georgia to be examined by Dr. Andrews in preparation for possible surgery, we had a day off, so I drove across the state of Florida to my home in Orlando to be with my family.

While at home, Frank and I talked on the phone about trading Jose Oquendo to St. Louis for Argenis Salazar, whom we had originally tried to get from Montreal in the Carter trade and who had ended up in a free agent compensation draft with St. Louis.

During our discussion I asked him the result of Ray's examination and what the instructions were going to be from the doctor. I was counting on somebody calling me and telling me what the test showed. Nobody called.

That night I went to bed about ten-thirty, tossing and turning, worrying about Ray and about the ballclub. After about two hours of lying there, staring at the ceiling, I told my wife, Mary Nan, "I'm going to get up and go to Tampa. If I stay here, I'll be awake until early into the morning, and I'll be shot for the day. A lot of things are going to be happening, and I don't want to have to rush to get to the ballpark."

In the dark I drove back across the state to St. Pete, and I got to the park around two-thirty in the morning, lay down and woke up around six. I still didn't know what had happened to Ray Knight. Frank Cashen was on the road in his car heading north, and nobody from the front office had called to tell me whether Ray was going to be operated on or not.

Around nine I finally saw Joe McIlvaine, Frank's assistant. "Are they going to operate or not, for Christ sake?" Mac said, "Yeah, they're operating this morning." I said, "What was the deal? Do we have any say in the operation?" I always want to have communication with the doctors, because you don't want them going ahead deciding in the middle of the operation that they want to do some additional surgery that might put him out for the year.

I said, "Did they use Dr. Parkes's X rays or did they take their own? Did Dr. Andrews make another examination, or what?" I was picturing in my mind getting the news that as a result of the operation Ray would be lost for the season.

Mac didn't have any answers. I said, "What time this morning are they operating?" He didn't know that either. I was acting too much like a mother hen. But it really worried me. Our doctors were handling it with Ray's doctors, but no club official was dealing with the surgeon. That concerned me.

Later I found out they had operated at three in the afternoon, that they had taken out three chips, and that Ray would be out, not two to three weeks, but three to six weeks.

The situation created two problems for me. Number one, not knowing any of the details added to my worry, and number two, if anybody from the press had asked me about it, I would have sounded like an idiot, because I didn't know, and I would have had to admit I didn't know. It was uncomfortable. Knowing is a lot better than not knowing. If you know, you don't have to worry. You can turn the page.

After getting nowhere with Joe Mac, I got to the ballpark for the game, and I saw Dave Cochrane walking around all upset. Dave is a switch-hitting young infielder we're high on who doesn't really have a position, so when we sent him down to Tidewater, Frank, Joe, and I decided he ought to play shortstop. Because that's what he wants to do. He sees himself as another Cal Ripken. Before I sent him down I told him, "Go down there and play shortstop, and if you do well, you'll come back up."

It remains to be seen whether or not he's ever going to be a shortstop, but it's the best position for the kid to play, because if he can play shortstop, he can play all the other positions. The main thing is for him to get a lot of experience in the field.

Cochrane came over to me, and the reason he was walking around so impatiently was that he wanted to talk to somebody, because for the last ten days he's been DHing. Now the worst thing you can do to a young kid who doesn't have a position is make him a designated hitter, because that way he never gets one. But Steve Schryver, the minor league director, decided on his own to make Cochrane a DH!

I immediately called Schryver. He said, "Nobody down here thinks he can play shortstop, so we're going to DH him." "Well, the National League doesn't have a DH," I said. "What are we doing, training ballplayers to trade them?"

I was also hot because I was embarrassed. If I tell a guy, "Go down and play shortstop, and if you do well, we'll bring you back," and then when he gets down there he finds himself DHing, then I've lost all credibility. Who's going to believe me the next time I send a kid down and tell him something? He'll say, "That Johnson, he doesn't know anything!" I can't live with that. Life is too short, and this game means too much to me. I have an obligation to Nelson Doubleday, Fred Wilpon, and Frank Cashen, and to the people of New York City to want this organization to run as efficiently and as well by communication as possible. And if that is not possible, then I will only be in this game a very short time with the New York Mets.

Then I was hit with two more problems, all on the same day. Ron Gardenhire came up with back spasms, and this was right after we traded Jose Oquendo to the Cardinals. If I had known about the back spasms, I might not have traded Oquendo.

And I got into another communications problem.

When I talked to Frank from home, he asked me if I wanted Argenis Salazar, whom we got for Oquendo, to come to Miller Huggins Field and train with the regulars. I said, "No, I've made my cuts. I'm through with picking the regulars. Please send him directly to Payson Field and the minor leaguers. If you want me to talk to him and tell him why he's my insurance in the minor leagues, I'll gladly make the trip to Payson Field and tell him. But please, don't have him show up at Miller Huggins Field and start putting on a uniform."

When I got through talking with Cochrane and convincing him that he was going to be playing shortstop at Tidewater, I looked up, and there was Salazar! And he was putting on a Mets uniform! Gardenhire was lying on the table with muscle spasms and hot flashes shooting down his leg, and I was thinking to myself, What is going on here? I had told Frank I didn't want Salazar coming over and putting on a uniform. What was I doing, talking for my health?

I was mad. Burning. Nobody was telling me anything, and people were unilaterally changing our plans. I went out onto the field, and I was met by a group of writers. I started holding court. I didn't mention names. All I said was, "Something's wrong here. Somewhere along the line in the chain of command there are some links missing." But I made sure to add, "Frank Cashen and I have a great relationship, and it could not be better." I was very, very specific about this.

The next day was one of the worst in my whole life. Ol' DJ got his butt chewed out by Frank Cashen. Frank was so mad he didn't want to talk to me at first. He told me, "You've insulted me in print. You're way off base. I don't like it, and I feel it wasn't called for."

Frank felt that I betrayed him. I did not betray him. I made a point with the writers to say, "I couldn't have a better relationship with a boss than I do with Frank Cashen." But that was not reported. Instead, to beef up the story, the reporters from the *Post* and the *News* twisted what I said. The *News* headline read, JOHNSON RIPS CASHEN. I apologized to Frank since, based on what they wrote, he had every right to jump me.

Two other writers, Dan Castellano and Marty Noble, understood what I was saying and printed what I said accurately. I told Dan, "I learned a lesson. I'll never again talk to the press when I'm mad. It's too dangerous. They twist what you say."

I don't mind if they rip me, but when they start undermining my relationship with my players or with Frank Cashen by taking things out of context or reading in what they want to or putting emphasis on what they want to write and not what I say and how I say it, then I'm very, very distressed.

I learned another valuable lesson as well: Don't ever be so sensitive that you commit your total being to doing what's right for the organization, because it hurts you when you do what you think is right and get jumped for it. Now maybe I didn't handle it properly by getting upset, but I honestly believe that things cannot continue like this if we are to have a championship organization. All I want is for our organization to work as one. I want us to be the best we can be, and it has to go from the top to the bottom. It has to work in harmony.

And being chastised by my boss and good friend, Frank

Cashen, hurts more than I can say. Because I'm too sensitive. Once I commit all my energy toward accomplishing something for somebody, in this case for Nelson Doubleday, Frank Cashen, and the New York Mets, that commitment has to be total. Or not at all.

I hardly slept a wink worrying about losing the credibility I had built up with Frank and harming my great relationship with him. I am very happy with my ballclub. I have my team just where I want it. I just hope Frank will kiss and make up with me.

12
OPENING

I HAVE NEVER started a season as manager when I wasn't optimistic about my chances, and this year is no exception. By nature I'm optimistic, but I'm not a dreamer.

On paper, I can't see how anybody can beat us. I don't think any team has a player with the potential of a Strawberry, the finesse of a Keith Hernandez, a catcher as good as Gary Carter, a runner with the electrifying speed of a Mookie, or an old slugging veteran like Foster. In addition we have Dwight Gooden, who's going to be the game's best of all time, plus some gutty side performers and Jesse Orosco in the bullpen.

For the fans there's going to be somebody for everybody, more so than any other team I've ever been associated with.

We opened the season winning eight out of our first nine. In our season opener, in front of 48,000 chilly fans, Dwight started and was protecting a three-run lead into the top of the seventh inning when he allowed two quick hits, a check-swing single by the Cardinals' Andy Van Slyke and then another single by Ozzie Smith. I decided to take him out. It was very cold, and I didn't want to push him. The game is not nearly as important to me as Dwight Gooden is.

Doug Sisk came in and got two quick ground balls, and we could have been out of the inning without damage, but Tommy Herr singled in the two runners. Doug got the Cards easily in the eighth, but in the ninth he reverted to last year's form, allowing a hit, a hit batter, and another single by Herr to load the bases with one out. I popped my first Rolaids of the year as Terry Pendleton, their third baseman, came up to the plate with the winning runs on base. I nervously kept my composure and remained in the dugout. I was leaving it up to Doug. I figured a double-play ball, and we would have our win. Pendleton struck out. Doug was one out away. Jack Clark was the batter.

Over the winter the Cards had acquired Clark, a premier power hitter, from the San Francisco Giants, who over the years seem to have traded most of their best players away. I had confidence in Doug. It was a perfect matchup, righty against righty, a free swinger against a sinkerball pitcher. and I was figuring we'd get out of it, but Sisk went to three-and-one on Clark and then walked him, tying the score. Darrell Porter, a lefty, was the next batter. Grimly, I went out and brought in Jesse Orosco, who got the final out. Opening day, and we're playing extra innings.

In the bottom of the tenth Gary Carter went up to the plate with one out. During the game Gary had had his problems. He allowed a passed ball, dropped a fouled third strike, gave up a stolen base to Joaquin Andujar, the pitcher, and also was hit by a pitch. He came over to me and said, "This isn't a very auspicious opening for me." We laughed. I said, "Gar, don't worry about it. Things'll get better." Sure enough, things got better.

The pitcher was Neil Allen, a high-ball, fastball pitcher. Allen had gotten out of a bases-loaded jam in the ninth and was throwing hard. He threw a fastball by Gary for a strike and then he tried to break a curve on the outside part of the plate. Carter went down and got it, and I can still hear the crack of the bat. There's a certain sound when you know it's going out. It resounds. For us it was a storybook ending. The new star hit a home run to win the first game for the home folks.

It was nice for the New York Mets fans to see him produce. Gary didn't have to impress me, or his teammates, but this win surely broke the ice with the fans, who are skeptics by nature, especially in New York. Now they'll say, "He's worth it. We could have given Montreal ten players for that guy."

The second game was also extra innings. Darling gave up one run through seven, normally good enough to win, except that John Tudor only allowed one unearned run through nine. I brought Jesse in to finish them off, and he would have, except we couldn't do anything with Tudor, and I had to use Sisk in the tenth to get the final out.

I was doing everything within my power to keep my young rookie, Roger McDowell, from having to come into a 1–1 game in the eleventh inning. I wanted very badly to break the ice a little easier for him. But I couldn't. I needed him, and so I put him out there, and all McDowell did was retire the meat of the St. Louis lineup—Clark, Porter, and Pendleton. He struck out Pendleton.

In our half of the eleventh, Keith Hernandez led off with a single off the left-hander, Andy Hassler. Whitey Herzog didn't want Hassler to pitch to the right-handed Carter, so he brought in Neil Allen again. Allen ran the count to three-and-two, and on the next pitch I had Keith running, and Carter fouled it off. Three times I ran Keith, and three times Gary fouled it off, until finally Gary hit a shot off the glove of third baseman Art Howe. Because he was running, Keith came around to third. Herzog then walked George Foster intentionally to load the bases.

My scheduled batter was rookie John Christensen, a righty. I needed a lefty against Allen, and I went with Danny Heep, a much-improved player this year. From where I was standing, it looked like all Allen was throwing was fastballs. Heep took three of them for balls and swung at two of them for strikes, and then Allen fired in another fastball, which Danny swung at and fouled back. Allen wound up and again let fly, another fastball, chest high, a ball, ball four, scoring Keith and giving us and McDowell the victory.

To me, Neil Allen is not a pitcher. To me, a pitcher is someone who can spot a fastball for a strike and throw a curveball over when he's behind. Neil Allen can't do either of those things. He's a thrower who relies on outstanding speed to get by. I still can't figure out why Whitey Herzog would have traded us Keith Hernandez for Allen. Oh, Keith does a couple little things that might annoy some managers. Keith has his own pace running down to first base on a hit, and he will never bust, even on a close play. Also, Keith isn't fond of taking infield practice, though I have asked him to do it early in the season so he and the other infielders become proficient working together. I told him, "It's like dancing with a girl. The only way to become a good dance team is to practice, otherwise you step on each other's toes." Keith has agreed to do that for me.

Keith likes to do the daily crossword puzzle before the game. So what? I read books. He does crossword puzzles. Supposedly, Whitey said Keith was traded because he concentrated too much on puzzles and not enough on baseball. I find that hard to believe. I know Whitey, and I doubt that he would be so intolerant over something so petty.

I know there was talk Keith was involved in drugs, but I have seen no evidence since he joined us. All I know is that Keith Hernandez is a fine man, hits over .300, is a great first baseman, and he will give you everything he's got, day in and day out.

We won the third game of the season 1–0, beating Cincinnati. Bruce Berenyi, whom we got from the Reds last year, pitched seven strong innings and got the win. Bruce has been criticized by the press for not being a complete-game pitcher, but I personally don't care. If I can get seven good innings out of him, or any of my starting pitchers, I'm satisfied. I'll take that, gladly. And Bruce is consistent doing that.

Bruce is a tough, tough cookie. Every time he goes out to pitch, he's in pain. He has an inflamed shoulder that was bothering him in the spring, and it's worse now. I've been trying hard to watch Bruce very closely, since he wouldn't tell me even if his arm were falling off. I suspect that somewhere along the line he's going to have to have an operation, but until that time I'm going to send him out there until he tells me, "No más." He's such a hard-ass, I have no alternative. As long as he says he can pitch, he's going to pitch.

The only run of the game was scored on a home run by Mr. Carter. It was our third one-run game, and after three games the job has taken its toll on my digestive tract. Which Doug Sisk does nothing to relieve. He gives me cardiac arrest every time he comes in to pitch, but I go and get my Rolaids, chew up four of them real quick, and wait for him to walk the first batter he faces.

I brought Sisk in to pitch the eighth, and he proceeded to walk the leadoff batter, Dave Concepcion, on four pitches. The next batter, Ron Oester, then grounded into a double play, short to second to first. Sisk's ball is like a slippery eel. It goes this way and that, sails up and down. He throws hard and erratic, and the batters more often than not hit it into the ground, and after a whole year of having to live with Sisk, I just assume that he's going to walk the first batter and throw a double-play ball to the second. The third batter in the eighth, Eddie Milner, singled to center. I took another Rolaids. Sisk then got a fly ball to end the inning.

In the ninth Dougie fooled me, striking out Eric Davis, but then the second batter, Pete Rose, hit a single up the middle, and the Reds again had the tying run on base with Dave Parker coming to the plate. Pete, who is managing the Reds this year, sent Gary Redus, a speedster, out to run for him. Even though Parker bats left-handed, I decided to leave Sisk in. Sisk's most effective pitch sinks, and he is just as effective against lefties as righties. Also, Cesar Cedeno was up next, and I didn't want to bring the left-handed Jesse in, only to have him face the right-handed Cedeno.

Parker swung, and he hit the ball deep into the right field gap, and the only chance we had was if Darryl Strawberry could catch up to it. Darryl came racing in toward center, and as the ball began to descend, he reached out with his gloved right hand and threw himself outstretched at the ball, landing hard on the turf with the ball in his glove, making a diving catch to save the game. Cedeno grounded out, and we'd won another laugher.

A manager can tell when a player's grinding, giving all out, totally concentrating on getting the job done. And you can also tell when the guy's just going through the motions. There were times last year when Darryl was just going through the motions. Not this year.

Darryl is also much more open to communication this year, even though he and I both know we don't need a lot of conversation. To communicate you don't necessarily have to have conversation. A player goes by you, and as he's getting ready to go out onto the field, you can hit him on the arm or tap him on the ass, or say, "Have a good one." Often that's enough.

Darryl knows that I care about him, even though I kept taking his money last year. He knows I admire his talents and that I'm counting on him. In St. Pete I told him, "Darryl, you're my security blanket. If you play well, I'll be around. If you don't, I'll be gone."

He said, "Skip, you'll be around a long time."

Our fourth straight win was another nail biter. The Reds scored a run early on two doubles off Eddie Lynch, whom I've brought from the pen to be one of my starters, and we got it back when Eric Davis dropped an easy fly ball in center field. We haven't exactly been hitting the cover off the ball, but our pitching has been solid, and after I took Eddie out after seven, I again brought in my bubble gum–chewing rookie, McDowell.

The score was tied 1–1 when Darryl got up to lead off the bottom half of the ninth for us. John Franco, who is left-handed, was on the mound for the Reds, a tough matchup for the left-handed Strawberry. As I said, Darryl has been concentrating with every at bat, which means that if a pitcher should make a mistake, Darryl will take advantage. Franco threw a fastball that was up in the strike zone, and Darryl got all of it, lining it just over the wall in right, giving McDowell his second win in his second game.

Though Darryl still has a tendency to uppercut too much, to dip and try to lift the ball, he is working to curb his bad habits at the plate. When he stays level and drives the ball, it's a most awesome thing. He can hit it out of any part of the park. And what's really scary is that when he gets all of it, the ball goes nineteen rows deep. Someday, I predict, he will hit the longest home run ever hit.

Pete Rose apparently is going to play himself at first base. Pete was the first guy who made a lot of money hitting nothing but singles. I admire him, but he's not going to have it easy, both playing and managing.

Pete is now eighty-nine hits short of Ty Cobb's record for most hits in a career. I wonder if he is going to be able to put his team before his personal goals. If the Reds stay down in the standings, Pete really shouldn't play much. He should be testing the rookies, finding out about the Reduses, the Walkers, kids like Eric Davis. Whether he will or not remains to be seen. It could be a very uncomfortable situation for the Reds organization.

Our fifth win in a row was, finally, a piece of cake. Dwight threw a shutout, struck out ten, and we won 4–0.

Somebody in the publicity department decided it would be fun to hand out big cardboard K's to every fan who showed up for the ballgame. It was billed as "K" Day, and every time Dwight would get two strikes on the batter, a zillion big red K's went waving around the ballpark. I thought the whole idea was bush. I don't like the added pressure being put on Dwight to go for strikeouts, and I don't like singling Dwight out for that kind of fan attention. Dwight knows the fans want him to strike out twenty batters a game, but I would hate to see him blow out his arm just to please them.

In any case Dwight Gooden is simply the best pitcher in baseball. At the start of the season I told Gary that I wanted him to be the boss in back of the plate. I told him, "When you call a sign, I want you to reinforce it, because you have a better idea than they do. Anybody, Darling, Berenyi, Lynch." I said, "Anybody, that is, but Doc. 'Cause I want to tell you about Doc. If he wants to throw a pitch, even if you think it's the wrong pitch, it's the right pitch. Doc'll make it right. So lean with him. With the other guys, push for what you want. But not with Doc."

Dwight is very inquisitive about everything. He'll ask Gary or Keith or somebody else about a pitcher, "What's he like to hit?" He pays attention. He's a student.

Doc, like most pitchers, thinks he's a great hitter. Before one game he said to me, "The last start I hit a ball to the wall. I just missed hitting it out." I said, "You hit it as good as you can." He said, "No, I hit it about five inches down the label. I didn't get it on the sweet spot." He said, "If I had, it would have been upperdeck." He talks like that.

Doc and Darryl are good friends. Doc has been a good influence on Darryl. They were standing by the batting cage, and I overheard their conversation—Doc was giving Darryl batting tips! Doc said, "Let me tell you your problem. You're wrapping that bat around your ear." Darryl couldn't believe it. He said, "Now what the hell do you know about batting?"

After we brought Doc up last year, I said to Joe McIlvaine, "You're worried about rushing him? You held him back a year. He should have been up here winning ten games when he was seventeen!"

My biggest criticism of Dwight is that he eats too much. He'll eat a big meal at home, come to the ballpark, order a Big Mac, and eat that too. And after the game, he'll devour a spread that was supposed to be for all the players.

Frank Cashen came by my office before we were scheduled to go on the road, and I asked him if he was going on the trip. He said, "Yeah, because the last time I left you on your own, you ripped the front office." I'm glad he can laugh about it. Frank has one quality I really admire. He can get angry, but he doesn't hold grudges. He knows I'm outspoken and that we're going to disagree about things, but he's smart enough not to try to squelch those characteristics, like some general managers try to do. Not to mention some owners.

With a 5–0 record, things were going smoothly indeed. Too smoothly. If you manage long enough, you know that some sort of crisis is never far off. In our sixth game, I had a one-player revolt on my hands.

We flew to Pittsburgh to begin a nine-game road trip. I couldn't use the guy I really wanted to pitch, Calvin Schiraldi, a right-hander, because of a rule I wasn't familiar with. Calvin was still at Tidewater, and I wanted to call him back up, only to discover that if you send a player down to the minors, apparently you have to wait ten days to recall him, and Calvin's ten days weren't up yet.

So I called up Bill Latham, and he did a decent enough job, holding the Pirates to one run when in the fourth he walked Tony Pena. He went to a three-and-oh count on Tim Foli, and so I had him walk Foli intentionally with the idea that I would bring Doug Sisk into the game to pitch to the Pirate pitcher, Mike Bielecki. I could see that Latham was tiring, and I needed relief.

I had instructed the bullpen, "Let me know when Sisk is ready," and I was waiting by my phone in the dugout for the call, which didn't come. I had no choice but to leave Latham in the game. Latham walked Bielecki to load the bases. Still no word from Sisk. Latham went to two-and-one on Bill Almon, the short-stop, when finally the phone rang with the call that Sisk was ready.

I slammed the phone down, because I couldn't very well bring Sisk into the game with a two-and-one count and the bases loaded, not as wild as Doug is. So I waited. Almon singled in two runs, and by then it was too late. Bielecki and John Candelaria shut us out the rest of the way, and we suffered our first defeat.

After the game, I went up to Sisk to ask him what the hell was going on out in the pen. "Why weren't you ready?" I wanted to know. "I was ready," he said, "but nobody asked me."

Well, a pitcher doesn't need to be asked. You get up to throw, and when you're ready, you say, "I'm ready." Sisk knows that. The way I see it, Sisk didn't signal because he didn't want to come into the game in the fifth inning. Last year he was a short reliever and in his eyes coming in sooner than the eighth inning is a demotion.

I should be angry with Doug, because his little rebellion probably cost us a ballgame, but I'm not, though I'm not sure why. Perhaps it was my fault. My communication with Doug perhaps has not been as good as it should have been.

In the papers the next day, Doug said, "I wish I knew what my role is." It's my job to make it clear.

Part of the problem with my determining exactly what his role will be is that it's going to take a little time to do that. It's going to depend on how well Doug continues to pitch. It depends on what McDowell can do. And of course, it also depends on Jesse.

The next day we scored two runs, but Ron Darling and Jesse gave up just one hit, and we won the game 2–1. Still, it was another Rolaids game. Ronnie pitched seven innings of shutout ball, but in the eighth he walked the first two batters and he looked like he was tired, so I brought in Jesse. Jesse proceeded to walk Lee Mazzilli to load the bases with nobody out, giving me acute indigestion.

I played the infield at double-play depth. Jesse's best pitch is a wicked slider that makes batters hit the ball on the ground, and I was hoping he could get us out of it. The next batter, Johnny Ray, popped out to shallow center. One out. I still couldn't relax, because Bill Madlock, who has led the league in hitting a few times, was the hitter. He's a smart hitter, and I knew he didn't want to hit into a double play, so I called for my third baseman, Howard Johnson, to move in to protect against a bunt.

Jesse threw, and Madlock hit a smash down the third-base line. If the ball got past Howard Johnson, it was in the corner, and two, probably three runners would score. But Howard dived toward the bag, knocked the ball down, picked it up, stepped on third for the force, and fired a strike to first, just barely missing Madlock for the double play as Almon scored the tying run. Jesse retired George Hendrick, and we went into the ninth.

With John Candelaria, a tough, tough pitcher, on the mound, Mookie Wilson led off by belting a triple into the left-center field gap. We needed a fly ball to score him, and Keith Hernandez, who's the best there is at scoring a runner from third with less than two outs, hit a fly ball to deep center, and Mookie scored easily. Jesse got them one, two, three in the ninth, and we won another one-run game.

That play Howard made at third tells me a great deal about him. It tells me that for what Sparky Anderson said about him, he's an outstanding fielder. He's been a Gold Glove for me.

I knew from day one of spring training from watching Howard field ground balls that he has good, soft hands. My guess is that Sparky put too much pressure on him by criticizing his defense, saying he couldn't handle the pressure. Sparky is one of those managers who will take a young player out, regardless of how it makes the kid feel about himself. Managers like that aren't concerned about their players feeling good about themselves. They only care about winning the game. Earl Weaver was like that too.

To Earl his stat sheet was God. It was the one major philosophical gripe I had with Earl. He abused his statistics. In other aspects of his managing, like strategy and how he used his pitchers, Earl was consistent. But when it came to batting, his stat sheet determined who hit. If his statistics said you shouldn't play, you didn't play. He didn't believe in the hot hand. Donny

Baylor would go three for four one game, and the next game Earl would have a stat saying he was two for ten against a certain pitcher, and Earl wouldn't play him. It used to drive Baylor nuts. Earl's stats were more important to him than the feelings of his players. He couldn't have cared less about how we felt. He prided himself on moving his players around like chess pieces.

Earl liked to be the puppeteer, and he expected his puppets to perform on demand. If he sent you up to hit, he expected you to produce, and he wasn't concerned about your preparation. He'd yell, "Grab a bat and hit," and you'd better do it. He would make us all so angry, but he was very successful, and who can argue with success?

I remember one time it was late in the game with the score tied, the bases loaded, and two outs. I was scheduled to hit and Earl whistled me back. He sent up Tom Shopay for me. He said to Shopay, "I want you to go up there and get a base on balls." He didn't want me to hit, and he didn't want Shopay to hit either. He wanted Shopay to get a walk! And Shopay did. And we won the game. But that was Earl.

I use a stat sheet too, but only if I feel a player needs a rest. In other words, if one of my players is tired, it makes more sense to rest him against a pitcher he has trouble hitting than against a pitcher he hits regularly. If he isn't tired, I leave him in.

I want my players under the least amount of strain possible. If I'm not going to start a player the next day, I always tell him. That way he can relax a bit, stay up late, eat a big meal, have some fun, instead of working himself up for a game he isn't going to play.

If your players always know what you expect, they produce more. I don't want a player fighting me. Let him fight the other team.

It's just not in the best interest of a player's future for a manager to be overly critical. With a young player you need to be even more consistent and show even more confidence in his ability, and you show that by the way you use him. I can tell a player, "You're going to be a great fielder," but if I keep yanking him in the eighth or ninth inning every day, it's going to be hard for him to believe that.

Howard Johnson knows that he's going to be platooning with

Ray Knight this year. He knows he's going to be batting mostly against right-handed pitchers, even though he's a switch hitter. But that doesn't mean I've given up on his hitting from the right side. Howard's been worried. He's upset that he hasn't been swinging well righty against left-handed pitching. I told him, "I still want you to keep working on your right-handed hitting. You have great tools, and you're going to be a great third baseman for me for a long time." He was all grins, and he promised that he'd keep working hard at it.

John Candelaria at one time was a fine starter, but Pirate manager Chuck Tanner has made him a reliever, and Candy has performed excellently, even though he has indicated he would like to leave the Pirates. I can see why Chuck would move Candy into the pen. He has a rubber arm. He can throw every other day, even every day. Tanner feels he has five quality starters whom he's comfortable with, and when you have five guys like that, you can afford to take a starter and put him in the pen. Which is why I never went along when the Yankees decided to make Dave Righetti a reliever. Yogi didn't have enough starting pitching to do that, and over the course of the season, it's only going to hurt them. They'll lose all those starts he would have gotten, and in the end Righetti's never going to be in very many save situations because the starters will end up collapsing. By the time they get Righetti in the game they'll be way behind.

The finale at Pittsburgh gave us seven wins in eight games, but emotionally it was one of our toughest days.

It started off before the game when Bobby Valentine came into my office to say that Rafael Santana's agent had called him. Bobby is my infield as well as my third base coach. The last couple of days I had opted to rest Santana, who had played so well in spring training that he took over Gardenhire's starting spot when Gardy went down with back spasms. I told Raffy, "I'm going to play Ron Gardenhire the next couple days because I want to keep Gardy sharp. Don't worry about it." Now Bobby said, "Raffy's agent is all upset and wants to know what's going on." I said, "Bobby, tell his agent that no, that isn't the case at all, that Raffy is still my number one shortstop, that I just wanted to give him a rest and keep Gardenhire sharp."

In the final Pittsburgh game, Darryl and Santana hit home runs to stake Berenyi to a seven-run lead going into the bottom of the fifth. I knew from the start Bruce was going to struggle because he was forcing the ball and wasn't getting his breaking ball over. Also, he's had trouble with the Pirates in the past.

Even so, we were going into the fifth leading 8–1, and Bruce proceeded to walk Tim Foli, the leadoff batter, and got a couple of outs that moved Foli to third. He was an out away from getting out of the inning when he walked George Hendrick and threw a wild pitch that let Hendrick get to second. Jason Thompson was the batter, and Bruce was trying to pitch to him carefully with first base open. Thompson lined a single to right to score two runs, and then it was 8–3. He walked Tony Pena and gave up a short single to left by Marvell Wynne to load the bases. I was squirming in the dugout, rooting for Bruce to get the next batter, who was Sixto Lezcano. Bruce needed only one out to have pitched five full innings and to be credited with the win. As manager, one of my basic philosophies is to try as hard as humanly possible to let a pitcher finish the fifth inning. To me, sometimes it's even preferable to lose the game than to give up on a pitcher too soon. I may take flak from the writers who will ask me, "Why didn't you take him out when he was struggling?" but I want to give him every chance to pick up the victory.

Having said that, I skated right onto thin ice with Bruce. I had given him several opportunities to get out of the inning, but he walked Lezcano to bring in the fourth Pirate run, and now the tying run was coming to the plate. I had to hook him, even though I didn't want to, and I had to bring in Doug Sisk, even though he didn't want to pitch this early in the game. My hope was that the prospect of an easy win would outweigh whatever problems he had about coming in in the fifth. I was handing Doug a plum. All Doug had to do was get one out and the win was his. Dougie came in, got Bill Almon to bounce out, and the inning was over.

In the next inning Doug gave up two runs, making the score 9–6. Then in the ninth he allowed a leadoff single to Tony Pena. That was as far as I wanted to go. Doug had done his job. He'd gotten me to Jesse. Jesse came in and struck out the side, ending the game.

It wasn't very pretty, but it was a win for Doug. I hope this erases any fear in his mind that I'm going to cost him money by bringing him into a game too early.

The next day I opened the papers. Again Doug was complaining about having to pitch long relief. "Listen, Doug," I said, "the reason I'm changing your role is that I have nine pitchers, including Roger McDowell, who I'm babying. As a result, I'm going to bring you in an inning earlier. Instead of the seventh inning, I'm going to bring you in in the sixth. In extenuating circumstances, I may bring you in with a lead to protect it even before the fifth inning."

"I'm not complaining," Doug said. "The quotes in the paper were taken out of context. I was just speaking off the top of my head and not thinking anything would be made out of it."

I'll accept that. I've had my own problems being quoted out of context. I also know Doug perceives himself as a short reliever, and the adjustment for him isn't easy.

The next day our bats went south again. We scored exactly one run. And we beat the Phillies 1–0 behind Dwight, who pitched the most awesome game of his life. During warmups, pitching coach Mel Stottlemyre and Clint Hurdle, who was catching him, saw that he was bringing something extra. Mel told me, "Doc missed the glove only twice during his entire warmup." I said, "He wants to prove something tonight. Last year he lost a game to the Phillies when he balked in a run. He's never beaten them, so he has something to prove." In eight innings he gave up three hits and no runs and struck out seven.

Unfortunately, we couldn't score any runs against Steve Carlton either, and so, in the top of the ninth, with the score 0–0, I sent Wally up to pinch-hit for Doc, hoping we could score a run and win it for him. I knew Doc could have gone a couple more innings, but I didn't want to push him so early in the year.

Wally responded with a single, and with Mookie Wilson up, I relayed the hit-and-run sign down to Bobby Valentine at third. Hudson pitched. Wally didn't run. Mookie didn't swing.

After the game, I asked Bobby what had happened. He said, "Mookie didn't even look at me. And neither did Wally!"

I don't like those things to happen. They were assuming that nothing would be on because of what I've done in this situation in the past. I tell them over and over, "Never take anything for granted. It's a losing attitude." I didn't fine them this time. But if it happens a second time I will.

Anyway, I changed the sign and had Mookie bunt, and he sacrificed Wally to second.

My next decision was a tough one. Here were my two choices: If I let Kelvin Chapman hit, Phillie manager John Felske was going to let Hudson pitch to Chapman, and then intentionally walk the left-handed Hernandez and pitch to the right-handed Carter.

On the other hand, if I sent Rusty Staub up to pinch-hit for Chapman, I figured Felske would bring in his left-hander, Don Carmen, a rookie whom I don't know anything about, to pitch to Staub and Hernandez, who hits lefties as well as righties and led the league in game-winning hits.

I decided to send Rusty up to hit. And, sure enough, Felske brought in the unknown Carmen. Rusty grounded to second, getting Backman to third. Keith was up with two outs. Carmen threw heat, but Keith battled him, fouling off five balls down the left field line. Carmen then threw a fastball inside, and Keith got jammed, but he hit a little humpbacked bloop just over the head of the first baseman, and Wally came home with the lead run.

I brought in Jesse to pitch the bottom of the ninth, and he started my indigestion off with a three-and-oh count to Juan Samuel. Carter called time and went out to the mound. He was hollering at Jesse, "Wake up, man. Let's go. We got a ballgame to win. Throw some strikes. We don't want this guy on base." And Jesse responded. He threw a strike, and then Samuel flied out. He got the next two guys, and it was one, two, three. Dwight got a win, Jesse got a save, everyone was happy, and I looked like a genius.

It's only April, and we're eight and one, but already I feel like I've been put through a meat grinder.

13
UNCERTAINTY

IT'S BEEN a very trying week. We blew games we should have won. I lost starting pitcher Bruce Berenyi and center fielder Mookie Wilson to arm injuries, and even Dwight got beat. I blew my stack at Eddie Lynch after he decided to pick a fight with me in the newspapers, and we finished the week two and four. The one glimmer of optimism is that we were able to sign free agent Joe Sambito for our bullpen, but whether he's going to be ready to help us remains to be seen.

Against the one-and-ten Philadelphia Phillies we lost a heartbreaker. We went into the ninth trailing by four. Darryl led off with a home run against their starter, John Denny, to make it 7–4. Danny Heep bounced one up the middle, and Howard Johnson walked. With the tying run coming to the plate, John Felske brought in Larry Andersen, a right-hander, to face Rafael Santana. I decided to let Rafael Santana hit, and he drove a two-hopper to their second baseman, Samuel, who let it ricochet off him. Samuel hits better than he fields.

Now it was 7–5 with runners on first and third. Even though

my bullpen was depleted, I sent up George Foster to hit for the pitcher, hoping with one swing he could end it. George bounced out to the infield and our sixth run scored. He beat out the relay to first, and I put in Kelvin Chapman to pinch-run. I figured we still had a heck of a chance to get back in the game, because our next two batters, Wally Backman and Mookie Wilson, don't strike out much. Wally struck out. Mookie struck out. We lost the game, 7–6.

After the game I told Eddie, "Today you fell in love with your fastball. You pounded away with it and you forgot to change speeds." I said, "You've got to throw more than one pitch. You have a great change-up and a good slider. You have to use them."

The next day Ron Darling did the same thing. He tried to overpower everybody, and he was no more successful than Eddie. That's what you have to live through with young pitchers. They're going to be inconsistent.

I had to bring in Doug Sisk, who came in, threw the ball up, and got rackytacked real quick for four runs. He took the loss.

The next morning I had to read in the papers about how unhappy he is. "Saves are where the money's at, blah blah blah." I've got to get it through his thick skull that I'm doing what's best for the team.

When we went to St. Louis to face the Cardinals, we continued to play sloppy, uninspired baseball. Once again we got off to a great start, scoring six runs against John Tudor. I was hoping the barrage would help my newest arm, Calvin Schiraldi, to relax and give us a strong game.

Calvin did admirably for his first start of the year. The Cards reached him for three runs early, but he settled down until the seventh, when he started the inning by walking Ozzie Smith and giving up a single by Willie McGee.

I hooked him and brought in Roger McDowell, who let two runs score and then got us out of the inning. I decided to let my righty phenom go back out in the eighth and pitch to one batter, Jack Clark, figuring Roger would get him out and then I'd bring in Jesse when their lefties came up. Clark doubled. So much for my phenom. I brought in Jesse, who got us out of it with a big assist from Howard Johnson, who made a brilliant backhand stop and a long throw for the third out.

We still had to get through the ninth against a very pesky team. The Cardinals have more speed than anyone else in the league, they steal bases, they hit-and-run, drive you crazy, and if you don't keep them off the base paths, it's time to hit the Rolaids bottle.

Jesse opened the ninth walking Ozzie Smith. The winning run, McGee, came up. He singled up the middle. Smith stopped at second. The winning run was now at first base. There were no outs. My guts were churning. Vince Coleman popped up a bunt that was catchable by either Carter or Orosco, but Carter waited for Jesse, and Jesse waited for Carter, and the ball dropped foul, and Coleman had another life. The pain in my gut became more acute. On the next pitch Carter threw through to second base to pick off Smith, and Smith was dead on his feet, but Rafael bobbled the low throw, the ball got away, and Smith went to third. I called for trainer Steve Garland to bring me more antacids.

Finally, finally, Coleman grounded to second. It looked like it might be a double play, but the throw to first was an eyelash late, and the run crossed the plate.

Now our lead was down to 7–6, there was one out, and the tying runner was on first in the person of Vince Coleman, who's the fastest runner in the league. Whitey Herzog sent up right-handed hitter Brian Harper to hit against Jesse. I was rooting hard for an out. Harper sent a foul fly down the right-field line, Wally was chasing it, Darryl was racing after it, and they both lunged, and the ball fell only a few feet from their reach. Another "almost out." Harper then lined a single between short and third, sending Coleman to second. The tying run was now on second with one out, and I was chewing on my antacids furiously, wondering what else might happen.

Nothing else happened. Jesse got two fly balls to end the game. I sucked in my gut, took a very deep breath, and raced out to the mound to shake Jesse's hand. Calvin Schiraldi didn't watch the end of the game. He sat on the bench, his head buried deep in a towel.

The next day I lost Bruce Berenyi, for how long I don't know. I suspect he's going to have to go onto the disabled list. He hadn't pitched in six days, as I was hoping the extra day's rest would help his arm, but when he went out against the Cards, he was behind on every hitter, and gave up two quick runs on three hits and a walk before I hooked him.

After he came out, Bruce insisted his arm was okay. How could he say that? Did he think I was born yesterday? I said, "Bruce, listen. We have to tell each other the truth. You have to tell me exactly how your arm feels. Let's be perfectly honest. Let's tell it like it is. If it hurts a little, tell me. If it hurts a whole lot, tell me. I don't need a hero."

I said, "I can tell right now you're going on the disabled list, even before you go to a doctor. The only way you're going to come out of this is if you undergo treatment."

He promised me he would cooperate, and not try to romance me once he returns. If he returns.

An April game is supposed to be as important as a September game, and with a veteran team, that's usually true, but with these young players, I use these early-in-the-season games to fish for a starting combination. I had been working to develop a fifth starter, and now, with Berenyi out, I'm looking for a fourth *and* a fifth starter. Eddie Lynch has pitched very well. He's number three behind Gooden and Darling, and I may try an experiment to see whether Roger McDowell might be my fourth starter, which still leaves me without a number five, assuming Bruce can't come back.

The day after losing Berenyi, I had to play the finale against the Cardinals with Gary Carter and George Foster on the bench with sore knees. I had intended to rest Mookie Wilson, who has been bothered by a sore shoulder all spring, and play George, but George told me his knee had swelling in it. I didn't want to play the game with Carter, Foster, and Mookie all sitting on the bench, so I decided to rest George and keep Mookie in there. And now Mookie may be lost to us for quite a while, because with a runner on third, their catcher Lavallierre hit a fly ball out to center, and when he threw home, late, something popped in his arm, and I suspect it's going to be serious.

We need Mookie. As a person, he's a gentleman, the perfect player. He'll do anything you want him to do. He never complains, and you never have to tell him to practice. Mookie is my catalyst. He's our speed on the bases, the guy who makes my offense go. Without him, it's going to be a much tougher road for us.

Dwight ended up with the loss, his first of the year. He told me afterward that his arm was tired. Still, in seven innings he only gave up two runs. Roger McDowell allowed the other three in the eighth. On offense we were able to score only one run against Andujar.

St. Louis didn't get much attention at the beginning of the season, but their new leadoff batter, Coleman, is so fast, steals so many bases, that every time he gets on, it's tantamount to his hitting a double. Whitey likes a speed game, and he has Coleman, McGee, Herr, Van Slyke, and this young kid Pendleton, and they can all run.

I finally had a good day when Ronnie Darling pitched a five-hit shutout against the Pirates, mixing up his pitches and throwing the ball over the plate. He struck out eleven.

Part of the credit has to go to Gary Carter, who calls an outstanding game. We're two weeks into the season, and Gary is starting to get a really good feel for the pitchers, and the pitchers for him. The game Darling pitched today is evidence of Gary's influence. Right now, other than Eddie Lynch, none of my starting pitchers has more than one year of experience. And if Eddie should falter, it's conceivable that I would have four starters, Gooden, Darling, and Schiraldi, none of whom have pitched more than a year, and McDowell, who has pitched just two weeks in the majors. Gary makes my job that much easier because he knows what he has to do. He's a consummate professional.

The other noteworthy event of the day was that we were able to sign pitcher Joe Sambito. I need another healthy arm in the pen. I just hope Sambito can return to his old form.

Joe had been a star reliever with Houston, was credited with 72 saves over a seven-year period, and then he injured his arm and had a serious operation. When he came back this year, Houston bit the bullet on his $750,000 salary and released him.

When Frank Cashen asked me if I had any interest in Joe, I said, "I don't know how he's throwing, but I used to like him a great deal." At one time he was one of the premier left-handed relievers in the league. Frank was thinking he would sign him and send him to Tidewater. I'm desperately hoping he can contribute something to the Mets. He certainly has the experience to be a stopper. And it's a good gamble. He's making $750,000 a year, but we're only obligated to pay $40,000 of it. Who knows? If he gets his arm in shape, he may come back and make all the difference.

Ray Knight played with Sambito at Houston, and Ray told me that Joe's a very hard worker and that he did a good job for them last year. Ray said, "He's a great guy to have on a club, he'd adjust to any role, and he's a tough competitor, a tough cookie." On that recommendation alone I'm inclined to give him the chance.

When I started Eddie Lynch against the Pirates the next day I was really hoping I could get five or six solid innings out of him. He had pitched three days earlier against the Cards in relief, and he didn't do very well. The trainer told me Eddie had some tenderness in his biceps, so when he went out there, I was looking for signs, ready to make a quick hook if I had to.

Eddie surprised everybody, really mixing up his pitches beautifully, keeping the Pirates off stride, and after seven strong innings he was pitching a three-hitter and had a two-run lead.

While we were hitting in the bottom of the seventh, Mel Stottlemyre asked Eddie how he felt, and Eddie told him, "I'm bushed," and so when it was our turn to go back out onto the field for the eighth, I said, "Eddie, that's enough."

I sent in a rested Jesse Orosco, but Jesse blew the game. By the end of the eighth inning the Pirates had three runs. I had considered using Doug Sisk, who had warmed up in the seventh. The Pirates have a lot of right-handed pinch hitters on their bench, and Dougie might have been a better choice, because he would have frozen all those righties on the bench, but with Dougie having problems with his control, I had to go with my best, and that's Orosco.

Afterward, though, a lot of writers were leaning on me. "Why did you take out Lynch?" The man had thrown 115 pitches. His previous high had been 104. He was pooped. But I didn't say any of that to the writers. Their greatest joy is in second-guessing, writing; "Lynch had a three-hitter, and that dummy Johnson took him out."

The toughest part of my job is coming back to my office after the game and rethinking strategy after everyone has gone. One thing you have to avoid doing is saying to yourself, "What if I had kept Lynch in?" It's wasted energy. Why bother thinking about what you could have or should have done? I made the right decision. I brought in my ace. They got to us with pinch hitters. If you're going to worry about pinch hitters beating you, you're in a whole lot of trouble. If they had been good enough to start, they would have started. But my guy had a bad day. How could I have let Jesse get two guys on, be one run down, and then made a pitching change, bringing in a pitcher who hasn't been pitching well? I couldn't have. Which is why I shouldn't lose sleep over it.

And yet, I still feel bad, because we lost. I feel bad because Jesse didn't save it. I feel bad because Eddie Lynch deserved his win and didn't get it. And I feel bad because I have to listen to the writers trying to second-guess me, and then read about it the next day in the papers.

I felt even worse the next day when I opened the papers to read that the writers had asked Eddie Lynch, "How were you feeling when Johnson took you out?" and that his answer was "Fine. I really wasn't tired at all." They said they asked him, "What about your sore arm?" and he shrugged, saying, "That's news to me." I knew damn well he was pooped. He told Mel he was tired. He told the trainer his arm was sore. But in the papers he changed his tune, making me look bad.

I called Eddie in for a meeting, along with Mel Stottlemyre.

"Is it or is it not true that you reported soreness to the trainer before the game?"

Eddie got a little belligerent. He said, "Nah, I didn't say that. I didn't mention anything about my arm to anyone."

"The trainer was right there," I said, "and three or four other guys heard you."

After we went through that, I asked him, "Didn't you tell me you were tired?"

He said, "I didn't say that." It was apparent that he didn't want to agree with me on anything.

I said, "Other people heard you say those things."

Then I brought the trainer in. "Eddie, didn't you tell the trainer your arm was sore?" I damn well wanted to get this out into the open. I said, "I'm doing my best to pitch you in situations where you will do well."

But Eddie was tough, tough, tough. He showed no remorse and refused to admit what he had said.

I was more than a little hacked off. "Two or three bad outings, and your ass is going into the pen."

"What difference does it make?" he countered. "With Schiraldi and McDowell the third and fourth starters, I'm the fifth wheel around here."

"Who told you that?" I asked. "I never said that."

"Klapisch wrote that in the *Post*."

I said, "I don't care what he wrote. I didn't say that, because you're my third starter."

He shrugged his shoulders. "I'm not going to worry about it." He was still very belligerent. We were having a tough time communicating, and I was really beginning to get upset.

Later I went to Klapisch and said, "Did you make some speculation on your own that Eddie's the fifth wheel and McDowell and Schiraldi are in?"

He said, "Yeah, I wrote that, but it was my own speculation."

I said, "Would you mind saying that to Mr. Lynch?"

He promised he would.

I have a very high boiling point, and my players don't ordinarily cause me to reach it. I don't ever like to reach it, because it's not pretty to see. Eddie had pushed me closer to exploding than I'd been at any time since Tidewater.

The player there was Rusty Tillman. I had had him at Jackson, where he helped us win the championship with two home runs against the San Antonio Dodgers. During the celebration, in the excitement he hit my wife over the head with a champagne bottle. I told him, "That's not a good way to stay in baseball."

At Tidewater Rusty wasn't playing as hard as I knew he could. He hit a ground ball to the pitcher and didn't run it out. I fined him. A short time afterward he hit a ball to the shortstop, and again he didn't run. I blew my stack.

After the game we went into my office, and I said, "I've had it with you. I have three options, to send you down, suspend you, or fine you. I want to do one of the first two. I really do. You're wasting a lot of talent, and I won't stand for it." If he had shown an ounce of disrespect, I would have punched him. My patience had been used up. In the end I just fined him.

But Eddie Lynch showed no respect at all. When I left our meeting I was having trouble controlling myself. I've always liked Eddie, liked his competitiveness, and I decided to let it lie for a while, to wait and see what would happen.

The next day Eddie asked to see me. He said, "Skip, I've had time to think over what you said, and I want you to know that you were right. I was wrong. I apologize. We should be trying to help each other, and I didn't hold up my end of it. I'm available for relief, or whatever you need me for."

I breathed a sigh of relief. I said, "Eddie, forget it. It's water over the dam. Turn the page."

14
RUSTY AND CLINT

ON THE LAST SUNDAY in April we played an afternoon game against the Pirates, and before it was over, we had played one of the most entertaining five-and-a-half hours of baseball I have ever seen. The game went eighteen innings. Pirate manager Chuck Tanner used twenty-three players, I used twenty, and as I sat watching, I could only shake my head as one crazy thing after another happened.

Darryl opened the game by hitting a grand slam in the first inning. I was figuring it to be an easy day. I was very wrong. For the next ten innings we didn't even get another hit!

Roger McDowell started. It was an important test for him. He was hurt most of last year, and though he had pitched well out of the bullpen, I was anxious to see how he would react to his first major league start. He didn't do too badly, got as far as the sixth, had good poise, and good command of his pitches. He made only one bad pitch, a hanging slider to Hendrick for a home run. I had been hoping to get four solid innings, and I got five, but when I tried to stretch it into the sixth, he got a little tired and gave up back-to-back doubles after one out.

I took him out and brought in another of my rookies, Calvin Schiraldi, to finish the inning. Calvin's a righty, and I figured he'd get out Hendrick and Pena, two right-handers. He struck out Hendrick, and he threw a fastball by Pena for a strike. Gary was figuring Calvin could do it again. Calvin fired it in there, and Pena hit it out for three runs to tie the game.

The next pitcher I called in was my new acquisition, Joe Sambito. I knew he wanted to break the ice. He got them one, two, three. I had Joe pitch just the one inning. Joe hadn't played much, and the last thing I need is for Doug Sisk to think that I'm auditioning pitchers to take his job away. The Pirates, moreover, have a predominantly right-handed lineup, tailor-made for Doug. Doug came in and walked the first batter in the eighth, and as expected, he got the next batter, Jason Thompson, to hit into a double play.

In the ninth the umps almost cost me the game. Sisk gave up a hit to Belliard, and with Doug Frobel up in an obvious bunt situation, Keith took several steps in from first as if to cover the bunt, and then rushed back for a pickoff throw. Harry Wendelstedt called a balk. Not on the pitcher, but on Keith! Hey, wait, you can't call a balk on a fielder. He was making that up.

I went rushing out to find out what the hell Wendelstedt was doing. Wendelstedt said that Keith couldn't fake in as if to cover the bunt and then come back for a pickoff throw at first. I said, "How can you call a balk on a first baseman, for Christ sake? You made the damn thing up to cover for a bad call."

He said, "It's in the rule book."

Like hell it's in the rule book. He made it up. If we hadn't later won the game, I would have protested, and I would have won. Anyway, Frobel went up to bunt, and Doug walked him, and I was eating antacid tablets by the handful. It was the ninth. Runners were on first and second. Nobody was out. Sisk had me crazy.

I went out to the mound. The next batter was their rookie outfielder, Orsulak. I said to Doug, "Go after him. If we get Orsulak at first, we can then walk Johnny Ray and try for the double play on Bill Madlock, who's a slow runner." Sisk said okay, and then he walked Orsulak to load the bases.

Nobody was out and the bases were loaded. We were in the ninth. Johnny Ray, a good contact hitter, was at bat. I played my infield in. Doug had to start Ray off with a strike, because if he didn't he was gone.

His first pitch was high and outside. I couldn't take any more. I went out to the mound and gave Dougie the hook.

I brought in Jesse. I was looking for a miracle. Jesse went right after Ray and struck him out on a wicked slider. Madlock then pulled one hard, but right at Raffy at short, and we had two big outs. I was beginning to feel pretty good.

Jason Thompson, their big first baseman, was the next batter, and I liked the matchup, the left-handed Jesse against a free-swinging left-handed batter.

With runners dancing off every base, Jesse threw Thompson a slider that glanced off Carter's glove and started to roll to the wall. Carter raced after it. Belliard, a fast runner, broke for home. Jesse covered the plate.

Carter then made a beautiful defensive play. He stopped the ball, perhaps fifteen feet from the plate, and with his back to the plate, instead of turning to throw, he flipped backhand to Jesse as Belliard started his slide. The ball arrived strong and low, and Jesse caught it and dropped his glove in front of the plate before Belliard got there. The umpire called him out. I took a deep, deep breath. We were out of the inning.

I was fired up now. I figured I had three more good innings left from Jesse, and we ought to have scored a run by then. Little did I realize that we had another whole game to play during this game.

We should have won it in the ninth. With one out, Raffy reached second when their shortstop, Belliard, threw his ground ball into the stands. The next batter was Jesse. Do I hit for him or let him try to get Raffy in? I would really like to hit for him, but I don't like my options. My one glaring weakness is a lack of a right-handed pinch hitter. On the bench this day my right-handed bats consisted of a gimpy George Foster, Mookie Wilson with an injured shoulder and a bad arm, and a green rookie named John Christensen who came into the game without a hit in seventeen at bats. I didn't want to hit Christensen in this situation. I couldn't hit George because he can't run well, and Mookie was having difficulty swinging the bat without a lot of pain. I let Jesse hit. Jesse's a good athlete, he swings a decent bat, and I was hoping Jess would hit the ball and win the game for himself. He hit it hard, but to second. Raffy went to third.

My next batter was Wally Backman. Wally grounded out, taking us into extra innings.

In the twelfth I was forced to do something very radical. I played Rusty Staub in the outfield. Rusty is forty years old, is carrying a couple of pianos on his back, and hadn't played in the outfield since 1983. But after having pinch-hit for Heep, I didn't have anyone else. I sent Rusty out into the field and held my breath.

I also made my last pitching change. I put in my lefty reliever with the charmed life, Tommy Gorman, who in '84 had a perfect 6–0 season. I had already used McDowell, Schiraldi, Sambito, Sisk, and Orosco. All I had left were starters. Tommy was my Horatio at the bridge, but he almost lost it in the fourteenth. The Pirates had runners on first and third with one out. Bill Madlock was up, and when he grounded the ball to Ray Knight at third, the runner at third, Frobel, tried to score. It was a slowly hit ball, and Ray had to hurry to get it. For the second time in the game a Pirate runner tried to take Gary's head off. Ray got the ball to Gary and Frobel leveled him trying to score, but Gary again held the ball and we were still alive. Two outs. And I could see that Gary was in pain. The Pirates, however, weren't finished with him. The next batter, Hendrick, fouled the ball back toward the stands behind home plate. From my spot in the dugout, it looked like the ball was going to be two or three rows deep into the stands, but Gary threw his mask off, raced toward the stands, and with his bruised ribs aching from the previous collision, he slammed into the railing, fought his way past the fans to the ball, and caught it.

Everyone was saying, "Great play, great play," but my concern was not only "great play," but "Are you okay?" The trainer insisted Gary see the doctor. Gary emphatically told him, "I'll see the doctor *after* the game."

On the game went into the eighteenth and its improbable conclusion. With two outs the Pirates had runners on first and second. Gorman was still out there, keeping us even. Tanner sent in pitcher Rick Rhoden to pinch-hit for Doug Frobel, who's an outfielder. Tanner had a strategic reason for doing this: Rhoden's a righty and Frobel's a lefty, and with the lefty Gorman out there, he wanted a right-handed batter. But it's a move I never would have made. I have to feel that when you pinch-hit a pitcher for a regular player, it destroys that player's confidence in himself.

With one out, the runners on first and second took their leads. I had shifted Clint into left field in case Rhoden should pull the ball, and Rusty had moved into right. They made that switch perhaps a dozen times during the game, and to this point Rusty hadn't fielded a ball, but I was sure he was exhausted just from having to jog back and forth between left and right fields.

Rhoden blooped the ball on an arc toward right field. Rusty saw it, started for the ball, picked up a head of steam, chugging like a locomotive, his arms pumping. As he reached a spot a few feet short of the foul line, he reached way out and caught the ball, saving at least one run from scoring. The fans gave him a standing ovation. So did we.

Gorman, my Horatio, got the next hitter, and we were out of the inning. We had played more than five hours of baseball, and it was still a tie.

We went up to bat in the eighteenth, and I had Ron Darling warming up in the bullpen. I was shooting all my aces. Two nights earlier Darling had thrown a complete-game shutout. I figured Gorman had about had it, and he was scheduled to hit fourth in the bottom of the eighteenth. If the four-spot batter got up, I had to pinch-hit for him.

Gary, whose ribs were on fire, went up to bat and drew an inning-opening walk. I had to find him a pinch runner. I figured Mookie Wilson's arm might have been hurting, but there was nothing wrong with his legs, so I sent him in.

The only players on my roster I hadn't used were Reynolds and Foster, and with Gary out of the game, Reynolds had to go in and catch if we didn't score. He started putting on his gear.

Darryl was the next batter, and he pulled a hard ground ball that just missed hitting Mookie and went into right field. Mookie alertly held up, letting the ball go by him, and he went on to third. Only Mookie could have done that.

Clint Hurdle was the batter. I had Foster standing in the on-deck circle pinch-hitting for Gorman should Tanner have chosen to walk Clint and pitch to the next batter. That would have been fine with me too.

Tanner chose to pitch to Clint. At the same time he pulled a Mickey Mouse stunt. He had all his fielders playing in the infield. The infielders were on the infield grass, the out-fielders were in very shallow. He was figuring a fly ball would beat him anyway, and I guess he figured this would improve his chances of getting a double play if the ball was hit on the ground.

Tanner's defense beat him. His first baseman was playing way in, and Clint pulled a shot that just got by him. Mookie trotted home. Darling stopped throwing in the pen. Reynolds took off the shin guards. End of game. End of long, long day.

The next day I opened the papers to read about our epic battle, and even though we had played one of the most exciting games I've ever seen, the Yankees got all the headlines because Yankee owner George Steinbrenner has fired manager Yogi Berra and brought Billy Martin back for another round.

What irritated me was the story in the papers in which Steinbrenner supposedly said to Yogi, "Johnson's getting all the ink, and you're nothing but dead space." And then Billy commented, "Davey Johnson is a nice guy, but what has he ever won?" I don't believe everything I read in the papers, but I know Billy well enough to know he said that.

I guess Steinbrenner has reason to worry about the Yankees not drawing the most fans in New York and about not being number one. It's obvious that if the Mets are pennant contenders, and the Yankees aren't, we'll lead them in attendance.

As for Yogi getting fired, it was very premature. Of course, Steinbrenner's relationship to his baseball team is different from any that I've been under. George puts all sorts of unnecessary pressure on his manager and his players, like saying in the papers, "If they don't do this, then . . ." or criticizing his players in the papers. Anyone who takes the Yankee managing job has to realize that George really wants to manage the ballclub himself. You also have to realize that when he hires you, it's not going to take much to get yourself fired. Look at Dick Howser. He won 103 games and was let go.

After a day off, Houston came to town, and for a while there it looked like we had reverted to our earlier, runless form, as Joe Niekro led Doc 1–0 going into the seventh inning. Doc gave up a home run to Dennis Walling in the first inning, and that was all they got, even though Dwight says he still doesn't feel like he's popping his fastball. All he did was strike out eight.

Gary started the game behind the plate, but he had to come out early. His ribs are still sore. It hurt him to breathe.

I put Clint Hurdle in for him, and in the seventh Keith Hernandez singled, and Clint came up. I had Clint bunt the first pitch, but he didn't get it down. I know he isn't a good bunter, so I took off the bunt sign, but he tried to bunt again. Later I asked him why, and he said, "I looked so bad trying to bunt the first one, I thought I would try to redeem myself." But he didn't get that one down, either. On the next pitch he redeemed himself. He slapped a two-strike single to center, sending Keith to third. It was the key hit in an inning in which we scored two runs and went on to win the game.

I am willing to admit it: Clint Hurdle is one of my favorites. That he is on the roster at all is a testament to his determination and his love of the game. When he first came to me two years ago at Tidewater, I had asked him to learn a new position, third base. He worked very hard and became an adequate third baseman. He didn't have the greatest range, but he made all the plays.

At the end of the year the Mets called him up, and he didn't have a very impressive debut. Nevertheless, when he reported to spring training last year he was hoping to be a shoo-in. When he arrived, the first thing I said to him, though, after hello, was, "Clint, I think you ought to put on the catcher's gear and go back to Tidewater for another year."

I told him, "If you can pull this off, next year you're mine."

It was again a question of faith. Not everyone would have agreed to spend *another* year in the minor leagues learning *another* new position. But Clint agreed, and he spent the rest of the year working on his catching skills. This year in spring training he amazed everybody. For a guy who had never been back there, he demonstrated major league skills.

No one was more delighted than I when Clint pulled it off. On cutdown day, Clint became one of my catchers. Clint's had his tough times, and he could have quit at a number of points along the way. But he hung in there, and I'm very proud of what he has accomplished. I gambled on his heart, and I won.

15

THE WALKING WOUNDED

AS WE WENT INTO MAY, my biggest problem was how to win despite all our injuries. It's like a curse. The minute Ron Gardenhire returned from his back problems he pulled a hamstring muscle, and now he's out, maybe for a month or more.

With Gardy injured and Mookie Wilson's shoulder still sore, I've decided I would like to bring up Lenny Dykstra from Tidewater. Lenny's been playing a lot of center field there, he's a switch-hitter, he's fast, and I could use him as leadoff in Mookie's spot. Lenny's mentally tough enough to handle it. The question is, will I be able to get him on my roster?

The first thing I had to do was get Gardy on the disabled list. I know if I rush him back into the lineup, he'll just hurt himself again like he did last year. Unfortunately, when Dr. Parkes examined him, he told Frank that Gardy'd be okay in a couple of days, killing my plans to bring up Dykstra. I couldn't live with that. Mookie has a bad shoulder, George Foster a gimpy knee, and Carter cracked ribs, and though Rusty Staub has been healthy, he runs too slowly to play in the field, which effectively leaves me only twenty-one healthy players, and that puts us at a bad enough disadvantage. With Gardy out, I don't have any flexibility.

Maybe Parkes is right. But I doubt it, and I can't afford to gamble. I need Dykstra up here, and I need him now. It would be different if I didn't have any other injuries.

I decided not to accept Dr. Parkes's diagnosis as final. I called him and said, "Doctor, I know you want to be nice to Gardy, but in the past when we've rushed him to come back, he's reinjured himself even worse." Dr. Parkes said, "Dave, I don't want you to rush him, but I feel it's not as severe as last year."

I then explained my predicament. Dr. Parkes agreed that even though Gardy might be ready in a week, to play it safe he would not object to my putting him on the twenty-one-day disabled list.

Dr. Parkes, a fine doctor and a gentleman, then called Frank. Two minutes later my phone rang. It was Frank. "Okay, Gardy's going on the DL. We'll have Dykstra here from Tidewater for tomorrow's game." I breathed a sigh of relief. Sometimes you just have to keep pushing in different directions to get finally what you think is in the best interests of the ballclub.

Getting Dykstra is a good deal in more ways than one, as who knows what might happen with Mookie? Maybe Mookie's going to need arthroscopic surgery.

I can't live with uncertainty. I am irritated with the status of both Mookie and Bruce Berenyi. Mookie hurts his shoulder, and the doctor prescribes rest. Berenyi has pain, and the doctor prescribes rest. "Christ," I told Mookie, "you had all winter to rest your arm. Five full months. You come to spring training, we take it real easy, and we still have a problem. Something has to be aggravating it. It can't be that you just need rest."

I said, "Having you as a pinch runner is a luxury I can't afford. If you can't play, then you're going to have to have your arm operated on." I should have known if he had a problem in the spring that rest wasn't the answer.

I told Frank, "I want to address the situation. Let's have a plan, one way or the other, that I can live with."

At my request Dr. Parkes reexamined Mookie and Berenyi. Mookie said his arm was feeling much better. Dr. Parkes said his arm was all right. We'll see. I think he, and Berenyi, are still going to need surgery. I said to Dr. Parkes, "If Mookie's arm is all right, then I'm going to go ahead and play him. If his arm acts up again after a week, as far as I'm concerned he's got to go to surgery." God knows I have enough day-to-day problems without having to play doctor.

I'm now comfortable with the Mookie situation. He will play until his arm falls off, and when that happens, he'll be operated on.

As for Berenyi, he took it at his own pace in the spring. He pitched well for five innings in an exhibition game, and then was hurt for three more weeks. He came back and threw the ball hard against Cincinnati the second day of the season, and then was blown out for the rest. Either he has something in the arm irritating it when he's giving his best effort, or he didn't build it to its normal strength so that he could pitch.

I talked with Dr. Parkes and Frank about Berenyi. Dr. Parkes suggested I give him another week or ten days and then let him pitch. I said, "I have a better idea. Why don't we let him pitch in the twenty-day rehab program, at Tidewater? Let him start. He can go at his own pace. It'll give him a chance to build up his arm through his starts and avoid surgery. And when he's gone I'll have a chance to test Calvin Schiraldi and Sid Fernandez." They thought it was a good idea.

I know Bruce can pitch. There is no question in my mind. I just want him healthy, and I want to make sure he's healthy. If he pops in and out of the rotation, it disrupts the young arms trying to establish themselves. So this works hand and glove with that.

I came out of the meeting with Parkes and Cashen, and called Bruce into my office. I said, "When you feel you're ready to pitch, I'll send you down to Tidewater and let you monitor your own progress. If you throw three innings, that's fine, and if five days later you go four innings or five innings, fine. You can get back in shape without any pressure." Bruce is quiet and uncommunicative—the strong, silent type. He just nodded.

I said, "If it takes three or four starts for your arm to regain its strength, we'll know. And if it doesn't, if it regresses, you'll need to be arthroscoped." Again he nodded.

I feel comfortable at last. At least I know what's going to happen and what the time frame is going to be, and I can project what to do with the rest of my staff. I don't like uncertainty. I always want to have one plan, at the least, and a contingency plan off the main plan if possible. But I have to have one, or it makes me crazy.

16
DOUGIE

I STARTED Lenny Dykstra against the Cincinnati Reds, and in his first game, with a runner on first, Lenny pulled the ball down the line and over the fence. When Lenny got to home plate, he was so happy he stomped on it with both feet.

The next day I started Roger McDowell, still trying to determine whether he should start or relieve, and he pitched great ball. We were 2–2 going into the sixth when the bottom fell out. Eddie Milner led off with a single and he went to third when McDowell's pickoff throw was wild. Pete Rose walked, and Dave Parker, who has never hit so well, doubled in one run. I ordered McDowell to walk Cedeno to load the bases and set up a double play. Then I brought in Doug Sisk, hoping that finally, this would be his game. The fans at Shea have been booing him, and he's let them affect his pitching. I was hoping he'd get his composure back on the road.

Nick Esasky was the hitter. The bases were loaded. Doug's first pitch was a strike; the second, a high sinker, was hit foul; and the third pitch was thigh high, out over the plate. It began to sink, but Esasky pulled it over the left-center field wall for a grand slam. So much for my "this game will save Doug Sisk" move. He gave up another hit behind a triple by Cedeno that went all the way to the wall. In all six runs scored.

He got an out, finally, but the last straw was when he walked the pitcher. I went out to the mound, and I brought in Joe Sambito. Sambito walked the first two men he faced and gave up two hits. Out to the mound I went again. It was my third trip of the inning. I never had to do that before, and it was broadcast on national TV! This was swell. Calvin Schiraldi finally got us out of it after a ten-run inning. We lost 14–2.

In the clubhouse Sisk told reporters, "The water is lapping over the boat, and I'm bailing out with a shot glass."

After the game I went up to my hotel room at the Terrace Hilton to be alone. I watched the Kentucky Derby on TV, and then I watched the golfers compete in the Tournament of Champions and I drank a little wine. I said to myself, Our pitching is in need of a little juggling. Dougie's ineffective. I need someone who can get me to the seventh inning, to Orosco. What should I do? I can't live with this.

I decided to move Calvin Schiraldi back into the rotation and let McDowell take over Sisk's role. I asked myself, What should I do with Doug?

I can handle the walks. Doug's had 14 walks in 18 innings. I can live with that. But I can't handle the lack of sink or bite on his fastball. He hasn't really been successful since the first half of last year.

There's only one solution, I told myself. Doug's going to have to go down to Tidewater and work it out. He can start a couple of times, get in a lot of work, and then go to the pen. He's important to our success, and I don't see any other way to get him back. Except maybe shock treatments or strangulation.

I went downstairs to the peanut-and-beer lounge. My coaches, Bobby Valentine, Greg Pavlick, and Mel Stottlemyre were waiting for me. I asked Bobby what he thought I should do about Sisk. "Why don't you start him?" he said.

"No, I couldn't do that," I said. "Sisk is not a starter, and there's no logic to using him that way. Then I told them my plan: Sisk to Tidewater. "I really think this is something we have to do," I said.

I knew it would be hard for him. He's had two good years in the big leagues, and he's making a good salary, about $300,000. He also has a new attitude. He's more serious about everything this year. He's got a really pretty girl friend who's dressing him a lot better. He doesn't drink as much beer. He's like a married man. Unfortunately, his new attitude hasn't improved his pitching any.

I called him into my office the next day and told him of my decision.

"I'll go to Jackson," he said. "I don't want to go to Tidewater."

I said, "What do you mean?"

He said, "I don't like Tidewater." The Tidewater team plays in Norfolk, Virginia.

I said, "How would you know? You've never played there."

He said, "I've driven by there. I don't like it there." Doug wasn't making any sense.

"Why do you want to go to Jackson?" I asked. "What's the big deal about Jackson?"

He said, "That's where I last had a good year in the minors."

I said, "Doug, I'll be glad to send you there, but if I do then somebody from there has to go to Tidewater. The best solution is for you to go to Tidewater and pitch."

He said, "I don't want to go. I don't like that area. If you're sending me down, at least let me go where I want to go."

I said, "If you insist on my presenting your request to Frank Cashen, I will. But I tell you, I don't recommend it. You're going to aggravate me and my boss."

"I don't like Tidewater," he said stolidly.

I said, "I'll let you talk to Frank. But it's not what we have in mind." I wasn't going to make a big hard-ass deal of it, because, knowing Doug, I figured that in thirty minutes he'd rethink his position.

Doug went on to his other problems. "Even if I pitch well down there, how do I know you're going to bring me back?"

"Have I ever given you reason to doubt me?" I asked.

"You may not bring me back," he said, ignoring my question.

"Look," I said, "the idea is for you to get people out, not to worry about coming back. If you get people out, you'll be back. You're one of the best pitchers in either league when you're right. You need to build your confidence back up."

He said, "Let me do it in Jackson."

I said, "Here's the program: start a couple of times in Tidewater and then go to the pen."

He said, "I can do that in Jackson." Then he said, "How do I know you're going to bring me back?"

Finally, after about thirty minutes of this, back and forth, he left and the press came in to see me. I told them the situation, that Doug was going down, and Wes Gardner and Sid Fernandez were coming up. The reporters wanted to rush out and talk to Doug. I said, "No, he's not talking to people right now. Give him some time." Right away they were hot on the trail, sniffing a wounded animal.

I make decisions based on two factors, what's best for the club, and what's best for the player. It's a cruel business. If you don't perform, you're gone. The players are seeing that with Doug Sisk. They know that I'm not going to let something or somebody stand in the way of accomplishing what I want to accomplish for the team. I think the players will grow to respect that, because they know that if there's action to be taken, I'll do something, and that by and large my decisions will be right. That's the way a manager gains respect.

Other managers gain respect by stringent controls, by constantly reinforcing the fact that they are the boss by fining or shouting or demeaning the players. It's as though the guy in authority is daring his players to challenge his authority. He wants the friction so he can demonstrate his authority.

My feeling is, if you make the right decisions and are consistent, your players will respect you. Not that I am actively trying to gain their respect, but it makes it much easier for them to accept later decisions if earlier ones prove to be correct. There's a fine line a manager has to skate. You have very little room for misjudgments. If you misuse your players, you end up losing them.

That's what happened to Hank Bauer at Baltimore. Hank was my first major league manager. I was twenty-four, just a kid playing in his second full year, and I was struggling at bat because my back was bothering me.

But Hank, the tough old marine, didn't believe you were hurt unless the bone stuck out of the skin or unless you were bleeding. I wasn't hitting as well as I should have been, though I must say, neither was anybody else.

One afternoon he called me into his office. I didn't know what for. He said, "Johnson, I've decided that you're going to be a part-time, utility player. I want you to start taking ground balls at short and third as well as second."

I couldn't believe it. The bastard was benching me. I thought to myself, You're doing what? The Orioles were struggling because our pitchers had sore arms and nobody was hitting, and here he was, singling me out. Me, a utility player? It shook me up. I had been a regular the year before, and we had won the World Championship! I had driven in sixty runs. And I was going to be a utility player?

As Hank was telling me this, I was saying to myself, But Skip, you're looking at All-Star material. And boy, was I down. This was traumatic! Aside from its not making any sense.

I sat for about a week when Hank called me up to pinch-hit against Sam McDowell, one of the toughest left-handers in the league. He threw a ninety-five-mile-an-hour fastball and a curve that fell off the table. He was also wild enough to keep you on your toes. I remember thinking to myself, That SOB Bauer's trying to bury me. And then I went up and I hit one nine miles out of the ballpark for a home run. My name was in the lineup at second base from that day on. Hank didn't say another word about my being a regular player after that.

Hank didn't have a lot of tact, and he was probably thinking he was doing me a great favor by shaking me up. "I'll tell this kid he's a part-time player, not a regular, and work his butt off taking ground balls," as though that would shake me up and somehow help me. But my problem wasn't mental. I had a bad back. But I knew Hank's mentality. It was rough, blunt, maybe even brutal. I was on the verge of throwing darts at the man.

Hank could probably say, "It worked, didn't it? The sucker came back and pinch-hit a home run, and now he's my everyday second baseman. He wouldn't have done it if I hadn't shaken him up."

Who's to say which of us is right? Except that Hank was taking a chance. If he had done the same thing to another player, Hank might have buried him.

Hank wasn't a very good manager. In '66 he had been lucky. Everything he did worked. He would bat Chico Salmon, a right-hander, against a right-handed pitcher, and Salmon would double. Moe Drabowsky, a good but not a great relief pitcher, would come in and strike out six in a row in the World Series. Frank Robinson would drive in runs or make a great catch so often it was unreal. Hank could do no wrong that year.

The next year, the confusion began. The pitching staff went to pieces, and his moves started to go sour. Hank was just hanging on, waiting for the ax to fall. You can try to stay on for the money, but your sanity has a price tag too. Hank had no intention of quitting, but deep down, I suspect Hank wanted to be fired. He was just going along, waiting for that other shoe.

We were losing, the players were grumbling, and Hank was not helping the situation any. I remember we had won four or five games in a row, and we were in Minnesota, and the Minnesota North Stars were playing the St. Louis Blues in the Stanley Cup playoffs. We had played a day game, and thirteen of us went to the hockey game. The game let out about eleven-thirty at night, and because we had trouble getting a cab back to the hotel, we got back around twelve-thirty, a half hour after curfew. He fined each of us a hundred dollars. I got a note that one of the coaches had called the room at midnight and that I wasn't in it. That didn't endear him to us. A hundred dollars was a lot of money then. We were only getting six dollars a day for meals. I was furious. It was such Mickey Mouse. Earl Weaver replaced him a few weeks later.

17
HOJO AND RAY

DURING THE COURSE of a season I have to let certain players lose the little battles, until they gain enough confidence to win the war. This year the player I've been nursing through a tough period is my new third baseman, Howard Johnson.

Howard is really feeling the pressure of playing in New York, and for the moment it's affecting his hitting. Playing in New York is tougher than playing anywhere else. The fans want instant results. The press demands instant greatness, and Howard, like all competitors, puts too much pressure on himself to succeed.

When he was with Detroit last year, Sparky Anderson platooned him all year, and then when they got into the playoffs and World Series, he sat Howard on the bench and played his veterans. Sparky's another one of those managers who prefer to go with veterans, who don't want a kid's inexperience to lose him a ballgame.

Howard told me he felt he never belonged in Detroit, that he never felt a part of the team. He also said he felt Sparky didn't like him, and for a kid as sensitive as Howard, that makes playing well that much harder.

When the Tigers traded Howard over here for Walt Terrell, Sparky bad-mouthed him in the papers, saying that Howard couldn't play in the clutch, which is about as bad a comment as you can make about a professional ballplayer. First he buried Howard, and then he said he can't play in the clutch. I thought that was pretty rough when I read that.

When we played the Tigers in spring training, Howard had a big, big game and helped us beat them. He was very nervous. He was trying to prove to Sparky that he's a big league ballplayer. The first time up he hit a line-drive single. Then he doubled one hop to the right field wall. The third time up he singled to left. Then I took him out, making sure he ended with a perfect day, and he was one happy kid.

I said to him, "Did you have a nice day, Howard?"

He had a big grin on his face. "It couldn't have been better."

After the game I ran into Sparky. I said, "Howard Johnson is a good kid."

Sparky said, "I don't have nothing but good kids." Then he said, "Or I get rid of them."

Huh?

Believe me, Howard is a good kid. He works hard, never stays out late, never causes a problem, and is all business. When Howard came to us, he had a good-hit, no-field reputation. Howard says that every time he made an error, Anderson yanked him out of the game and the press jumped all over him. "I felt he was putting me out there to fail," Howard told me. To my eyes, he's going to be an exceptional fielder. He has caught everything hit near him, he's quick, and he's got a real good arm.

Now all he has to do is start hitting, and he will as soon as he stops pressuring himself. The pitcher we traded to the Tigers for Howard, Walt Terrell, has already won five games, and that's got to be on HoJo's mind. Every time he goes up to the plate he tries to impress everyone with his power. Last year playing part-time Howard hit twelve home runs for the Tigers, but he hasn't hit one for us, in part because he's trying so hard. Nevertheless, I'm going to keep putting him out there against right-handed pitching, building him up, telling him, "Hey, don't worry about it. The job is yours no matter what." I've been taking a lot of heat from the fans and from the press, but my judgment tells me that Howard Johnson's going to be fine.

Making it easier to be patient with Howard is the fact that Ray Knight isn't hitting very well either. Together they are hitting .300, .150 each, but I need them both.

For a guy who's been in the big leagues for ten years, Ray is a real worrywart. Ray always has a bat in his hand, and he's always looking for advice. During one bus trip in the spring, he and Gary Carter were discussing Ray's swing. Carter told him, "I see something you're doing wrong," and in the middle of the ride, Ray got up in the aisle with his bat. "Is this what you mean?" "Yeah." "I think I've got it now." He's always looking for tips. He'll talk hitting with anybody who'll talk to him. Even the batboy. The other players kid him, "This is your ninety-third stance of the year, Ray." He changes his stance a lot, changes his swing, tries different bats. And it works against him. He ought to just go up there, see the ball, and hit it. His mind is so filled with tips that I don't know how he can possibly concentrate on the ball.

When Ray isn't playing, he's miserable. During the game he'll walk around the dugout with a bat in his hand and damn near hit me every time he walks by. Then when I send him in he hasn't been getting on base. He's so confident as a hitter he doesn't understand it. "How can that guy get me out?" he'll say afterward.

My problem is that I have a kid who has to play in order to improve, and I have a veteran who needs to play in order to get on track. I end up having to reassure both of them all the time. I kept Howard out for two days against right-handers just to let Ray play a little more, and when Howard found out he wasn't playing, he got all upset. He said, "What's my situation?"

I said, "Just relax. I want to get Knight going. I need you both. I rest people. You need a rest. Step back. Watch a few ballgames. Take it easy. And come out smoking." That night Ray got a key hit and played very well defensively, and a couple days later hit a home run to tie a game.

The next day I had a real dilemma, but against a right-hander. I went back to Howard, because I don't want to lose Howard emotionally. I need Howard Johnson. Of course, Ray didn't understand. I'm sure he was saying to himself, God, I helped you win, and now you're not playing me? But I had to get Howard back in there. It's a tough situation, believe me.

18

DARRYL'S THUMB

WITH MOOKIE WILSON playing as well as he has, and George Foster's knee on the mend, I decided to call up Sid Fernandez to strengthen our pitching and to send Lenny Dykstra back to Tidewater so he can play regularly. I've been told that Sid's throwing the ball much better, that his fastball is alive and his breaking ball better. They say he looks more confident and relaxed than he was in the spring.

On a Thursday I announced that Sid was returning the coming Saturday. That afternoon Lenny Dykstra came to see me. "I have to talk to you," he said, making it sound urgent.

I said, "What about?"

He said, "I have some close friends coming in Friday."

I said, "Yeah, so?" I thought he was going to say, "Let me play." But I couldn't get him to say anything.

"They're coming in Friday," he repeated, "and they're *real* close friends."

I said, "What are you trying to tell me, Lenny?"

He said, "Sid is coming up Saturday, isn't he?"

I said, "Yeah."

He said, "Somebody's got to go down. If it's me, will I be sent down Friday or Saturday morning?"

Now I understood. I said, "When do these people leave, Lenny?"

He said, "Sunday morning."

I said, "If it is you, how about going down Sunday?"

He said, "That would be great!"

I told Lenny, "You proved you could play up here, and I appreciate what you did. You won two games for us. I don't know what's going to happen in the next few days. Mookie's arm might go back out, something might happen, in which case you'll stay." I wish I hadn't been so prophetic.

On paper I sent Lenny down to Tidewater on a Friday to make room for Sid Fernandez, who pitched a one-hitter the next day. In reality Lenny was still in New York, spending the weekend with his friends as I had promised. He was to return to Tidewater Sunday. On the day that Sid pitched his gem against the Phillies at Shea, and something did happen, only it wasn't to Mookie. It was to Darryl Strawberry.

In the third inning Juan Samuel hit a liner to Darryl's left. Darryl got a real good jump, and as the ball began sinking, he threw himself at it. But it was an awkward play because he's left-handed, and he had to twist his glove backhand to try to catch the ball. He dived, made the catch, rolled over, and came up holding his right thumb. The diagnosis: torn ligaments. The cure: surgery.

After the game I sat with Darryl, pleading with him to have the thumb operated on immediately. I said, "If you wait and try to play with it like it is for a couple of weeks, the tendon will shrivel, and then it will be necessary to do a graft, a much more difficult procedure."

Darryl didn't want even to discuss an operation. The idea of it scared him. "I'm going to wait and see how it feels in the morning," he said.

The next morning Darryl's hand was swollen. I went right over to see Dr. Parkes, who informed me that the hand specialist, Dr. Dick Eaton, could only do the operation the next morning. He would be unavailable the rest of the week.

Darryl had to have it done. But the idea of the operation still scared him. Darryl had never been hurt before. He said, "I need a few days to think about it." But a few days would have meant his having to wait a week to ten days to have the operation.

I said to Darryl, "If you wait three days, that's three days you're going to miss at the other end." Nevertheless he was determined not to have the operation.

After batting practice I brought Darryl over to talk with Frank Cashen and Dr. Parkes. Dr. Parkes explained it again, saying that if you wait, the procedure will be more difficult. Parkes said, "I recommend having it done as soon as possible. And I need to know right away, because I have to make the appointment with Dr. Eaton, the hand specialist."

Darryl said, "No, I'm not going to do it." He wouldn't listen to reason.

Before our noon chapel I called Keith Hernandez and George Foster into my office, explained the situation, and asked them to help talk Darryl into having the operation done now. They both understood. George said, "Bill Madlock won a batting title after being operated on by Dr. Eaton." They said they would talk to Darryl individually.

After chapel, I also enlisted Tom Jeffries. Jeffries, a large black man, is an accomplished inspirational speaker who has conducted services in such diverse forums as prisons and stadiums. I asked if he wouldn't mind talking to Darryl and helping him to get over his fear.

Jeffries met with Darryl. He said, "I've seen doctors reconstruct whole hands. I've seen football injuries where the wrist was severed, and the doctors put the hand back together again." He told Darryl, "Football players had hand surgery and were back throwing a football in six to ten weeks. It's miraculous what they can do now."

In the first inning of the game, Darryl came over to me and said, "Did you hear?"

I said, "No."

He said, "I decided to let them operate tomorrow." I shook his hand and told him I was very glad.

It's the first time he's ever been cut on, and it's not easy trusting a stranger to correct an injury. But I'm happy the way this worked out. At least I know we'll have Darryl back before the year's over.

The operation on Darryl's hand was a success. He'll be in a hard cast four weeks and in a soft cast for two. We're going to have to manage without him.

Frank Cashen and I talked about a possible replacement for Darryl outside the organization. I asked him who was available on other teams. "There isn't much out there, Dave," Frank said bluntly.

We could probably pry a Tito Landrum loose from the Cardinals, but we'd have to give up more than he's worth. We could probably get Barry Bonnell. But you're talking about guys at the end of their careers, and I'd rather go with Danny Heep and John Christensen. It's something I'm going to have to piece together.

I decided that with Darryl out, I'd start Danny Heep in his place. Danny runs the bases well, and is hitting the ball hard to all fields. He already has more ribbies than he had all last year. He's playing the outfield much more aggressively. In the field, he catches everything he gets to, though he's still a little tentative charging the ball. It takes him a little too long to get off the throw. He's also tentative on ground balls, as though he's a little afraid of making an error, but he'll improve as he plays more.

Danny has always wanted to play, and now he has that chance he's happy as a lark.

Right from spring training, Danny's been a different player. All last year Bill Robinson was pushing him when he hit to speed up his hands and drive the ball, and apparently the lessons have finally paid off.

As a person Danny's usually very quiet, but he got into some habits last year I didn't like. He was part of a little group that calls itself the "scum bunch" and sits in the back of the bus horsing around, and it may have affected his play.

Bill Robinson got all over Danny about it. "You have a chance to make some money in this game, but you won't if you keep clowning around all the time. You're always in the back of the bus or the plane making funny jokes and talking loudly, and you don't need that. Just do your job. Until you get serious, you're not gonna be the ballplayer or the hitter that you can be."

This year he's quieted down, and he's letting his bat do the talking for him.

Vern Hoscheit, my bullpen coach, fills out my lineup card for me before we get to the ballpark. He likes to do that because if I say, "That's correct, Vern," he thinks he's read my mind. If I say "Tear it up," he thinks I'm crazy. He's happy either way. The day after Darryl hurt himself, Vern came in with the lineup of Dykstra, then Backman. I said, "Wrong. Dykstra's going back to Tidewater. It's going to be Backman, then Mookie, and Heep is playing for Darryl."

Danny Heep is very valuable to me, and I'm not going to lose him mentally because I'm playing a rookie. He feels he deserves to play, and he would not understand not playing. I don't want to take the chance of ever telling him he's not valuable to me.

You would think team morale would have been hurt by Darryl's injury, but it hasn't been. The team really acts like a team. Everybody feels important. You can say "This guy is a key player," or "That guy gets paid more," or "That's my fourth-hole hitter." But *everybody* is key. When Darryl went down the other guys just said, "Well, we're just going to have to pick up the slack."

There was no need to hold a team meeting and pump them up with a phony rah-rah. My ballclub doesn't need a lot of pep talks, because we're grinders. We haven't been blowing anybody out, but we do wear them down and beat them. We're in first place, one game up on Montreal. Our work is cut out for us to stay there.

19
MORE OF THE SAME

WHEN I MOVED Roger McDowell into the pen to replace Doug Sisk, I was counting on twenty-two-year-old Calvin Schiraldi to win himself a spot in the rotation. I started him in mid-May against Atlanta, and in the first inning the very first batter, Claudell Washington, hit a two-bouncer back up the middle that nailed Calvin on the right toe. Calvin insisted he was all right, and for four-and-a-third innings he pitched very well. Then his foot really started to give him problems. At that point, I had to take him out.

When he was hit, Calvin said his toe was just "numb," but I suspected that it might be broken. My experience is that when you break your toe, it doesn't hurt much at first but then the pain can be excruciating. Going into the fifth, I knew he was in a lot of pain, but he had a 3-0 lead and begged, "Let me try to get through the inning." I went with him. He gave up a home run to Washington, got the next batter out, and then walked a batter throwing nothing but breaking balls. With the tying run at the plate, I felt I had to hook him. Roger McDowell came in and retired the last fourteen batters to end the game.

I'm figuring that Calvin probably won't be ready for three weeks, maybe a month, and I don't want to rush him on a broken toe. Dizzy Dean came back too soon after breaking a toe on a line drive, and when he tried to favor the toe, he injured his arm and ruined his career.

I remember what happened when I broke my toe. In 1966 Gates Brown jumped on me trying to take me out of a double play in Detroit. I turned the double play, but he left a big spike mark where he squashed it. I needed fifteen stitches and my little toe was cracked.

About a week later, when they took the stitches out, I was back in the lineup, but because of the pain in my toe, I began putting all my weight on the right side, and that leg just about blew out. It didn't come around until World Series time. So I know what it's like to have a broken toe and keep trying to play.

The question is, who's going to take his place? Perhaps Bruce Berenyi if he's ready. But that's a big if.

I've also decided to call back Ron Gardenhire. Hopefully, he's recovered from his muscle-pull problems. Maybe I'll be able to get through without anyone else getting hurt.

The writers keep asking me, "What are you going to do when everybody starts coming off the DL?" Those are wonderful problems. I should have such problems.

Meanwhile, there's more unsettling news. Frank Cashen called. He said, "Texas asked for permission to talk to Bobby Valentine about managing the Rangers." Bobby is my third base coach. He's been my right-hand man, my friend and confidant. We really work well together. He can read my mind so well that most of the time he knows what sign to give without my having to tell him. On top of everything else, I don't need this.

The Rangers are in last place, and I guess they're thinking about firing Doug Rader. When I heard the news, I tried to convince myself that Bobby wouldn't take the job. I made some pretty good arguments. Unfortunately, I wasn't very convincing.

Tomorrow Bobby Valentine is going to see Eddie Chiles, the president of the Texas Rangers, and Tom Grieve. He came to talk to me before the meeting.

Bobby said, "Tommy Lasorda suggests I take the job, that not that many of them come along."

I said, "Bobby, you have to ask yourself two things: One, can you do a better job than the guy who's in there? Two, if you do take the job, what will your situation be two years from now?"

Bobby told me he asked for a three-year contract and he wants some veto power on player moves. He's demanding a lot of say-so, and it looks like they're going to give it to him. I guess the Rangers feel they don't have any choice.

I sat around, waiting for the news, and it was like waiting to get hit in the stomach. By the time the punch came, I was already resigned. My feeling is that Bobby might be making the move a little bit prematurely, but he's intelligent, and he'll be able to handle it.

Replacing a third base coach isn't as easy as it sounds. The players were comfortable with Bobby. They respected him, liked his aggressiveness, worked well with him. My two possible replacements are Buddy Harrelson, who's managing the Columbia, South Carolina, team in A ball, or Sammy Perlozzo, who's managing Jackson in Double A. My first thought was to call Perlozzo. I figure we have good chemistry on this ballclub, so let me keep things the way they are and replace an Italian with an Italian. Also, Cashen and everybody in the organization say Sammy's our next best managerial prospect. I thought they would want me to give him some big league experience coaching. That way, if they want to fire me, they'd have Sammy right here.

When I asked Vern Hoscheit whom I should get, he said, "Hire Yogi Berra." He was serious.

I said, "Dad, I don't know that Yogi would come, and even if he would, I don't want to get involved in George Steinbrenner's contest as to whose town it is."

After discussing the question with Frank and some of the other organization men, the consensus was that they preferred to keep Perlozzo where he is. Darrell Johnson, whose opinion I respect, told me, "You only have one choice, and that's Buddy Harrelson."

Darrell said, "Buddy was an outstanding shortstop with the

Miracle Mets of '69, he had major league experience, and he'd be popular with the fans." He's been managing and coaching third base for the last two years. I made the choice, and I called Buddy.

As the rest of the Mets were leaving Houston to return to New York, Bobby Valentine stayed behind. His next stop is Dallas, where he will meet his Rangers. As I was walking out to the bus, Bobby jokingly let out a loud yell, "Aaaaaargh!" as if to say, "What the hell am I getting into?"

I've lost Darryl for a month or so, I've lost Calvin Schiraldi, and I've lost my third base coach to Texas. I am undaunted. Things like that you have no control over. They happen. They are part of baseball. After putting the injured player on some kind of recovery program, you concentrate on how to cover the loss of that player. You say to yourself, Now that this has happened, how can I solve this problem?

And you turn the page. You can't dwell on it. Because it doesn't do you any good. Nothing constructive can come out of worrying about things over which you have no control.

20
GOADING THE KID

IN BUDDY'S FIRST GAME his newness almost cost us the win, but thanks to Gary we ended up beating the Giants in extra innings.

With the score tied in the eleventh, we had runners on first and third, one out, and our shortstop, Rafael Santana, up. It was a perfect time for a squeeze bunt, but I could see that a squeeze was exactly what San Francisco was expecting. Giant manager Jim Davenport had his third baseman playing in. I signaled for Raffy to hit away, and on the first two pitches catcher Bob Brenly called for pitchouts. It was a good thing I didn't order a squeeze. The runner from third would have been a dead duck.

Raffy fouled off the next two pitches, making the count two-and-two. Now, I figured, was the time to squeeze. I was thinking to myself, They won't be expecting it, not with two strikes on the batter. I relayed the sign to Buddy coaching over at third.

Buddy got the sign and gave it to Santana. Santana looked down at Buddy, and I know he saw Buddy give the sign to him, but Raffy didn't return the mandatory answering sign.

He hadn't played with Buddy before, and he didn't trust Buddy enough to know whether he was giving the right sign. So

Santana didn't answer, killing the play. The pitcher threw, and it was a perfect pitch to squeeze on, a breaking ball down, and we could have ended it right there. Instead, Raffy popped out and we didn't score.

After the game I said to Raffy, "Buddy gave you the bunt sign."

He said, "But I had two strikes on me."

I said, "You would have won the game right there."

Buddy and I discussed it afterward. Buddy said he didn't know what to do after Raffy brushed off his squeeze sign. I said, "You should have called time and then gone through it again. The Giants might have thought we had the squeeze on but were taking it off."

It was frustrating. I don't squeeze much, and when I did, it was on a day when I had a brand new third base coach, so my player wasn't really sure he knew what the sign was! I felt like punching the wall.

Gary Carter won it in the twelfth, despite himself. Gary has this macho thing about pulling everything down the left field line. I wish just once he would go to right field. All the fielders know he's going to try to pull the ball to left, and when he gets up, opposing managers stack the left side with fielders. Early in the game Carter said, "LaPoint always gives me trouble. He throws me that little screwball." I said, "Why don't you drive it to right field?" He said, "Naw, this time I'm going to drag one." He went up and got a bunt base hit down third.

Next time he was up I said, "Why don't you just drive it to right field?" He pulled the ball to short. Then in the ninth he popped up with Mookie running. Before the twelfth inning started, I said, "Gary, damn it, I'm going to make you win the ballgame. This is an order. When you go up there, I want you to hit the ball to right field."

Wally Backman got on in the twelfth on an error—left fielder Jeff Leonard dropped a line drive hit right at him—and with Keith up, I started Wally on the pitch. Keith singled and Wally went to third. Now it was Gary. On the third pitch Gary lined a hard shot to right field, bringing Wally in to score. I said to Gary, "I told you I was going to make you win the game."

Carter, who played every inning, has been getting beat around. Foul tips are hitting him with regularity. He gets four or five foul tips beating on him a game. After the game he came over to me, mugging as if he were punchy.

"I'm all right, Skip," he said, flinching.

I said, "Gary, how about me giving you off tomorrow? You caught twelve innings and it's been drizzling."

He said, "Nah, nah, I'll be in there. I'm all right."

21
LOOSE

ROGER MCDOWELL is the sunflower-seed kid. He cannot sit in the bullpen without flicking them, and he loves to hit bullpen coach Vern Hoscheit right in the nose with them. He is very good at it. During the game Vern left his coffee by the bullpen phone unattended, and Roger, from ten feet, flicked the sunflower seeds into the cup until it was half-filled with seeds. When Vern returned, he put the cup to his lips, took a long sip, and swallowed a mouthful of seeds.

The next day Roger came out to the pen early. He was drinking coffee. Vern sat down next to him. After a few minutes, Roger set his coffee down and walked to the other end of the pen. Quickly, Vern reached down and picked up a handful of dirt and gravel and dropped it into Roger's cup. Later Roger took a sip. Roger said, "Boy, is this bad coffee." Then he started sputtering and spitting.

Since Vern is not a practical joker, Roger accused the security cop. Roger was ready to throw the rest of the coffee at the cop when Vern stopped him. "Whoa, wait a minute, you'll get the man's uniform dirty. If you want to get even, think of something else." But Vern wouldn't admit he did it, either.

Later in the game Jesse Orosco took to impersonating Tommy Gorman. He put on Tommy's warmup jacket, took a huge wad of bubblegum, and stuck it on his face in the shape of a big nose. Jesse grabbed a ball with a split-finger grip and went around saying, "Who am I?" He had the entire pen in stitches.

To show how loose this team is: the other night we were riding the bus to the Houston airport when the players held a rip session. Tommy Gorman started in on Ray Knight. "Hey, Ray," he said, "you don't need to play." Ray said, "What do you mean?" Tommy said, "Nancy has all the money in the family. You can go one for twenty, and it won't make any difference if she wins a couple of tournaments." Everyone went, "Woooooooooo." Ray is married to golfer Nancy Lopez. Keith Hernandez, who's a real agitator, shouted at Dwight Gooden, "Hey, Doc, you now a six-inning pitcher? I guess you can't finish what you start anymore, huh?" Doc had beaten the Astros for his sixth win but I had to hook him in the seventh. Someone then ragged Rusty Staub about his weight, and Darryl about the rap music he listens to. Then someone gave Wally Backman a jab about being short. The guys are always making jokes about Wally's size. If someone throws his luggage on top of the bus, another player will say, "Don't throw it up there. That's Wally's bed." The radio once was playing "Small World," and someone yelled out, "Hey, listen, that's Wally's song."

Keith then started calling Gary Carter "Camera Carter," alluding to the fact that somebody or the other is always asking Gary to pose and that Gary never turns down an interview. On this team nothing and no one is sacred. Everyone gets on everyone. Carter said to me, "Everyone used to talk about me in Montreal, but behind my back. Here, everyone does it right in front of everyone."

What his Montreal teammates had against Gary I can only guess. Jealousy is a terrible thing. It wasn't Gary's fault that whenever a company needed an Expo to do a commercial, it chose Gary. Gary's a PR man's dream. He's a genuinely nice person, and he not only cares about playing, he knows he has a responsibility to the press that he cares about too. He does work for the Leukemia Society. He is a very caring person. He's been accused of being a phony, but he's not. He's just a nice person, and if being nice is bad, then so be it.

They call Gary "the Kid" because he loves baseball, loves to play, and is very enthusiastic. He's often kidded because of his exuberance. After road games he's always the last one on the bus because he doesn't refuse anyone for interviews. When he finally shows up, the players yell at him, "That's all right, Gary, we don't mind waiting for you—as usual." Players can gauge whether they're late for the bus by checking on Gary. "I got time to get dressed. The Kid isn't dressed yet. He has to give another interview."

22

THE WOLVES

EDDIE LYNCH has had the worst luck. In his last start he was beaten by the Braves 1–0. This time he gave up only two runs to the Giants but had to come out after eight without a win. The score was tied, and in the bottom of the eighth I went for the win and pinch-hit for Eddie. We didn't score, and in the ninth I sent in rookie Wes Gardner to relieve.

I went with Wes because my bullpen is in shambles. I had used Jesse for two innings two days before, and his arm is a little tender. I had used Roger McDowell yesterday, and I didn't want to use him a second day. I couldn't go to Tommy Gorman, who was scheduled to start the next day. My choice came down to Wes and Joe Sambito, who hasn't been throwing all that well.

Wes got in a jam in his first inning of work, but somehow we got out of it; in his second the dam broke loose. In the tenth inning Wes had runners on second and third, so I had him walk Jose Uribe to load the bases to try to get the double play with Gary Rajsich up, but Rajsich hit a seeing-eye grounder through the infield. He ended up giving up six hits and six runs before he could retire the side.

After the game all the writers kept asking me, "Why didn't you bring someone else into the game to keep the score closer?"

The writers weren't the only ones second-guessing. The next day I received this letter in the mail:

Dear Mr. Johnson,

I have been a major league fan for over forty years. That display of managing I saw on channel 9 on Saturday night, May 18 in the 10th inning was a disgrace to baseball.

With your team tied 2–2 and a good chance to win, you left pitcher Wes Gardner in the game that 10th inning to take a fearful beating, giving up six runs and six hits and losing the game.

The beating you made Gardner take on that mound was inhuman. Don't give me the story that there were pitchers on the teams who had worked in prior days and could not work anymore that night. At least that is the lame excuse the "house men" announcers on TV who shill for the Mets came up with.

Wes Gardner could have blown a major league pitching career thanks to you; he must have thrown 75 or more pitches in less than two innings as he was battered in that embarrassment.

If you thought so little of the pitcher, why did you put him into the game? You sure as hell didn't try to win the game. If I didn't know better, it seemed like you were trying to lose the game on purpose. I know if I were the National League president, you would answer some questions.

The public must be nuts paying money to see you bunch of dopers in major league baseball to start with. Add to it managers like you who don't know what they are doing, and you have made big league baseball a laughing stock.

I love the commissioner's idea of drug testing; he should start with you. Because after that exhibition of managing on Saturday night at Shea Stadium in the 10th inning, I would like to know what the hell you're on!

Truly yours

I also got this one. I left the punctuation and spelling as it was written.

Davie Johnson its a dam shame the way you handle that
club That you should they are not hiting no game that they
play why dont you bring them out in the morning and make
them practis hitting and get on them once in a while in the
club house.They are to relaked, & dont even look like they
try to hit.You cant run a ball club like that man you should
know that.You are so dum and stupid.Get on those fellows
and make them get on the ball and snap out of that slump.
make them have bating practice often dont be so stupid as a
manager you are so stupid we have to talk to the oners and
ask that you be removed and replaced.at once we cant stand
it much longer and you better keep that in your mind.

Fans.

Isn't it nice to have the support of your fans?

The next day the rightness of what I did was borne out. Because of the injuries to Berenyi and to Calvin Schiraldi, I was
forced to start middle reliever Tommy Gorman. I can only ask
Tommy to give me six good innings. Tommy was heroic against
the Giants, allowing only two runs. We were leading 3–2 when I
brought in a fresh Roger McDowell to relieve in the seventh. Had
I pitched Roger yesterday, I couldn't have used him in this game,
and who would I have thrown out there then? Not Jesse. He's
hurting. No one else has been sharp. But I had a rested
McDowell, and he shut the Giants out the last three innings, and
we ended up winning the game. That's why I didn't bring him in
yesterday. It's as simple as that. Kenny Harrelson, who used to be
a professional golfer, once asked Jack Nicklaus after a moderately
hit drive, "How come you didn't hit your driver all the way out?"
Nicklaus told him, "You have to keep a little bit on your hip."
And that's the truth. You have to hold a little bit back.

Second-guessing the manager is one of baseball's great pas-
times. Getting second-guessed by people who don't know all that
much is a constant aggravation for me. But it's something you
have to live with if you want to survive the job. You get it from
all sides, from the fans, from the writers, and sometimes even
from your friends.

In a recent game I sent Ray Knight up to pinch-hit for Howard
Johnson. Even though Ray hasn't been hitting much lately, I had

several very good reasons for doing it, the best one being that the opposing team had substituted a lefty pitcher, and I wanted a right-handed bat. Ray was my best choice. He popped out.

My hitting coach, Bill Robinson, happened to be back in the clubhouse for some reason, and he said to me, "I've been watching the game on TV, and Tim McCarver has just gotten into your kitchen." Tim McCarver is a Mets TV broadcaster and a good friend of mine. I said, "How's that?" Bill told me, "McCarver said, 'Johnson put Ray Knight in the game because he's worried about Ray's feelings more than about winning or losing this ballgame.'"

For McCarver to say that I'm not concerned about winning a ballgame, them's fighting words. And I will let Timmy know it when I see him. But it just goes to show you that in this town, even your best friends will say things that may undermine what you have going. We're two games in first place, so can you imagine what they'd be saying if we were playing .500 ball? It's a constant reminder that there are a lot of wolves waiting to tear you to pieces at the drop of a hat. The lesson is to stay on your toes.

23
DOUG GETS THE CALL

AFTER THE WES GARDNER DEBACLE, I knew that I needed to bring up another relief pitcher. I decided to call back my old heart-attack and Rolaids kid, Dougie Sisk, and I hope he's in a better frame of mind and that his fastballs are sinking better.

In fourteen innings of pitching for the Tides, Doug has allowed 15 hits and 13 walks. He is 0–2 with an ERA of 6.60. Not exactly encouraging statistics.

I called down to Triple A and talked to Tidewater manager Bobby Schaefer, who told me, "Tonight Sisk went into the game in the sixth inning with one man on, gave up a bunt single, and got the next two batters. The last seven pitches he threw were strikes." I said, "That's good enough. I need him. I want you to hold him there. We'll make travel arrangements as soon as I can find Frank Cashen." Frank had left the ballgame about the eighth inning and I needed clearance from him. They finally ran him down, and Frank okayed it.

The next day my scheduled starting pitcher, Sid Fernandez, came to the ballpark early and hobbled over to see the trainer. He said his Achilles tendon on his left leg was killing him. "I can barely walk on it," Sid said. The trainer says he has about a seventy-five-percent chance to make his next start five days from now. I don't believe this!

My options are to piece together a start using Sambito and Sisk, and then if Sid needs to miss a second start, to use Gorman. Or I can call up somebody from Tidewater. One choice is left-hander Bill Latham. If I go to Latham, that gives me five left-handers and five righties, and I'm not comfortable with that because most of my left-handers are finesse-type pitchers, and their being left-handed doesn't give me much of an advantage. The other choice is to call up Tidewater's best young pitcher, right-handed Rick Aguilera.

Frank Cashen was for getting Latham instead of Aguilera, but I had done my homework before I went to see him. I said, "Let's look ahead to San Diego and Los Angeles. How do those clubs do against left-handers and right-handers?" Frank called up to publicity director Jay Horwitz's office, and Dennis, his assistant, told Frank what I already knew; LA's record against left-handers was 16–9 and San Diego's record 11–10; against right-handers LA was 3–9 and San Diego 4–9. So Frank said, "The right-hander it is."

Frank's mood has improved greatly over what it was last year. Last year our 90–72 record proved that Frank's five-year plan was right on schedule, and so this year the pressure on him isn't so great, and Frank has actually loosened up. He smiles more, and he's a lot easier to get along with. Through the spring during the games, he'd joke with me. He'd point to the area of the press box where he always sits, and he'd say, "I'll be right up here, and you can look up anytime you need some help."

Last year Frank questioned my decisions much more. Once he came in after a game and said, "I don't want you to use Orosco today. You used him the last two days." I got hot under the collar and said, "You want to manage this ballclub? 'Cause if you do, you go ahead and manage it, and I'll leave." He said, "No, I'm paying you a lot of money to manage it."

Since then his suggestions have sounded less like orders, and a lot of times he's right, too. For instance, he'd tell me, "You can rattle Soto if you bunt on him or yell at him." Different things like that. Because he wants to win.

Sometimes it rubs me the wrong way that Frank feels he has to give me help, that I'm missing something in trying to win a ballgame. It's offensive to me that he feels I haven't thought of everything. What I end up saying is: "Thank you, sir, I'll try to do that."

Nevertheless, as I get to know him better, I admire him more and more, to the point where I consider him a friend. I hope he thinks of me the same way.

When I called Doug Sisk back up, I had to send someone down, and the one I picked was Wes Gardner. Wes, I feel, is still an outstanding young prospect, but he needs to pitch, and he's not going to get much work sitting on our bench.

No player is ever happy when he's sent down, but I try to be honest so he'll understand why I'm doing what I'm doing.

When we activate Aguilera, I'll have to send Ronn Reynolds down too, which is a problem since they already have two catchers at Tidewater. When I told Bobby Schaefer what I was planning to do, I said, "I hate to do all these things to you, but I have no choice but to look after my own up here. If you're below me, and I get to pick from the cream of your crop, you're in deep trouble."

He laughed, knowing I wasn't lying. He said, "One time let me choose from you." We both laughed.

24

FEELING THE WEIGHT

THE LOSS of Darryl Strawberry is making itself felt. Before, we were scoring a couple of runs and our pitching was keeping us in games. Now we aren't scoring any runs at all. Dwight gave up two runs and lost to the Padres. We got four lousy hits against LaMarr Hoyt and didn't score once, even though Hoyt made some bad pitches. He was mixing up his pitches enough, however, to keep the guys off stride. There's a joke going around the dugout when we're up at the plate. One player says, "What's the count?" "Three and one." "Hey, a rally."

I have asked Frank Cashen to get me a veteran right-handed bat for the bench. With the guys not hitting, it would ease the tension if I had a veteran bat to come off the bench to hit against left-handed relievers. Ray Knight is out with vertigo caused by an inner ear infection, and Gardenhire is out. That leaves Wally Backman when Kelvin Chapman starts, and a rookie, John Christensen, who has had outstanding years in the minor leagues, but which were compiled by playing every day, against righties and lefties. With us he's playing part-time and pinch-hitting only against left-handers, and not very often, and it's an alien role to him. For a youngster trying to establish himself in the big leagues it's tough, because it's a role—a very difficult role—he's never performed before. He's facing only left-handers, and he probably didn't hit them that well in the minors. Plus, he's a slow starter to begin with. And so he's 4 for 34, hitting .118. He's not giving me much production. If Frank could get me a veteran right-handed bat I would send John back to Tidewater, where he'd be better off.

I told Frank how I was feeling about John's situation. I said, "I don't think John's going to be able to handle that situation, and I need an experienced right-handed bat."

Frank got on the phone and talked to a number of general managers. We're looking for a veteran right-handed hitter like a Tom Paciorek, a Barry Bonnell, a Steve Henderson, a Ron Roenicke, a Dusty Baker. But some of these guys are making as much as $800,000. In the American League these guys can DH. In the National League, we're talking about a part-time pinch hitter. So certain players are not worth the price tag.

Frank knows how important it is. He just hasn't been able to do anything, which is very frustrating for me.

The other day I told Frank, "You know, with your inability to make a deal, our two kids, Blocker and Christensen, will be veterans." He laughed. He said, "You stole the words right out of my mouth."

I was in my office when Frank came in all excited. He said he had been talking to Al Campanis, the LA Dodger general manager. "Al says he's willing to deal Bobby Bailor," Frank said. I got excited. I said, "Bailor would be the perfect right-handed bat. What do they want for him?" I asked.

Frank said, "The Dodgers don't need him. They have Dave Anderson coming back and a bunch of middle infielders. Bailor's making a lot of money. I think we can work something out."

The next day Frank came back looking grim. Frank had called Campanis to work out the deal, and Campanis gave Frank a list of all the top prospects in our organization: Schiraldi, McDowell, Aguilera, Mars, Jefferson! All our number one picks! In exchange for a utility player making big bucks whom they're thinking about unloading! It's a joke and I sympathize with Frank. I really feel for him. I don't blame him for not wanting to deal with Campanis anymore. I wouldn't deal with Campanis either. I wouldn't call him back, and if he called me, I wouldn't return his calls. Because I don't like somebody leading me on and saying to himself, I've got a live one. I'll set a hook on him.

You have to be up-front and straightforward from the git-go. Obviously Campanis is not. I wouldn't even bother thinking about making a deal with him. The only way I'd ever make a deal with him is if he said, "I'll trade you so-and-so for so-and-so," and then he would have to sign it, seal it, have it notarized, and then leave it open for me to close the deal.

Frank also said he was talking to other clubs about bolstering our pitching. We need a starter and a reliever. He was talking to the Pirates about acquiring John Candelaria, but the Pirates want too much. They're asking for a couple of young arms, plus a bat. Bringing Rick Aguilera up seems to be the best way for us to strengthen our staff.

I'm upset because Joe Sambito hasn't worked out. When we signed Joe it seemed like a good gamble. We only had to pay $40,000 of his $750,000 salary. Unfortunately, Joe hasn't made it back far enough from his arm injury. Gary Carter confirmed my doubts.

"He just doesn't pop the ball. He doesn't have any velocity at all."

I finally had to tell Frank that I didn't think Joe Sambito was going to help us. I feel bad about it. But I'm getting pretty impatient. The Mets can't seem to firm up any new talent before we go into June. It seems to me that if you have a need, you ask a lot of people about the commodity you want and get an asking price, and then you relate the asking price to what you think the player's worth, and then make a deal or not make a deal.

Anyway, we are shorthanded. And I am short-tempered.

I went into our finale against the Padres pissed off. At Shea Stadium we have a large satellite, and the reason we have it is so we can pick up other games around the country. I can scout any team in-house, tape them, study them. I have an arrangement with the head electrician that I made through Frank Cashen. Any National League East game takes precedence over anything else.

I came to the ballpark early to watch the Cardinals play the Atlanta Braves in St. Louis. But I couldn't get the channel tuned in. Either my TV set was out, or they didn't have it tuned to the right satellite. The game began, and I couldn't get it. The electricians weren't there. No one was there. I was getting very frustrated because I had come to the ballpark early specifically to watch the game.

I complained to Frank Cashen and to Bob Mandt, the stadium manager. Finally, at 3:45, miraculously, the Cardinal game came on, and I got to watch a half an inning, because at 4:05 I felt it more important to watch the Cubs game. When that game didn't come on, I was even more frustrated.

When I complained to Frank, he turned a deaf ear. I didn't understand. Say, "I can't do anything, Dave." Or tell me, "We're doing the best we can, but it won't work because of such-and-such." I can accept that. But don't walk away from me like it's a pain in the butt to you.

I was ready to quit. I'd have fired the whole damn crew. It's a detail, but it's important. I don't think that I have to be aggravated over something like this. I have enough aggravation in my job without being aggravated over something like this.

The game itself was a toughie. Ronnie Darling was in total command, and in the sixth inning San Diego's tenacious hitters made a couple of hits. We had a three-run lead, but with two on and two out, Ron made a bad pitch to Terry Kennedy, and Kennedy hit it out of the ballpark to tie the game.

That was Ronnie's hundredth pitch, and I didn't want to push him so I brought in Roger McDowell. He shut them out for three, but we couldn't score either, and we had to go to the tenth. I brought in Jesse Orosco, and Kennedy got a base hit off a curveball to drive in the winning run. It was our fifth straight loss.

The outcome of the game may have been aggravating, but the overriding thing that pissed me off was the problem with the satellite before the game. I went home one very unhappy man.

25

SEEING BLUE

AT SHEA WE BEAT THE DODGERS in the final two games of our homestand. McDowell starred in relief and then Darling pitched a complete game, allowing only one run. The Dodgers made two errors in each game. They've been making a lot of errors and losing games because of it. Right now they are in fourth place, five back of San Diego, but I still think that potentially they have one of the best teams in baseball.

After flying cross-country to begin a West Coast road trip, we opened with an afternoon game at Candlestick Park. Eddie Lynch gave up three quick runs after he failed to cover first on a grounder to Keith Hernandez and then when Ray Knight lost a pop-up in the sun. Lynch didn't give up another run through the seventh, but we didn't score.

In the eighth we scored a run, and Keith came up with Chappie on first and Mookie on second. I noticed that the new Giant pitcher, Mark Davis, wasn't paying enough attention to the runners, and so I called for a double steal. With the count one-and-one Mookie and Chappie took off, and they slid in safe.

Now we had runners on second and third. Keith stepped in,

and with the count two-and-one, just before Davis went into his windup, Keith waved for time and stepped out. The umpire, Jim Quick, ignored Keith's request and called the pitch a ball. Keith was furious. He knew he'd asked for time early enough, and he was figuring that Quick was jobbing him because he had complained about the very first pitch thrown to him.

That pitch had been five inches inside, and Quick had called it a strike. Keith had told Quick, "This is the critical point in the game. Don't put me in a hole."

So Keith was figuring Quick was jobbing him just because he had complained. This time Quick said, "You're lucky it wasn't a strike." Keith said that Quick was smirking at him. Keith then struck out, and called Quick a cocksucker and a horseshit ump. Quick told him, "You can take it to the clubhouse," and he threw him out of the game. I ran out there and so did Bill Robinson from the first base coaching box, and it was all we could do to stop Keith from ripping out Quick's throat.

Gary Carter, who's been in a slump, was up next, and to my surprise, Giants manager Jim Davenport let the left-handed Davis pitch to Gary. Against the Giants back in New York, Davis had thrown Gary nothing but curveballs, and so this time Gary went up there looking for the curve. When Davis hung one at the letters, Gary lined a double to left to tie the score. Davenport took Davis out and brought in right-hander Scott Garrelts to face George Foster, who drilled a single to center to score Gary with the winning run.

I had asked Doug Sisk to warm up in the seventh and was going to have him come into the game to mop up, but when we tied the score I had him sit down and got Roger McDowell up. I felt bad because last year Doug had been my number one right-handed short man, and now I was telling Doug that he's not anymore. Roger came in and pitched two shutout innings for his third save of the year.

After the game I talked to Doug. He said, "You took me out of the game before you even put me in it." I said, "Yeah, Doug. Sorry about that." I felt bad for him, but there are times when a manager has to put the team ahead of the individual player.

After the game Keith was still talking about Quick. He said, "When I go out there tomorrow, I better not have any check swings," figuring that a check-swing call, or any other call by Quick would go against him.

I certainly didn't expect that of Quick, but the next day Keith certainly got it from two other umpires in the crew. Early in the game Keith checked his swing, and the home plate umpire, Bob Engel, called it no swing, and when the Giants didn't appeal, it was called a ball.

Over by second base I could see Runge, the second base umpire, walk over to Quick, who this day was umping third, and I could read their lips to see what they were talking about. Runge was asking Quick, "On the check swing of Keith's, would you have rung him up?" meaning, would you have called him out? And then Runge made a sign with a circular motion indicating that he damn sure would have. Runge was grinning. At the time I figured they were fooling around.

In the fifth we had runners on first and second, nobody out. Keith was up with a count of two balls and no strikes. The Giants' Jim Gott pitched, and it was so low I didn't even check the umpire's call. I *knew* it was a ball.

I looked to Buddy Harrelson, my third base coach, and gave him the take sign, indicating that I didn't want Keith swinging at the three-and-oh pitch with nobody out and runners on first and second against Gott. Buddy saw me, but he didn't relay my sign! I was perplexed, and then I looked at the scoreboard and saw that it was two balls and a strike. Engel had called that grounder a strike! Because I missed it, I didn't have time to give the hit-and-run signal, and Keith hit into a double play.

At second Runge made it worse by ruling that the runner, Wally Backman, had interfered with the fielder. It was a ridiculous call because Backman never touched the relay man. Runners slide at the fielder all the time, and if they don't actually hit him, the umpire never makes an interference call. I bitched a little bit with Engel about the call, but I really came out because I was beginning to think that the umpires were conspiring to get Keith!

I said to the guys on the bench, "One more call against us, and they're going to have to run me." It happened in the eighth. Mookie swung at a ball, and it hit the ground and jumped up in the air five feet behind home plate. Engel called it fair. I came out, saying, "The ball is five feet foul, Bob."

He said, "No. It was fair."

I said, "It was five feet foul. I was looking right at it. If you can't see it, get some help."

He said, "I saw it. It was fair."

I said, "Let me tell you something. You blew that call. But let me tell you why I'm really here. I had more respect for you before you tried burning Keith today because of yesterday."

He said, "What do you mean? That was with Quick yesterday."

I said, "You guys stick together." And then he threw me. And I had a few choice multisyllable words for him.

This game is too big to let what happened yesterday influence our judgment today. But it does. And it was obvious it was happening today against Keith Hernandez. So I had to make sure that everybody knew that I knew. I had to get thrown. Because I don't want this to linger over us all year. And because I want my players to know I'm out there fighting for them.

That was one of Earl Weaver's most endearing qualities, though, like so many things he did, Earl took it to extremes. During a game no one baited an umpire harder than Earl. He would scream, rant, rave, throw dirt, and one time he got so worked up over a call he pretended to faint on the mound. He was telling the world, "You're not going to take advantage of my team." And we felt, If he really cares that much, if he's competing so hard to win this ballgame, we owe him nothing less from ourselves than that kind of effort.

After I was thrown out by Engel, I told Buddy Harrelson he was in charge. My one concern was whether Dwight could finish the game. The only run he gave up was a home run to Trevino, and Doc had a 2–1 lead going into the eighth inning. I had Jesse warming up. The one Giant batter I was worried about was Chili Davis, but Doc struck him out on four pitches.

Going into the ninth Doc had thrown 126 pitches, which is a lot, and Mel Stottlemyre asked him, "Dwight, how do you feel?" He said, "I feel fine." Mel said, "Dwight, you've thrown a lot of pitches." He said, "That's okay, I feel fine." Mel said, "Dwight, if anybody gets on, you're out of there." Dwight's eyes got real big. He looked back at Mel, smiled, and said, "That's fair."

In the ninth, with that thought in his mind, he faced Jeff Leonard, Chris Brown, and Trevino, and struck them all out.

26

LOSE ONE, WIN ONE

SOMETIMES the other manager outfoxes you. You hate to admit it when it happens. We were playing the San Diego Padres in what might well have been a preview of the League Championship series.

We went into the bottom of the eighth with the score tied. I brought in Doug Sisk instead of Jesse and McDowell for several reasons. One, I wanted to put Doug in a game situation to build his confidence, to tell him I still had confidence in him. I also wanted to give Roger one more day of rest, sensing that he might need it. Also, even though Jesse was well-rested, I didn't want to bring him in to pitch two innings with the score tied. I want him in there when we're ahead to save the game.

What happened wasn't Doug's fault.

Steve Garvey started off the Padres eighth with a bouncer up the middle, and Kevin McReynolds bunted him over to second. Graig Nettles grounded to second, moving Garvey to third, and with two outs I was feeling pretty confident that Doug would get us out of it.

The batter was Carmelo Martinez, whose home run put the

Padres ahead in the sixth. He'd hit three home runs in the last two games. I fully expected him to be hitting away.

Howard Johnson at third moved in a little bit, but Keith over at first yelled for him to move back. The pitch was a ball. HoJo moved back in but again Keith yelled for him to move back. It was ball two. And I had to agree with Keith. It wasn't a bunt situation.

Doug had run the count to two-and-oh, and now Martinez had Dougie right where he wanted him. With two outs, I was figuring him to be swinging the bat.

If Howard had learned to speak Spanish, we might have been prepared for it. Ozzie Virgil, their third base coach, yelled something that sounded like "dejasela," which HoJo later learned means "drop it down." Dougie pitched, and Martinez laid down a blueprint bunt. HoJo came running in, and he fired the ball past Keith as Garvey scored the winning run.

The next day I got Dick Williams back. I started Clint Hurdle behind the plate, moved Carter to first to rest his knees, and batted Ray Knight, who's hitting .180, third. Mark Thurmond, a tough lefty, was pitching, so I gave Keith the night off.

We scored three in the sixth, with Chappie and Knight singling, and Carter and Hurdle both getting walks as we took the lead on a bloop by Rafael.

Follow the rest of this closely. It's a little complicated. In the top of the seventh I pinch-hit Keith for Ron Darling, who had either hit or walked the leadoff batter so often I wanted to hit him.

Keith, hitting in the pitcher's number nine spot, struck out. Mookie doubled to left field, and Williams brought in a right-hander, DeLeon, to pitch to Kelvin Chapman. Countering, I sent up Rusty Staub, who singled down the right field line and drove Mookie home. I pinch-ran Blocker for Rusty. Then Knight hit into a double play.

Blocker and Staub were now out of the game, and the home plate umpire, Dutch Rennert, was figuring I wanted to stick Wally Backman, my new second baseman, in the number two spot, where Kelvin had been.

But no, I put Hernandez in the game, my regular catcher behind the plate, took Hurdle out of the game, and put Backman in the seventh hole, where Hurdle had been hitting. I had the pitcher, McDowell, hit number two, in Blocker's spot.

Later on in the game we ended up getting an insurance run when Backman doubled, stole third, and scored on a groundout. We won 5–3.

After the game Frank Cashen said, "You managed a great game." I always take offense when somebody tells me that. I said, "You must think that I'm terrible in all the other ones I managed." He said, "No, I really mean it. You really managed great today." But again, I said to myself, If you're going to compliment me on one game, maybe you don't like the way I manage the others.

27
DOWNHILL

LATELY OUR BULLPEN has been erratic, and as Eddie Lynch's luck would have it, it seems to be most erratic when he's pitching. Earlier in the season Eddie and I had had our little blowout, but despite his adversity, since then Eddie has tried hard to keep his emotions under control.

I can remember last month Eddie pitched his first career shutout against Atlanta, and at the end of the game Gary ran out to give him a bear hug, and when Gary got to him, Eddie pushed him away. Gary didn't know what to make of it, but what Eddie was saying was, "I don't want to get caught in the hype. I want to keep my emotions on an even keel."

The next game out he lost 1–0 on a bad call, and then in his next outing he took the Giants in a 2–2 game through eight innings, only to see Wes Gardner give up six runs in the tenth. After that there was a loss to the Dodgers because of poor support, and then again against the Dodgers, I had to take him out after five innings losing by the score of 2–0. Jesse Orosco allowed two runs in the ninth to tie, and in the twelfth we made a couple of fielding errors behind Doug Sisk and lost it.

He was unlucky again at Shea after pitching brilliantly against the St. Louis Cardinals. Eddie never pitched so well. He kept the Cardinal runners off balance, nipped the corners, changed speeds, a casebook demonstration of pitching. He only had to make 88 pitches as he held the Cardinals to no runs and two hits.

In the bottom of the eighth, in an attempt to break the 0–0 tie, I pinch-hit for Eddie, and we didn't score. In the ninth I brought in Tommy Gorman, a lefty, against the switch-hitting Tommy Herr. Gorman threw him a fastball, and like a rocket, Herr sent it over the left field wall to win the game. I was feeling terrible despair, but what could I do?

I had gone with Gorman because I had run out of options. Doug has been ineffective, Jesse isn't right either, and against the Cardinals the day before Roger McDowell tripped over first base, spraining his ankle, and will be lost for a couple of weeks. I can't say enough about how important Roger is to our bullpen. Here's a guy, 5–1, who has three saves and has pitched extremely well. You're talking about eight games in a very short time. And now he's walking around on crutches.

In the game we had exactly one chance to score. Keith was on second, and with two outs Gary lined a hit to center, but my new third base coach, Buddy Harrelson, held Keith up at third: The next batter, Foster, made out, and we didn't score.

After the game I said to Buddy, "Hey, let's take more chances." Buddy said, "I thought he would have been dead by thirty feet." I can't really argue with that. The only thing is, the ball was hit fairly deep, and the outfielder fielded it awkwardly so that his throw was going to be off balance, and I don't care, you've got to send him on a two-out single up the middle. Shit, with Foster not swinging the bat well and up next, you have to send him.

Buddy is too conservative, but that's all part of my having to break in a new third base coach. He feels that the baserunners are his responsibility, and he wants to play it close to the vest. Bobby Valentine learned to gamble because he had the benefit of our being together in the spring, when the games don't mean anything. I don't like conservative baserunning, and I've been trying to get that message across to Buddy.

I told him, "Let's be aggressive. Don't worry about the guy getting thrown out. Make him take the extra base. Let's not play station-to-station ball." I said, "I want you to get so comfortable that if you read something out there, I want you to send a guy to second on a steal on your own." That's the way I had it with Bobby. "Let's not be conservative. Don't let me be conservative. We want to be aggressive."

We have too many rookies on the bench, which is not conducive to our winning. I've always said that the two things that make a difference between a championship club and one that doesn't win is the strength of the bullpen and the bench. A weak bench is even more glaring after you lose one of your regulars, because you're then forced to use one of your bench players as a regular, and that means you end up with even more rookies on the bench.

Of course, the way we're hitting right now, you could say that there wouldn't be much drop-off anyway. Every once in a while we hit a home run, but when we do there's never anyone on base, and it's very difficult to manufacture anything when you don't have anybody on base.

I had a meeting with Frank Cashen, Al Harazin, and Joe McIlvaine before the game, and they gave me a list of people who were available, and to be honest, none of the players they mentioned could help us. As far as I was concerned, these were people other clubs were trying to unload.

The next day we played a doubleheader against the Cardinals. Dwight won the first. He didn't have his good stuff, but managed to pitch his way out of about everything, holding them to one run.

In the second game their third baseman, Pendleton, hit a grand-slam inside-the-park home run when rookie Terry Blocker collided with Danny Heep on a fly ball. Blocker has a severe bruise above the kneecap. He had to be carried off the field on a stretcher, and it looks like he'll be out for a couple of weeks.

Pendleton's grand slam should have been caught, but it was hit right in the seam between two young outfielders. A veteran center fielder would have called off the right fielder, but I have a young center fielder, Terry Blocker, and he and Heep haven't played together much.

A few days later I had the worst night I ever had in baseball, as player or manager.

We got beat 26—7. I know. It sounds like a football score.

Tommy Gorman started, and when you start a reliever you can expect that your pitching is going to be short. I've been using my bullpen, namely Sambito and Sisk, quite a bit the last couple of days. I don't have Roger McDowell, who's out with a bad ankle. Jesse is my short man, and I don't like to use him when we're behind if I can help it.

Gorman went out to the mound to pitch the first inning, and I had barely settled myself at the end of the bench when the first seven Philly batters either walked or hit the ball like a rocket. Before I knew it, we were losing 4—0, the bases were loaded, and the eighth-hole hitter, Garry Maddox, was up.

Gorman had retired one batter. I went to take him out. He said, "Sorry, Skip." Well, hell, he did the best he could. He ran into a buzz saw. I brought in Calvin Schiraldi. He had thrown 55 pitches in a start two days ago, but he said he was fine. An inning and two thirds later, we were losing 16—0!

Because I didn't want to wear out my short guys, I was going to let Calvin go the rest of the way no matter what, but after ten hits and ten runs, I had to hook him. I couldn't let it continue.

And so it was still the second inning and I had used two pitchers and I was losing 16—0, and now I had to go back to my pen. I knew I was in deep trouble, apart from our losing 16—0. What was I going to do for arms?

I called in Doug Sisk, and Doug pitched very well. He gave me two-and-a-third innings. I took Sisk out after four. I said to myself, "Joe Sambito is fresh, and this will give me a good opportunity to see him pitch a few innings." Well, I stretched Joe out all right. He gave up another ten runs!

At the start of the seventh inning, after he had allowed six runs, I went out there and asked if he was all right. I had Rick Aguilera warming up, but I didn't want him to have to pitch. Joe said, "No, don't worry. This game is over. Let me get them out." So I sat Aguilera down, and even though they got four more runs, Joe saved me.

It's tough to lose 26—7. First of all, it's embarrassing. Everybody's laughing at you. "You missed the extra point," that sort of thing. Also, the pitchers' ERAs get jammed up, and that's what they get paid on. Relief pitchers especially have to spend the rest of the season overcoming that one bad performance.

After the game I called a little meeting. I was not mad at the players, only that we could get beaten so badly. I said, "We needed a good ass-kicking like this to wake us up. We have to be a little meaner to win this thing."

I told them, "We've hit the bottom. Don't forget this one, boys. This is the one to remember. So whenever you're feeling a little tired, think about the ass-kicking we got tonight."

28

NO RELIEF IN SIGHT

AFTER OUR 26–7 DRUBBING, we rebounded against the Phils and beat them in eleven innings. But we were still in trouble and lost the next two, the first on a home run in the eighth off Jesse. In our first game against the Expos, Dwight went into the bottom of the ninth leading by a run. He had thrown 147 pitches, which is a lot for an outing, and I decided that Doc's arm is more important than any game. Once again I went back to my bullpen.

I had used Jesse two days in a row, so I finally decided to give Doug Sisk a chance. Sisk has pitched terribly all year, but he's thrown decent ball the last couple times out. I knew it was a gamble, but it seemed like an educated gamble.

Well, Doug walked the first guy, Wohlford, on a close pitch. It was drizzling rain. He walked the second guy, Raines, and hell, if he'd have thrown the first one over to the next batter, Vance Law, I still would have stayed with him, but he threw a ball.

Now I had to get Schiraldi. He threw the ball over all right, but Law, who's swinging the bat exceptionally well, singled in the tying run. Calvin then got Dawson to hit into a double play. We had two outs. A runner was still on third.

The batter was Dan Driessen, a tough lefty, so I figured that the smart move was to bring in Jesse and let him come in and get the one hitter. Then in the tenth I'd go to Gorman and hopefully we'd win on a run in extra innings.

Driessen looped a high pop fly into shallow right-center field. Mookie from center came running in. Christensen in right came running in. From second base Chappie went running out after it, and so did Keith Hernandez. They all met—after the ball had dropped for a base hit. The runner on third, Tim Raines, stomped on the plate, and we lost the ballgame.

These are the games that try managers' souls. We're struggling along. It would have been nice to have won this game. I hate to lose. I really hate to lose.

The New York fans and the media have lost confidence in Doug Sisk, and Doug has lost confidence in himself. He's become shell-shocked. When we're playing at Shea, Doug's scared to death to come to the ballpark. I told him, "Doug, hey, don't let it bother you. Get earplugs, cotton, whatever. If I have to use you, just do the best you can."

I received an anonymous letter that read, "The next time you bring in Doug Sisk, we're going to shoot him and shoot you too on the way out." I won't start worrying until I get a note with the individual letters cut out of a magazine so there's nothing to trace. I said to myself, The FBI won't be able to run the guy down, and the bullet will probably be from the bore of a stolen gun!

Doug acts like it doesn't bother him, but things bother him probably more than any other player on the ballclub. As to what's going to happen: There isn't anybody who can take his spot, so I'm going to have to wait and let him come around, or not come around.

The next day Sid Fernandez pitched a great game, struck out eight, didn't walk a batter, and had a 2–1 lead going into the eighth when Driessen hit a long home run off a fastball to tie it. Sid went into the ninth and got the first two guys easily, and then Dawson hit a double. In my mind I knew he was tiring, but after the events of the last couple of days, I was determined not to let someone else come in and give up the run. I said to myself, Sid is either going to get out of the inning or he's going to stay in and give up the base hit.

With Dawson on second Sid threw Hubert Brooks a pitch down low, and he hit it over my left fielder's head. Ballgame.

Afterward Gary said, "I know Brooks likes the ball down. I should have gone out to the mound and made him throw the ball up." I said to myself, I should have gone out and said the same thing.

It's very tough when you get beat in the ninth because you don't trust your bullpen, and when before that your ace reliever gave up a two-run homer with two outs in the ninth when he should have been fresh, and when your other short man, Sisk, is throwing high sinkers. And when McDowell's on a good roll and he goes down, and you can't use him for two weeks. You have to make adjustments, and sometimes you don't get them.

Gary and I were talking. He said, "I just can't stand it. We wasted a game. We should have won."

I said, "Gary, we haven't tried to waste it. We tried to do the best we could. Things are going to get better."

He said, "I just can't stand it now. I want to open a lead."

I have to look at this over the long term. My injured players are coming back. Despite everything that's going against us, we're only two-and-a-half games out because the Cubs have lost four in a row. We've stumbled along but managed to stay in there.

The toughest part of my job is sitting after a particularly horrible loss with Arthur Richman and publicity director Jay Horwitz and feeling their misery. Arthur and Jay are two of my best friends, and I sympathize, because they do feel deeply—too deeply—and it shows on their faces.

I always feel a little down when we lose, and sometimes there is some carryover, but I do not want my feelings or concerns to reflect the picture of a distraught manager. I can't afford to be walking doomsday, a billboard that says, "Boy, are we going bad!" The next day I have to come to the ballpark smiling. "It's a new day. Let's go get them! Let's have some fun."

Eight guys have the blight, three guys lost their right arms, but you still have to give the appearance that, "Hey, everything's fine. Let's go get them. Come on. Great day for a ballgame!" A reporter asks you, "Are you ready to play this Cub series?" "Hey, yeah, we're great." Strawberry won't be ready for another three weeks. Neither will my best short man. Mookie can't throw, and

Foster's in a slump. But let's go. You have to psych yourself up, and sometimes it's tough. Sometimes I want to say, "We ain't going higher than tit. We're going south. These guys can't play!"

We have a saying, Vern Hoscheit will tell you, "KP." Kaint Play. But that doesn't do any good. You keep trying to look on the bright side of things and sometimes you look at the .230 team batting average and the injuries and the decimated bullpen, and it's very difficult to stay optimistic. And you try to salvage a Doug Sisk, and then you get a letter: "Kill Doug Sisk, and if you keep putting him in, we're going to kill you." It's rough. Winning is important to everybody who's on my team. I have guys who care. It tears our hearts out to lose a tough one. I have thoughts of, If this doesn't change, I'm glad I only have one more year on my contract. I'd rather be fishing than go through this mental anguish. There's a saying, and I've been saying it a lot more than I have in many years past: Things happen for the best. Even the 26–7 game. I keep on telling each player, "Things happen for the best. Make it work for you, son, make it work for you." "Well, so what if Orosco gave up a two-run homer and got beat in the last inning? So what if they came back and scored two in the bottom of the ninth? It happens for the best." But that sentiment starts to run to where you don't believe it anymore. I feel like shouting, "The hell with what's happening for the best. Let's start making it happen *my way* for a change."

29
DECISIONS

THE TRADING DEADLINE was midnight last night; it has come and gone, and we weren't able to do anything. Frank is still working at it, as is his assistant, Al Harazin, and probably the whole office. It's very difficult to pick up somebody, or even to make a major trade.

At one time I thought we had a good chance of getting Tom Paciorek of the White Sox. Originally the White Sox were asking for a player like a Christensen or a Blocker, or another youngster who hasn't done anything on a major league level, and I thought we really had a chance to get him. And then nothing happened. They decided they didn't want to make a move at this time. And then another name came up, Joel Youngblood of San Francisco, and Frank asked me about him and I said, "Man, yeah. Go get him!" I said to myself, There's my veteran right-hander off the bench—he can play third, second, the outfield. I talked to my coaches, and they all wanted him. I wouldn't have thought the Giants wanted much, because the Giants have a lot of young outfielders, four, perhaps five, and Joel is way down on the list. I

really thought Frank was going to do something there, but evidently he couldn't.

Padres second baseman Alan Wiggins is available, but I don't think anybody is going to touch him right now. He has a drug awareness situation. Here's a guy making $2.5 million over four years, and he's not able to play because of a cocaine habit. Drugs can have a permanent affect on a player, and unless you know for certain a player's clean, nobody wants to take the chance. Of course, if he goes to the minors and plays very well, shows that he has a clean bill of health, clubs who need a second baseman of his caliber might be interested.

I called Frank Cashen and we discussed sending Sambito and Schiraldi down to Tidewater about the time McDowell's ankle heals, and calling up Terry Leach. They tell me Terry's pitching very well down at Tidewater. I had him a couple years ago. He has the heart of a lion. He's an underarm pitcher, throws a sinker and a slider that moves up. At Tidewater he hasn't given up a run in thirty-something innings.

Schiraldi needs to pitch a little more, and Joe Sambito needs regular work, pitching three times a week. I think it will be best for them both to go down to Tidewater. With that in mind Frank said, "That's fine, talk to Sambito," and rather than let grass grow under me, I told Joe to meet me in the bar of the hotel. I said, "I appreciate the effort you're giving me. I think your arm is coming back and your stuff is improving, but it would be best for you to go down to Tidewater and pitch regularly for a while."

It's a tough blow for any player, but especially for a guy like Joe, and I understand that. He wants to pitch in the big leagues. He's been here, and he's been a star, though for the last three years he's had trouble.

"I want to trust you," he said. "How do I know that you'll be interested in taking me back?"

I said, "Joe, let me tell you this. Last year I released three pitchers—Torrez, Tidrow, and Swan. I'm telling you that I would release you if I didn't think you had a chance. You need to work down there. If you're successful, you'll be back."

Joe said, "I'll talk to my wife and my agent about it." We parted amiably. I can understand his talking to his wife, but I always wonder why a player feels he has to talk to his agent.

The toughest thing about our situation right now is that my one-two table setters are not getting on base for Keith and Carter and Foster. Wally was on base last year about thirty-six percent of the time, and Mookie was on base about thirty-two percent. This year they're both under thirty percent, and that's hurting us. Aside from the fact that the other guys are not hitting either.

I have to make a decision concerning Mookie. He cannot swing left-handed because his shoulder is swollen from an inflammation. I told him that I'd platoon him. For the time being it'll be him and Heep in center, Hurdle in right, and Foster in left. We'll have Darryl back in a week to ten days.

With Mookie only available part-time, I'm thinking about bringing back my little leadoff hitter, Dykstra, and maybe platooning him with Mookie instead of Heep.

I still think we're going to win it and that we're just being tested right now. We're at the point where we're hardening up the steel, so we can cut through at the end. I have to think that we just went through a bad period. Once we get healthy and win a few ballgames, we'll be right in it.

30
FIVE IN A ROW

JAY HORWITZ, our publicity director, came barging into my office all red-faced. He was waving what looked like a newspaper clipping. "Uh, Davey, read this, read this," he said. "How could he have said this?" Who? What?

It was a Chicago newspaper article in which Cubs pitcher Rick Sutcliffe, last year's Cy Young Award winner and the guy who pitched the Cubs to the division title, was doing a little bragging and at the same time putting us down pretty hard.

I started reading the article. In it Sutcliffe stated, "Maybe in spring training it was the Mets, but now I'd say our biggest competition is the Cardinals and the Expos." He went on to say, "I wouldn't trade any one of our guys for any one of theirs—with one exception. I think we'd be able to find room for Dwight Gooden." Blah blah blah. He said he wouldn't even take Gary Carter over their catcher, Jody Davis, because their catcher does all the things Gary does and calls a better game. For a guy playing on a team with a five-game losing streak, you'd think he'd have the sense to keep his feelings to himself. Especially when his team is in town to play us.

I took the article and posted it on the bulletin board. Everybody read it. I couldn't have given a better speech to pump them up any more. To Gary, those were fighting words, and against Sutcliffe he hit one harder than Chinese trigonometry over the left field wall. It was the game-winning hit.

In that game Ron Darling pitched a five-hit shutout, went all the way to win, and the next day Eddie Lynch went out and beat them, allowing only one run. The only Cub batter I was a little worried about was their first baseman, Durham, who swings the bat really well against Eddie. I said to myself, The only way Eddie is coming out of the game is if Durham comes up as the tying run late in the game. But it never got to that.

My one and two hitters finally got on base like they're supposed to. Keith, who's in a terrible slump, even got an inside-out broken-bat hit and drove in a run. But the principal hero again was Gary Carter, who drove in the first run, and then a second off a guy who's been awfully tough against us, Steve Trout.

Late in the game, there was a pop-up between home and first, and Keith came running in, a little late, and he had to grandstand to catch it. Gary and Keith have run together on some pop-ups because Gary likes to catch them, and so does Keith. When Keith saw this one go up, he started calling for it real early, way before he got there, and he had to jump to get it.

This thing between Keith and Gary is a kind of in-house joke, and as they came into the dugout we were all teasing Keith for hogging the ball. When Cubs manager Jimmy Frey saw everybody laughing, it pissed him off. He started yelling from the bench. At first I thought he was yelling at the umpire. But Jimmy was yelling at us, "Yeah, grin, you suckers. You'll pay. It ain't going to be this funny later on. Enjoy it while you can, you suckers." Jimmy was hot.

I understand where Jimmy was coming from. We both came into the series bad, we won the first game, and we were about to win the second—we were enjoying a four-run lead—and Jimmy was trying to fire up his troops.

As far as I'm concerned, we should be grinning. It was nice to be ahead and beating the Cubs for a change. They beat us twelve out of eighteen last year. We've had enough frowns on our faces lately from the injuries and losses. There's nothing wrong with a little laughter.

Before the game I came into the training room, and Bruce Berenyi was on the table. Ron Darling and a couple other players were sitting around him. Bruce had just returned from Columbus, Georgia, where he was supposed to see the doctor who last month performed his arm surgery.

I couldn't hear everything, but I did catch Darling saying, "That's got to be the dumbest thing I ever heard." There was more talk, and Darling again said, "Nobody is that dumb." Berenyi was lying there, not saying anything.

Then Ron said, "How can you get on an airplane going to Columbus, Georgia, and end up in Columbus, Ohio?"

So that's what Berenyi did! As a result, he couldn't get a checkup from the doctor who did his arthroscopic surgery. When I heard that, I stopped laughing.

The next day Dwight pitched a shutout, our third complete game in a row. Jim Frey started a strange lineup against him. He didn't play their best right-handers, and none of his lefty subs got a hit.

Dwight pitched out of a tough jam in the ninth. Ahead by only 1–0, he had a runner on second and had three left-handers coming up. Normally in this situation I would bring in Jesse Orosco, but I never take Doc out of a game unless he says he's tired. Beside, there were 51,000 fans filling Shea, and if I had taken Doc out, they would have strung me up. I never would have made it back to the dugout alive.

The fourth game of the Cub series featured the return of Roger McDowell. It was comforting to have him back. During a season, you lose players at bad times. And sometimes you get them back at the right times. This was one of those times.

Sid Fernandez, who is improving with every game he pitches, pitched a great six innings and struck out ten.

We scored all five of our runs in the third inning. The batting star was George Foster, whom everybody, including the fans and the sportswriters, has written off. With the bases loaded, George hit Ray Fontenot's second pitch way over the center field fence, just missing the big red apple out there. And no sooner had George come into the dugout when John Christensen, my rookie right fielder, also hit one out.

Sidney tired after six, and I hooked him and went to Roger McDowell, who recorded the save. Ahead by two runs in the ninth, Roger allowed a one-out double, but he got Steve Lake to pop to short. With the fans chanting, "Sweep, sweep, sweep," Roger was one out away and had to retire only Jody Davis, Sutcliffe's "Catcher Who Is Better Than Gary Carter." Mr. "Better Than Gary Carter" grounded out to short to end the game.

The next day we moved into a first-place tie when the St. Louis Cardinals beat the Cubbies, handing them their tenth straight loss. That may be the last interview Sutcliffe gives this year.

31
MENTAL MISTAKES

WE WON OUR FIRST GAME against the Expos. In the second we were getting beaten 2–0 by David Palmer going into the bottom of the seventh, when Raffy led off with a single. Palmer got the next two outs, but with Wally Backman up, Montreal manager Buck Rogers brought in his ace reliever, Jeff Reardon.

Wally bounced a hit behind second base, putting two runners on, and with Lenny Dykstra the scheduled batter, I decided to pinch-hit Rusty Staub.

The best matchups for Rusty are pitchers like Reardon and Goose Gossage, guys who really throw the ball hard. You hope you can get Rusty in a situation to drive in a run from second base, getting you a sacrifice fly or a base hit. I love to try to create those situations, because Rusty's a formidable equalizer against those hard right-handed throwers.

Reardon threw a fastball, and Rusty pulled a long drive deep, but it just did go foul. I was praying Reardon wouldn't come back and throw him a hard slider down and in. I was saying to myself, Challenge him with another fastball, Jeff. Let's see you throw it by him; and that's what Reardon tried to do, and Rusty hit the ball farther than the other one, way over the outfield fence deep to right-center field, a three-run home run to give us a 3–2 lead. Three batters later, Heep singled in Keith to make it 4–2. It was Nostalgia Night, and we had a packed house of fans wearing Brooklyn Dodger and New York Giant caps, but they are all Mets fans now, and forty thousand of them cheered the roof off.

I brought in Jesse Orosco, and he gave up one run in the eighth. In the ninth Jesse gave up a cheap Texas League double off Santana's glove, a bunt base hit, and then a double by Nicosia off the chalk in right to tie. The air had gone out of the crowd's balloon. I brought in McDowell to stop the rally.

We got out of that inning, but they beat Roger in the tenth when Driessen doubled, Wallach walked, and Wally booted a double-play grounder.

I'm concerned about Jesse. He doesn't have the real sharp breaking ball. It's not consistent. He isn't as aggressive with the hitters as he was last year. Everybody thinks he's hurt. I don't. It looks to me as if he's throwing his breaking ball differently, but I'm not sure what it is that he's doing. I'm going to have to get Mel and some other people to go over his films and look at him, because we sure as heck need Jesse.

For the moment all I can say to my players is, "Hey, our backs are against the wall, but we have enough talent here to win, so let's kick ourselves in the butt and get our act together."

The next game was even uglier. We played poorly and lost. We made mental mistakes. There's a big difference between a mental and a physical mistake. Mental mistakes are unacceptable. We deserved to lose.

Our most costly mistake was a play in which the Expos' Tim Raines, who is a fast runner, was on third base. We had one out. Their second baseman, Vance Law, hit a pop fly to shallow right. Our second baseman, Wally Backman, went back after it. Our right fielder, John Christensen, was coming in under it. This was a routine play. Even little leaguers know that on this play the outfielder is supposed to call off the infielder because he is moving toward the plate and is in a much better position to throw out the runner trying to score from third.

What happened? Christensen stood by as Wally caught the ball flat-footed. He had no forward momentum for the throw home, and Raines scored easily.

When I saw this, I said to myself, Wally has no business catching that. But the blame lies with Christensen. Christensen should have called him off.

Why didn't he? Perhaps because he's a rookie. Maybe he was feeling, I don't want to mess up. Let him mess up.

There was another mental error in that game. With runners on first and second, their pitcher bunted the ball right back to Eddie Lynch, who went for the double play via second base. Eddie made a bad throw to second, pulling Raffy off the bag, and Raffy threw to first base, except that no one was covering first, and the ball went rolling out into the outfield as the Montreal runners went wild, though not as wild as I was.

The reason no one was covering first was that when the batter squared to bunt, Wally stopped thinking—what I call "vapor lock." He should have realized that Keith would be charging in and that he would have to cover first. Instead, he was standing uselessly at second. Afterward I told him in no uncertain terms that he had mugged it. "Don't tell me where you should have been. You were wrong. After you think about it, you'll realize how wrong you were." I told Raffy it was his mistake too. "You can't throw the ball if nobody is there." It was a comedy of errors without the comedy.

I don't usually criticize my players during a game. I prefer to wait until the next day, but I was so upset by the Christensen-Wally mix-up that I spoke to them right there in front of everybody. After the messed up double play, there were so many screwups I just said, "Boys, let's get our heads out of our butts. We're playing like Ned in the first reader. Let's play a little hardball."

Christensen knew he was wrong. Backman, too. They all knew they were wrong. There's a fine line between winning and losing, and mental errors cost you ballgames. It's not the way we played the first two months of the season, and it's not the way we are going to play the rest of the season.

32

TOO MANY DOCTORS

IT'S BEEN FIVE WEEKS since Ronnie Gardenhire pulled his hamstring. As far as I'm concerned, he's ready to play, but the Mets doctors say that they want him to wait another week, a total of six weeks. The last time Ron came back only three weeks after pulling his hamstring he pulled it again. So maybe the doctors are right. I don't know. It used to be that if a guy was ready to play, you didn't have all this medical science saying he couldn't.

Darryl Strawberry's doctor put a little plastic splint on Darryl's hand and told him to take it real easy. He said, "The ligament doesn't fully heal until six weeks, and it's only been five weeks. Have him take it real slow so there won't be any setbacks." But the doctor admitted that Darryl's about a week ahead of schedule.

We're taking Darryl down to the batting cage for controlled hitting. The pitching is underarm and only from thirty feet, and if he doesn't have any swelling from two days of that, we'll lob the ball from sixty feet. After a couple days of that, he can take regular BP, and I would say he might play by the end of the month. That's good news. Darryl is chomping at the bit. And I am too.

The only one who's nervous is Frank Cashen. He had told me, "Don't let him play pepper. Don't let him do anything until the doctor says it's okay." My goodness. I don't need a degree in medicine to know that when he's able to go through a regular workout, he should be able to play. As long as he doesn't have any excruciating pain, he can play. The rule is: Do anything you want to do, but back off if it hurts you.

When Frank saw that Darryl had graduated to regular batting practice, he came to see me in the dugout. "We saw Darryl Strawberry hitting, and the doctor said he's not supposed to do that, blah blah blah. If you use him too quick, you might lose him all year."

I kept my mouth shut, but I was pissed. Players like Darryl are my livelihood. Those guys are my bread and butter. I'm not going to treat a guy who's injured improperly. It's an insult to my intelligence.

33

ROCK BOTTOM

WHEN A CLUB is going bad, bad things happen to it. The Cubs are going worse than we are. When we came into Chicago the Cubs had lost twelve games in a row. We were playing at Wrigley Field, and Lenny Dykstra started the game by hitting a fly ball to right. Keith Moreland stood under it but then lost it in the sun, and it went for a triple. Keith Hernandez sacrificed him in. Had Moreland made the catch, Keith's sacrifice fly would have been the third out. Gary Carter then hit a home run.

In the fourth Howard Johnson hit his second home run of the year into Sheffield Avenue. On the mound Dwight's curve wasn't working at all, and Dwight isn't supposed to do well when his curve isn't working. But he did. The Cubs ended the day with their thirteenth loss in a row.

The next day it was our turn. In our second game at Wrigley, we were winning by a run on another Carter home run, but after breezing through the fifth inning, Sidney started the sixth by giving up two little dinky line-drive base hits to Sandberg and Matthews. Sid had already thrown 90 pitches, the wind was blowing out to left, and Moreland, a powerful right-handed batter, was up, so I figured it was time to make a move. I brought in McDowell, my most successful relief pitcher.

Cubs manager Jimmy Frey was also figuring Moreland couldn't hit McDowell out, because he ordered Moreland to sacrifice bunt—twice—but both times Moreland didn't get it down. With two strikes Frey took the bunt sign off, and Moreland swung away and hit a three-run homer! And we got beat.

In the Cubs finale Ron Darling gave up three home runs, one in the first inning to Ryne Sandberg on a high fastball, one to the first baseman, Bull Durham, and one to the rookie center fielder, Billy Hatcher. Those were all the runs he gave up, but we only got two against Sutcliffe. Wrigley Field is supposed to be a hitter's paradise, but we just couldn't score.

Darryl's going to play tomorrow. The question is, who to send down? I've been tossing it over for about three days in my mind. I think it has to be Lenny Dykstra. He hasn't played much, but I just don't think he's the answer right now. He's a "Punch-and-Judy" hitter, and as long as we're having trouble getting our number one and number two hitters on, I might as well lead off Wally Backman and platoon Heep and Christensen. At least I'll have the threat of someone hitting a double in the one and two spots.

With Darryl starting for the first time in weeks, I'm also going to play Mookie Wilson, even though it's going to be his last game for a while, since they've finally decided to operate on his arm. I just want to see what my lineup would have looked like if everyone had stayed healthy. Call me a sentimentalist.

Frank Cashen and the doctors duped me. Last week they told me Darryl had been out for five weeks and that this would be his sixth week. I never bothered to check on it. It turns out that this is really his seventh week! Frank and the doctors really got me there. They decided to play it on the conservative side, and as a result I didn't get to use Darryl against the Cubs, when I needed him. Darryl has been hitting long home runs in batting practice, and now that I realize he's been out the seven weeks, he's going to start playing again against the Cardinals. I pray he can give us some offense. As a team we're hitting .229. Only the Giants are worse. The Cardinals have scored 69 runs more than they've allowed. We've allowed more runs than we've scored. If we don't do something to change that, the Cardinals are going to be long gone.

We flew to St. Louis to play the Cards three games, and in the opener lost another tough game when Darryl made a mental error.

He led off with a walk, and when George Foster got a hit, Darryl went to second. There was nobody out. Ray Knight then hit a deep fly ball. I was waiting for Darryl to tag up and go to third, but he was anchored at second. The next batter hit another fly ball, and if Darryl had been on third, he would have scored. We lost by a run.

Again, our bench was a problem. Our right-handed pinch-hitting has been so bad that in the ninth I used Danny Heep, a left-hander, to face a left-handed pitcher with a runner on first. We can't compete with the Cardinals and Montreal and the Cubs as far as bench strength is concerned. We don't have the horses.

The next night we got shut out by Joaquin Andujar. It's really upsetting me that we're just not hitting. After the game I called a team meeting.

I said, "It takes twenty-five guys to win, and the only way twenty-five can play up to their potential is if every man in here takes a good, long look at himself and says to himself, Am I doing the things that I need to play my best?" I looked at Keith, who's in a dreadful slump. "Is the pitching that tough this year?" He said no. I asked Gary and George what they had to say, and it wasn't much. I said, "I'll tell you what I think the problem is. I think everybody is looking to the other guy to get them going, instead of each individual saying, 'I'll be the one to get this club going.' I've tried to make excuses for you guys all year—injuries, umpires. Maybe I need to get thrown out more. What do I need to do? As far as I'm concerned, we've all been horseshit. But I still think we can win this thing. We just have to get mad, at ourselves, and go out there and play like we're capable of playing."

You try to say, "Listen, boys, this is just a bad time we're going through. Don't get your dobbers down. Let's have some fun. Get a base hit, slide hard, take somebody out, have a few laughs, and we'll come through." You tell them why they're going through a bad period. You let them know that when you're in that dark tunnel, that though it doesn't look like there's any light at the other end, there is. Our club is very sensitive to these things. No question about it in my mind. The slightest little tremor, and we go south. And I don't mean that we don't play a hundred percent. We get frustrated. We get a little more cautious.

The critics are saying we don't take chances anymore, but that's not the big problem. We aren't getting on base. We're getting one hit every other inning, making it difficult for me to steal a guy or even hit-and-run.

I went to bed that night hoping my pep talk would do the trick. In our finale against the Cardinals, we scored exactly one run. It was unearned. In our last seven games, we've scored twelve runs. We're five games behind St. Louis, and dropping.

After losing five straight on the road to contenders, we flew back home to Shea to play the Pittsburgh Pirates. Sid Fernandez pitched a truly outstanding game. He gave up one run, and that came on a double that followed two walks. The problem was that we didn't score any.

Gary is really frustrated. He came into my office and told me, "I came over here with high hopes, and we're not playing as well as we should." He's tougher on himself than anybody. He said, "Skip, I don't know what to tell you. I know I'm letting the team down."

I said, "Let me explain the way I see things. Here's an analogy. I'm renovating my house in Orlando. I'm the general contractor building a house. Managing a baseball team is like being the general contractor of the house.

"As general contractor I have to hire electricians, plumbers, and finish carpenters. Say I'm building cabinets in the walls, and my finish carpenter gets sick for two months. I can't go out and hire another finish carpenter away from somebody else, because the other top finish carpenters are all working, so to replace him I have to use an apprentice finish carpenter or even a regular carpenter to do this work, and the end result is that the product is not as good. I don't care how much enthusiasm you bring to the project, the end product just won't be as good. That's what happens when your bullpen gets sick, when your starting pitcher comes up with a bad arm, when players like Mookie and Darryl can't play. The substitutes are not going to be as good and the team won't be as good. It's wishful thinking to feel that it will be, but it's just not going to be as good, so the product is suffering, and what happens is that the other players on the team begin to feel that.

"There's a snowball effect. At first you feel, Boy, we lost Berenyi, but maybe these other guys will pick us up. Then you lose Mookie. He's really been lost all year. He's been ineffective from the left side and hasn't been able to throw from the outfield. And then Darryl is out two months. It begins to wear on a team. The guys get to thinking, We're just not as good as we were."

I told him no one was playing his best, but that we can't worry too much. I said, "We have to realize that we can still do it, and if we can't do it now, we'll get them next year. Gary, don't make it life or death, just because the New York fans and papers say it is. The fans say, 'If you don't win, I'm going to die.' Or worse, 'You're going to die.' And you can get wrapped up in that, and sometimes it causes you to press." I said, "Don't let it affect you."

Gary didn't say much. He nodded his head a lot. It relieved his mind knowing I had a bigger perspective of it.

Keith is hitting in a 6-for-80 slump, and I don't really know what's causing it. It may have something to do with his personal life, though I doubt it. He's in the middle of a bitter divorce and custody battle with his wife. The money she wants doesn't bother him nearly as much as her trying to stop him from seeing his children.

I don't believe his marital problems are related to his problems at bat, but they are affecting his psyche. He's so tense; he reacts to the slightest little thing. I really feel for him, though there isn't much more I can do than put his name in the lineup and let him take out his aggression on our opponents.

Fortunately for Keith, Rusty Staub, whom he rooms with on the road, is there for him. They have developed a close bond.

Rusty is Keith's confidant. Rusty also keeps Keith on an even keel. Keith can become very moody, get very down, and when Keith feels sorry for himself, Rusty quickly talks him out of it. If Keith gets too boisterous on the bus, Rusty tells him, point-blank, "Keith, that's enough." And Keith will stop, because he knows Rusty is telling him for his own good and because Keith respects Rusty so much.

Still, Keith is a professional. I probably should stroke him more, but I always feel that the stars don't need a lot of stroking. They get stroked all the time by the public. I talk to Keith. I tell him, "Look, Keith, I know you're living in Manhattan, and there's nightlife, but you have to make sure it doesn't affect you, that you don't burn the candle at both ends. Take care of that body. It's got you here and made a good life for you." And he'll agree. My concern is always that players play to the best of their ability for as long as they can.

I've been trying to get Gary to stop pulling the ball so much. He keeps pulling the outside pitch to the shortstop. Or he hits cans of corn to left. Gary really needs to use the whole field more than he does. He should be patient enough to be able to slap the ball to right field.

I said to him, "Why is it you never look for the curveball and if the pitcher throws a fastball, hit it the other way?" He said, "I don't know why." I said, "I know why. It's your ego. You can't stand to be beaten by a heater at any time. You always want to go to left field, because that's where you can hit it the hardest and farthest."

He shakes his head and nods, indicating that I'm right. We've had this conversation a hundred times.

Whenever he does slap one to right, usually because he doesn't get around on an outside pitch, I tell him, "See, it is possible for you to hit a line drive over there." He grins at me and I grin at him, because each of us knows what the other one is thinking. I'm thinking, Do it, and he's thinking, I won't.

I've decided to bench HoJo and play Ray Knight full-time, but I still think HoJo is going to be one heck of a player. It's like other guys who came over from the American League, Von Hayes and Glenn Wilson. The first year they were duds. The second year they came alive and became stars in the league. HoJo too will become a star. Meanwhile, I'll play him at short occasionally to rest Raffy.

It's really unfair to Howard. When you do this, you seem to be singling out one player, as if to say, "It's your fault." It's not HoJo's fault, and I told him that. I said, "Howard, I'm not singling you out. It won't hurt you to have a little rest and play some at short." HoJo understood. He says he is feeling a little bit better with every game he plays.

The one guy who's been hitting when everyone else is slumping is George Foster. George can be like that. Last year about this time, his batting average was rather low, and I had a little chat with him. I said, "Don't worry, I'm not going to give up on you. I'm not going to platoon you." He went on a tear the rest of the year. Who knows whether my discussion helped? Maybe it was just that time of year.

George can look forbidding, but that's not the way he is. He's a nice guy. I like George. He works hard. He takes very good care of himself. If everybody took as good care of their bodies as George does his, we'd all be in great shape until we were fifty. And live to be a hundred.

I kiddingly threatened to fire batting coach Bill Robinson because of our batting slump. I said, "Bill, I've gotten a couple letters here saying, 'Fire Bill Robinson.' What do you recommend I do about it?" He said, "No, Skip, don't do that!" I said, "Bill, my only recourse is to fire somebody before they fire me." I was just kidding, but he was a little worried there.

I agree with the way Bill teaches hitting. He wants the guys to hit the ball down and through, he's a hard worker, and that's all I can ask.

A couple days later I told him, "Bill, you better be glad I'm not George Bamberger." He said, "Why is that?" I said, "You know, I know a little something about hitting, and George knew a little something about pitching, and when he had a little trouble with his pitching, he fired Bill Monbouquette, the pitching coach, and handled it himself." I just let it sit there. Bill didn't say much. He didn't know quite how to take that.

I know it's not Bill's fault. But it is true that when guys do not

play up to their ability, somebody has to pay. On all of the ballclubs that I have ever had, the players overachieved, and this year they are underachieving. From time to time I do consider making a change. Because this hitting slump isn't easy on me either. If they keep hitting like this, I'll be glad to go.

I've thought of rearranging my lineup. I've thought of putting different guys in different places. I've thought about asking some of the writers to give me a lineup. But an illogical move doesn't make a lot of sense to me. Hit Strawberry leadoff, or hit Hernandez and Carter eighth and ninth. Shake it up. For what?

I've heard all that BS about Casey Stengel pulling a lineup out of a hat. I think a batting slump is a lot like having a cold. You can take every kind of drug in the world, but if it's a two-week cold, you're still going to have it for two weeks.

You can pull all kinds of theatrics. If I bat Gary Carter leadoff, I'll get the big headlines, JOHNSON HITS CARTER LEADOFF. And then the game begins, and the bases are loaded, and my cleanup hitter is up and I have Backman hitting, and he hits a ground ball to second. Then they say, "What an idiot? How can he do that?"

One happy note: They finally got my satellite dish working. Now when I want to watch a ballgame anywhere around the country, it's on. But when I came back from the road trip, I sat down at my desk to make a phone call, and the phone in my office wasn't working. I'd call upstairs, and the operator would answer, but they couldn't hear me. For two days. I kept picking up the phone, saying "Hello," but they couldn't hear me. These days I'm very reluctant to drive my car. The way things are going, a tire might fall off.

34

MOOKIE GOES UNDER

I HAD MY regular outfield of Foster, Mookie Wilson, and Strawberry intact for one game, but now Mookie's going to have his
arm operated on and will be out until September, at best. Even
after this operation, he may still have real problems. They'll
know more once they go in and look around. But there is no
question that there is something wrong. His arm hasn't been right
for a year and a half.

I thought he should have had the operation in April, and to be
honest, I'm having mixed emotions about his having it now. I'd
rather let him platoon for the rest of the year and help me win a
few games, but Frank feels he should have it done, and in the end
I just let Frank, the doctors, and Mookie hash it out.

So just when I'm getting Darryl back, we're going to be without
our center fielder. Maybe now if I can find a set lineup, it may
have a settling effect on the rest of the players. I hated to be
hodgepodging around, not knowing whether Mookie could play
or not. It was always, Is Mookie going to play today, or is he sore?
It's one thing to rest a player, but it's a lot tougher on everybody

when the rest of the players are wondering, Who in the heck is going to be out there today? You can't prepare mentally.

One piece of good news for a change: Despite what the writers are saying, Jesse Orosco does not have a serious arm problem. About a week ago I said to Mel Stottlemyre, "There's something wrong with Jesse's motion. He's hanging too many sliders." Mel studied some films of Jesse pitching, and he noticed that Gary Carter kept setting up outside, not inside, where catchers usually set up for the hard slider, and that Gary was signaling for what we call "backdoor sliders."

Jesse's been cutting his slider, trying to shut off its break and just drop it over the outside part of the plate. That was never Jesse. Jesse was always a power pitcher, throwing the fastball up and away, and then the hard-biting slider down and in. The backdoor slider is a good pitch to throw to a left-hander, but it's something Jesse has never done. And shouldn't.

I'm not blaming Gary for calling it. Maybe Jesse hung a few inside, and they hit them downtown, or hard, and Gary started thinking, Let's throw this breaking ball on the outside part of the plate. A new catcher has to get to know the pitcher, what works and what doesn't, and sometimes it's not always standard or obvious.

In any case, Jesse now should regain his old effectiveness and save us some games.

We can use his help, too, since it doesn't look as if the Mets will be able to pick up any players from other clubs. From day one I told Frank what I would like, a veteran right-handed hitter, but it doesn't look as if any will become available in time to help us this season. It's become a moot point.

35

SOME LIGHT

AGAINST THE PIRATES starting out July we ended our six-game losing streak and broke out of our hitting slump. At one point in the game we even had a four-run lead. During the game Gary got a hit, and then Darryl Strawberry stroked a long double, driving in Gary from first. After Gary crossed the plate, he came into the dugout and said to me, "This is more like it." I said, "See, there is light at the end of the tunnel."

That's the lift we get when Darryl is playing well. After Darryl's double, George Foster drove him in, which was the way the offense was originally structured. But in how many games have we had that? We haven't. Darryl hasn't been out there.

The next day Eddie Lynch pitched himself a complete game, and George Foster got the big blow, a three-run home run. Keith drove in a run, Gary drove in a run, and Darryl hit another double and stole a base, and again we won. We're starting to look like the Mets of old. It's an intangible thing. All year it's been Gary carrying the club, with George and Keith unproductive and Darryl out. For the last two or three weeks George has been alive and well, and now with Darryl and Keith coming around, it's taking a lot of pressure off Gary, and as a result we'll score a lot more runs. Everybody'll hit better.

After a long discussion with Frank, we called up Lenny Dykstra a second time from Tidewater to play in Mookie's spot. I don't know if Lenny's going to be the answer. Frank thinks he is. Frank came down to my office yesterday with a stack of computer printouts on Dykstra's hitting. He suggested I lead off with Lenny and bat Wally Backman second.

I said, "You know, Frank, Christensen's coming along, and Danny Heep's done a credible job. I think we would be stronger offensively with Darryl in center and either Christensen or Heep in right. Dykstra to me is a little overmatched right now. He's got a little bit of an uppercut, and he doesn't have a center fielder's strong arm. Also, I'm not that comfortable with two little ping hitters, one and two. But the difference between going the way I want to go and the way you want me to go is not that big. You want to make a decision, I'll be glad to do it."

He said, "No, I'm paying you to manage."

I said, "This could be your chance, go ahead."

I asked Gary how he felt about it. Gary said, "I like Dykstra against the right-handers and Christensen against the left-handers." I could do that. It means Danny Heep becomes a utility player, playing for Foster when I rest George, but Danny has tapered off. He isn't pulling the ball with authority like he did earlier. Maybe that is the best way to go.

None of the choices seem really great. It's not concrete in my mind. I'm more comfortable with Strawberry in the middle, and Heep and Christensen platooning in right, but what I may have to do, at least until the All-Star break, is play Dykstra. I have to find out if he can do it. He's not going to have the opportunity to prove himself sitting on the bench.

36
NINETEEN CRAZY INNINGS

ON INDEPENDENCE DAY I started Dwight Gooden with only three days' rest. This way he gets three starts before the All-Star break, and because he pitches right before the All-Star Game, it keeps him out of it. The All-Star Game really takes it out of a pitcher. You're talking about two or three innings that you really have to be up for. Every hitter's a star, and you're all excited, and it can drain you. I'd rather Doc save it for the regular season.

Doc warmed up, and it started raining, as it often seems to do in Atlanta. He stopped. The ground crew pulled the tarp. Ten minutes later, they pulled it off, and a ground-crew guy came over and told Doc to warm up. The umps weren't even on the field! Who are the ground-crew guys to be telling my pitcher to warm up? I went out there and firmly told Doc to stop. Even if the ump had told him to warm up, I would have stopped him. Until the managers and umpires meet at home plate and exchange lineups, the decision to call a game is in the hands of the club officials. I wasn't taking the chance that Doc would pitch his game on the sidelines.

An hour and a half or so later, when the game looked like it would get underway, I told Doc, "Warm up late. Let's make sure the tarp is off and we're going to play. I'll get you five more minutes if you need it because we bat first."

When the game was set to begin, Doc wasn't ready. I told the umps, "My pitcher is going to need another five minutes, because these ground-crew guys have been yo-yoing him. This'll be his third time warming up, and I want to make sure that this is going to be the real thing." They said, "Dave, don't worry. We agree. There's always a problem here in Atlanta."

We started the game. We scored a run, and they got one off Doc. We were in the bottom of the second inning, and Oberkfell got a base hit, and then the rains came again. Holy mackerel! I had my franchise out there, it was only the second inning, and there was another rain delay.

I asked Mel, "What would constitute a delay so long that I can't let Dwight continue?" He said, "Sometimes a long inning is fifteen minutes, so if you wait ten or fifteen minutes more than that, it wouldn't be excessive." I said, "Yeah, Mel, but I'm bringing this kid back on three days' rest for the first time in his career. He's warmed up three times. If something happens to this kid's arm, I'll hang myself. And I'll have to do it quickly, before they run me out of town or worse." I said, "I'm not going to take a chance. I'm going to scratch him."

We waited another forty minutes before the next pitch was thrown. I got up my best in the bullpen, Roger McDowell. I was thinking, The weatherman says we're going to have a dry hole for an hour or an hour and a half, and then the rain is coming again. Hell, the game may only go five innings."

Umpire Jerry Crawford called me out and said, "Dave, we're going to start in twenty minutes." I said, "I may make a pitching change. I'll let you know."

He said, "I don't care what you do. Twenty minutes. Send your pitcher out."

I said, "Jerry, just have the ground crew fix the damn mound."

He said, "Send the pitcher out, because I want the damn mound fixed for him. I want them to have it right."

I said, "Okay, you got it." I told Roger, "Go out to the mound, and you can throw from there. They want you throwing from the mound."

The tarp was still out, and while the ground crew was piddling around on the field, Roger went out there and started warming up.

Now, remember, I hadn't told Crawford I was definitely making a pitching change. I had told him that if I made a change, it would be McDowell. Also, Crawford had demanded that I send my pitcher out to check the damn mound rather than have him throw on the side.

McDowell went out there and threw about eight pitches. I went out, and I said to Jerry, "Okay, it is going to be McDowell, but he's going to hit seventh, and we'll make a double switch. Howard Johnson will come in for Ray Knight and hit in the ninth spot." Our number eight hitter was scheduled to bat, and by double-switching I kept McDowell from having to hit in the middle of the next inning.

Crawford said, "No, Dave, I've already written McDowell down ninth."

I said, "I don't care what you wrote down. The tarp is still on the damn field. You asked me to get him out on the mound. Now you're telling me he can't hit seventh?" I said, "We're twenty minutes away from playing. You're telling me he can't hit seventh?"

He said, "I wrote it down. Eddie Haas will protest if I change it."

I said, "Hold on. Let's go back a little bit. They had a ruling in Philadelphia. Koosman's leading eleven to nothing, he goes in the clubhouse in the top of the ninth inning to change his sweatshirt, and a relief guy comes running in from the bullpen and is warming up on the mound with their players playing catch behind them, actually warming up. Koosman comes back out to the mound, chases the guy off, and he stays in the game and pitches, and he's allowed to.

"Now you tell me about actual and announced. Roger has not been announced. We are in a rain delay. There's nobody behind him. Because you've asked me to warm him up on the hill and not on the side, you're figuring he's an unannounced announced player. And now you're telling me that you will not allow me to make this switch?"

He said, "Yes, Dave, that's correct."

I said, "And the reason is that Haas will protest?"

He said, "That's right."

I said, "That's fine, because I'm protesting the damn game."

Then the umpires got hot at me, even though all they had to do was say, "Dave, we haven't told anybody anything. We'll put McDowell in the seventh spot and the other guy in the ninth spot. We won't worry about it."

My pitcher warmed up for a while and came off the field. They still hadn't taken the tarp off. The ground crew worked about ten more minutes on the field. We went back out, Roger got in his seven warm-up pitches, we started the ballgame, and the Braves rackytacked him for two runs. So now I was looking at a situation in which my best pitcher was out, and my best reliever would have to come out because he was struggling and we were behind, and I was going to have to pinch-hit for him. Hell.

The only consolation I had was that I thought I was going to win the damn protest, but big deal, I wanted to win the game.

We rallied, but I had another run-in with the umpires. Keith Hernandez hit a shot to center field. It was puddles everywhere, and Dale Murphy came running over, sending water in every direction, dived for it, trapped it in his glove, fell on the ground, scrambled up, and threw a pea into second. Gerry Davis, the second base umpire, ruled it a catch. Davis hadn't seen whether Murphy had actually caught the ball or not, but he should have called safe, knowing that Murphy, who is honest, would not have hurried to throw it in if he had caught it.

I ran out there to argue with Davis. I said, "It's very obvious to the world that you blew this call. You don't think with nobody on he'd come up throwing to second if he had caught it, do you?"

He said, "I don't know."

I said, "Why the hell do you think he threw it in?"

He said, "I don't know."

I said, "Well, I know. It was because the ball was rolling around out there. You didn't see it. I didn't see it. But I know he didn't catch it. Now why don't we ask for help from one of the umps on the corners?"

Davis said, "No, I ain't going to do it."

I said, "When they show it on camera, they're going to see the ball rolling around out there. But you don't want to get any help?"

He said, "No, I ain't going to get any help."

I said, "The hell with it then. You blew it, and you won't get help. That's really great. That's dandy. You're horseshit." Making an umpire change his mind is next to impossible, but I didn't get thrown because he knew I was right.

Umpires Jerry Crawford and Terry Tata, who was behind the plate, were mad at me to begin with because of my protest, and now Davis was mad at me too. We rallied to score four runs, and we were up 7–4, thanks to some great pitching by Terry Leach. In the eighth, Jesse came in. He should have ended it, but he was wild. He only gave up one hit, but he walked three, and I had to bring in Sisk. Sisk got us out of the inning, but not before allowing the go-ahead run to score.

At this point we could have lost it, but we didn't. In the top of the ninth Eddie Haas brought in Bruce Sutter, who for years has been the best reliever in baseball, but after he struck out the first batter, we scored a run to make it 8–8. I was shaking my head. There was no way the Braves should have scored eight runs. My relievers didn't hold them. We should have won it in regulation.

We also should have won it in the thirteenth, but didn't. Howard Johnson got up righty and hit one out with a runner on base to put us ahead 10–8. He should have been the hero.

In the bottom of the thirteenth Tommy Gorman was pitching. He had two outs, a runner on first, and an oh-and-two count on Terry Harper. I was standing in the dugout, waiting to rush out to congratulate Tommy on a nice job of pitching. I was figuring he was going to throw Harper a forkball and make him chase it. He threw the forkball all right, but he ran it inside instead of away, and Harper hit it deep, way up into the screen. A home run. Tie game!

I couldn't believe it. I had a veteran catcher, Carter, out there, and I had a veteran pitcher, Gorman, out on the mound. I shouldn't have to go out there and say, "Hey, don't let him hit this ball out of the ballpark." Nobody wanted him to hit the ball out. Twenty-five guys and five coaches didn't want him to hit it out. Because he can. You want to give him a pitch away. You don't want to walk the tying runner on base, but you don't want to give him something he can hit out. Well, he hit it out. So what are you going to do? You can't sit there and cry about it. You say, "Get the next guy, we'll come in and try to score some runs."

We didn't score another run until the eighteenth. By that time I was no longer around.

At the start of the seventeenth, the clock was showing it was three o'clock in the morning. There were still fans in the stadium, which has to make you wonder. Darryl Strawberry led off, and home plate umpire Terry Tata called him out on a pitch that wasn't even close. I saw Darryl arguing, and I didn't have that many players left, so I went out to keep him from getting tossed. But when I got to home plate, I found that Tata had already thrown him out of the game. I said, "What in the world? How in the heck can you throw a player out of a game like this? I don't blame the kid for bitching. The damn ball wasn't even close."

And then he said the same thing to me he said to Strawberry. "It's three o'clock in the morning, Dave."

I began sputtering. I said, "What difference does it make that it's three o'clock?"

Something in my brain snapped. I called him every name in the book, and I got a little more personal than I normally would. I made some derogatory comments about his heredity, and I don't even know what Tata's background is! I discussed his mother. I said a lot of things I would not have otherwise said, but I was really upset. I lost a player because Tata blew a call, and it was okay with him because it was three in the morning? That fried me. So he tossed me and I was gone.

I went back to the bench, and I was still red-hot, and I was waving a towel at him. He was telling me to get out of the dugout, and I was signaling with my fingers. "Three, eight, five, ten, five, what difference does it make, you . . ." And so I said my piece, and I went into the clubhouse. After storming around for a bit, I grabbed a beer, and the game went on.

I was sitting in front of the TV in the clubhouse watching our game with about eight other players who had already been in the game. Strawberry, pitchers, the pinch hitters I had used. There was only one fielder left I hadn't used, and that was Ronn Reynolds, our reserve catcher.

We went to the top of the eighteenth, and boom, my new center fielder, Lenny Dykstra, got on and ran the bases with abandon. Thanks to his heroics, we scored a run. We were cheering because we figured we finally had this game won.

We went out in the field. Tommy Gorman was still on the mound. Except for the home run to Harper, he had pitched beautifully. Tommy got the first batter, Harper, out, and got the second out, and we were one out away from winning the game. Gorman was facing Rick Camp, the Atlanta pitcher, one of the worst hitters in the game. Eddie Haas could not pinch-hit for Camp because he had run out of pinch hitters. Gorman got two quick strikes on Camp, and we figured we were sitting in smug city.

When Camp got up, Braves announcer Ernie Johnson started talking as if he were praying. He said, "What we need is a home run by Rick Camp. He hasn't hit one in his life. Would that be too much to ask, Lord?" He was sort of laughing.

Then, wacko, Rick hit one not just over the fence, but way over. Ernie said, "We're going to wake up from this dream in a minute. This is not really happening."

For me it was no dream. It was a nightmare. We didn't win it in nine because they came back to tie us. We couldn't hold the lead. Then we had a two-run lead with two outs and couldn't hold that. And then we even got a one-run lead with two outs and the pitcher up. They couldn't pinch-hit for the pitcher because they had no other pinch hitters left. And he hit a home run! What in the world could happen next?

At this point Gorman had pitched six innings and had given up only three runs, not a bad outing, even though the two home runs had kept us at the ballpark until four in the morning. He was my last available relief pitcher, but his day was done because he was scheduled to hit in the top of the nineteenth, and I had to pinch-hit for him. The problem was, we had run out of replacements.

Mel Stottlemyre knew it too, and he came running into the clubhouse from the dugout and said, "This is what the coaches want to do. We want to take Carter and put him in left field." I said, "Why is that?" He said, "Because we want to bring in Heep from left field to pitch." I said, "Whoa, back up. Run this by me again. What do you want to do?" He said, "We want to bring in Heep to pitch." I said, "No, no. I don't care whether we score or not, you're going to pinch-hit Rusty Staub this inning for Gorman and bring in Ron Darling. Get Darling hot. We've come this far. We ain't quitting now. Darling can give us a couple of innings, and if we have to, we'll go to Sid Fernandez next. We're not giving in on this one." Mel went running back to the dugout and got Darling up.

If they had gotten us out one, two, three, Darling would not have had time to warm up! But Gary singled, Christensen bunted him over, and with Gorman scheduled up, Mel pinch-hit with Staub, and that was the right thing to do, even though there was a base open. I suppose Mel and Buddy could have disregarded my advice. I'm glad they didn't. Atlanta walked Staub intentionally, Ray Knight doubled for a run, and then they walked HoJo intentionally to load the bases. Danny Heep was up, and he struck the big blow, a two-run single, and we ended up scoring five runs in the top of the nineteenth. We were leading 16–11. And I was really happy it wasn't Danny Heep coming in to pitch.

But the Braves weren't finished yet. Darling got an out, and then one guy got on, then another guy walked, and then a base hit. It had been Darling's day to throw on the sidelines. He had already thrown that day, and his arm was tired. His fastball was decent, but he didn't have a breaking ball. When the pitcher, Rick Camp, came up again, I got up from my chair in the clubhouse and said, "I can't watch this anymore. I'm going to take a shower. Let me know." As the water washed over me, I listened for either a roar or a groan from the guys sitting in front of the TV, and I finally heard a roar and figured we had held on and won, which we did.

After the game, Gorman came over to me and said, "Sorry, Skip, it should have ended a long time ago."

I said, "Tommy, don't worry about it. You did a heck of a job keeping us in there."

Riding the bus back to the hotel at five in the morning, we didn't have a lot of energy. We wore quiet smiles. We were happy to have won this ordeal. Winning it sure made it a lot easier than losing it. I couldn't help thinking how Eddie Haas and his Braves must have been feeling.

$\mathbb{37}$

FEELING GOOD

WE'VE WON nine out of ten and finally as a team we're starting to play with consistency. Contributing to that consistency has been the outstanding play of Lenny Dykstra, whom I've put in center field every day. When Lenny first came back up from Tidewater, I felt ambivalent about him, but Lenny has made me change my mind.

In my own defense, I had never really seen him throw in a game situation. When he's practicing he looks like a girl, but in the field he has cut loose two or three throws that were on the money. He's played the hitters well, and he's covered a lot of ground out there, which we've needed. So defensively, he's been as good as Mookie, and offensively, he has actually been better. His stroke is not ideal, and he hits too many fly balls, but he's a pesky little hitter, he has no strike zone, and he'll get you about a hit and a walk a game.

The first time he was here, before I sent him back down and he returned, he hadn't gotten a lot of walks, and his on-base percentage wasn't very good. But that isn't the case now. Lenny has been getting on base more than forty percent of the time and scoring runs. He's a good base stealer, not as good as Mookie, but good. I may be dumb, but I ain't stupid. He really has been a spark plug for our offense.

I like Lenny. He's a character. When he first came up, he was very nervous. He exaggerated his idiosyncrasies at bat—fidgeting all the time, constantly adjusting his hat and helmet, going up and down on the bat, driving everybody crazy. But he's a lot calmer now.

Sometimes Lenny is so cocky that he has a tendency to piss off the veterans. One time Bruce Berenyi was pitching batting practice, just trying to get in shape, and Bill Robinson, our batting coach, had to pick several batters to hit against him. Naturally you aren't going to send up your starters against a hard-throwing pitcher who doesn't have good control, and so Bill picked several subs, including Lenny. In front of everybody, Lenny started complaining. "I shouldn't have to hit against the guy." Lenny was offended he was being used as fodder. Bruce was offended by Lenny's attitude. He said, "The next time he comes up to hit, I'm going to drill the little SOB."

Another time coach Greg Pavlick was throwing batting practice, and his pitches were coming in low, so Lenny ran up in front of the batter's box to swing. That is also insulting to a pitcher. Greg told him, "You do that again, and I'll hit you in the head."

Bill Robinson, our batting coach, wanted to talk to Lenny about his arrogant behavior, but I told him not to. I said, "Bill, let it go. Lenny's an asshole kind of guy, very obnoxious at times, but I don't want him to lose that attitude. That's what motivates him."

I remember Lenny in the minors at Columbia, South Carolina. He drove around in a Porsche, and his teammates were always kidding about how he liked high school girls. He was twenty-one. I remember one day we had some gymnasts come out and perform before a ballgame. These gymnasts weren't but two feet high, and one of the other guys shouted, "Somebody tie Lenny down."

Lenny may look a little sleepy-eyed and like he isn't paying attention, but he doesn't miss much. In Houston my sister's two girls, who are sixteen and seventeen, came by to visit me, and he said, "Your sister's kids are really cute."

Someone said he was a California beach type. We're not really sure what type Lenny is. But he gives you everything he's got. He looks like he can hardly walk at times, and then he'll show you surprising quickness. You have to love him.

Keith has finally broken out of his deep slump, and he's hitting like I knew he could. I suspect he had been dropping his hands too low, maybe opening up his stance too much, which would slow down his bat more than usual. Keith says his daddy's the one who got him out of it. Keith told me, "My daddy was watching me play on TV, and he said, 'On TV, when I can't read the word "Mets" on your jersey, I know your hands are too low. You need to close up your stance and get your hands higher.'"

When you're in a slump, a lot of times your mental state will improve and you'll hit better just by thinking you've corrected the problem. I don't know much about Keith's dad. I know he was once a semipro ballplayer. Sometimes Keith gets annoyed that his dad is always trying to help him with his hitting. This time I guess he was glad to get the advice.

Darryl's return has been the catalyst, as I knew it would be. Before he got hurt, our record was 18–8, and we were just getting ready to go on a roll. When he got hurt, our hitting suffered. With Darryl's return, now Keith and Carter and George have all started to hit better. The pressure on each of them is less.

Against the Reds, we were behind 2–0 when Darryl hit his first home run since coming back, a monstrous shot over the left-center field wall. That picked the club up. George Foster then hit a two-run shot. Howard Johnson hit one out, and Keith had four hits in five at bats.

The next night we hit a couple more home runs, and the boys are starting to play the way I had expected them to. Having Keith, George, Gary, and Strawman all healthy and swinging is what's done the trick. We're really feeling good about ourselves. It looks like we will mount a consistent attack from this point on. It's making me look like a genius as a manager.

Ray Knight has also begun to hit. He helped us win four straight games, once again showing us what a great hitter he can be. Ray then pulled a leg muscle.

In his place Howard Johnson began playing regularly, finally started to relax and to hit. He even hit another home run right-handed to tie a game we would have lost. Once third base was a liability. Now I'm getting production at third.

And now poor Ray will be back in a platoon situation when he gets back. I feel sorry for Ray. It's been a tough year for him. He's a career .280 hitter with a lot of pride, and having to platoon with Howard Johnson has not been easy for him. During the season Ray has had sleepless nights because he wasn't playing as much as he thought he should. He was talking of quitting, but his wife talked him out of it.

Circumstances have kept him out of the lineup a good part of the time. Early on, I had planned for him to start the season as my regular third baseman, but then Ray had to have his elbow operated on. With Ray out HoJo played and struggled, and I finally decided that Ray would play full-time. The next day Ray came down with dizzy spells, and he wasn't able to go. Finally, I got Ray healthy again and got him into the lineup to play. He tore the cover off the ball, raised his average from .150 to .206, won almost all the games in Atlanta for me, and then pulled a leg muscle. All we can do is wait for Ray to get healthy again, and then we'll see what happens.

When the Texas Rangers came to the city to play the Yankees, Bobby Valentine came to visit me. Bobby mentioned that Baltimore had offered him two or three players he wasn't real high on for his third baseman, Buddy Bell. Bobby said, "You can get Bell if you want him." I asked Bobby what he wanted for Bell. He said, "All I want is Howard Johnson and Calvin Schiraldi." I said, "Bobby, no." He said, "You would have traded Schiraldi and Walt Terrell for Buddy Bell last year, wouldn't you have?" Terrell is who we sent to Detroit for Howard. I said, "Maybe last year, yeah." He said, "What's the difference?" I said, "The difference is that your guy is hitting about .240 and drove in 30 runs and my Knight-Johnson twosome has driven in about 36, and your guy is making about twice as much money and he's older. I'd like to have him, but I can't give you the guys you want." He said, "Think about it." I said, "Bobby, you know our organization. How about someone else from the system?"

I like Buddy Bell. But I have a twenty-four-year-old switch

hitter who I would damn sure not part with, even if he was still struggling with the bat. Because in Buddy Bell, you're talking about two more years of productivity and then a decline. And Howard's going to be a star. Howard has a lot of competitive spirit. He's struggled and struggled, but he has never quit. I'm still looking for the key that will unlock his hitting problems.

A few days ago I asked him, "HoJo, what are you thinking about when you go up and hit?" He said, "I'm thinking about waiting and being quick."

I said, "Listen, shitcan the wait and be quick. Do me a favor. As you see the ball come in, try to time it and hit it out front."

I could probably say anything and it would help, because what I'm really saying is that I'm paying attention and that I care. In any case he's been hitting the ball better, and I think he'll end up hitting .250 this year. You wait and see.

38
GARY'S KNEE

THERE IS SOMETHING WRONG with Gary. He has loose cartilage in his knee. Some of it loosened during the season, but it got really aggravated in Houston, and the Astro team physician thought it should be surgically repaired because Gary could hardly walk, much less squat. But our doctor, Fiske Warren, looked at his knee, and saw that it was inflamed and swollen. He said, "Let's get rid of the inflammation, and hopefully the swelling will go down, and then let's decide if we need to operate." He figured that would be better than panicking and going in right away.

Dr. Warren treated the knee for inflammation and let the swelling go down. Gary's seventy-to-eighty percent better, and Dr. Warren says Gary can play.

I agree with both doctors. I believe a surgical procedure is going to be necessary. The big question is when. If it's possible that Gary can continue to play with the leg brace he wore last year, I would prefer we not operate right now. Without him, we're going to be hurting, badly. If Gary insisted on the operation, I wouldn't stop him. I always listen to the player when it comes to an injury.

I remember in 1972 when I was with Baltimore and hurt my arm during the summer of 1971 after twice trying to run over catcher Duane Josephson of the Red Sox. The collisions tore up my left shoulder, and I could barely lift it. But Earl Weaver kept insisting I could play.

I kept telling him my shoulder was bad. But whenever the Oriole doctors would examine me, they kept saying there was nothing structurally wrong. They sent me to the Mayo Clinic in Rochester, Minnesota, and to a couple of other specialists in Minnesota, but nobody could find anything. No one could diagnose it. No one would confirm what I knew to be true, that I was hurt.

With all the doctors saying there was nothing wrong, Weaver would say to me, "You're jaking. It's in your head." But it wasn't in my head. It was in my shoulder.

That winter I was traded to Atlanta. When the trade was announced I called Eddie Robinson, the Atlanta general manager, and I said, "Eddie, I'm hurt. If it doesn't get better in the spring, I'm quitting."

Eddie sent me to see the Atlanta trainer, Dave Pursley, and Pursley sent me to see the Braves' orthopedic specialist, Dr. Wells, who immediately diagnosed what was wrong with my shoulder. Why they were able to figure it out when the Mayo Clinic couldn't I'll never know.

"You have subluxation," Dr. Wells said, meaning I had stretched the ligaments in the shoulder. I was elated. Once I knew what the problem was, I could now take steps to correct it. I exercised my shoulder endlessly, leaning my left elbow against a wall or car door and pressing as hard as I could for ten seconds. Within two weeks of treatment I noticed that the shoulder was getting stronger. By the spring I felt for the first time that I was going to be all right. My career was saved. That year I hit 43 home runs, breaking Rogers Hornsby's single-season record for most home runs hit by a second baseman.

My experience with Earl taught me a valuable lesson: Given the choice between believing one of my players who tells me he's hurt and believing the doctor who says he isn't, I believe the player every time. I've never known a player who didn't want to play when he was healthy.

So when it came to Gary's situation, I decided the best thing for him was to force the issue. I'd love for Gary not to have an operation, to take treatment and be able to play five games out of seven. I can live with that. But I'm not going to let him start and rest and start and rest, wasting the rest of the season and possibly taking the chance of damaging his good knee.

I said to Gary, "Since the doctor said it's okay for you to play, I'll play you. But we've done enough procrastinating on some other players—Mookie, Berenyi—trying to get them well. If you have a flare-up, like you did in Houston, you'll go under the knife."

I told Frank's assistant, Joe McIlvaine, "Gary may be better, he may not, but let's send Darrell Johnson around to look at our minor league catchers, Ed Hearn, Barry Lyons, and John Gibbons."

Darrell said, "Dave, Hearn is the guy. He's the best hitter, and he's a little better defensive catcher." I wasn't so sure.

"Darrell," I said, "don't you think you ought to check all three out again? Lyons has eighty ribbies and is hitting .320." Darrell said, "I don't have to see him. He chases too many bad pitches. He's eventually going to be better, but right now it's Hearn." I said, "You really don't feel you need to go in there?" He said, "Only if you tell me to." I said, "Not if you've already made up your mind." So okay, if we lose Gary, I'll take Hearn.

39

THE ALL-STAR BREAK

THE PLAYERS HAVE SET an August 6 strike date, but I intend to continue as though there isn't going to be one. It's analogous to a big black raincloud that hovers over a game in progress. You don't change strategy just because the cloud is overhead.

However, I'm not unaware of what happened back in 1981 when the teams who were ahead at the strike were given playoff spots. Mel Stottlemyre and I went over the rotation for the next couple of weeks, and the way it's working out, Dwight is pitching August 5.

On the strike issue, I am backing the players wholeheartedly. When I was a player, I was a player rep, and the issues are still, and will always be, important, particularly the pension fund. The older players who weren't making big money, like myself, participate in it.

The number one issue concerns the percentage of the TV money the owners will have to contribute to the pension fund. In the past it's been thirty-three percent, but in the past the dollar figure was about fifteen million, a third of forty-five million.

Today TV revenues have increased to around a billion dollars, and so the owners have offered the players about eight percent, which, they argue, comes to the same amount. The players, quite reasonably, are not buying that argument.

The other issue is that the owners want to institute a salary cap to keep an owner from paying two million a year for an Ozzie Smith. Frankly, I don't understand the concept. It seems stupid to try to tell a player, "Look, I'm paying you too much, so have an agreement with me to prevent me from paying you too much." That's the most ludicrous thing I've ever heard.

Quite frankly, if the owners were so hot on a salary cap, I don't understand why they just don't go ahead, meet among themselves, and institute a cap in secret. Why get the players involved?

I can tell you why. Because all it takes is for one owner to decide to pay more than anybody else. That's why they want the players to *make* them agree. It shouldn't be an issue. Nobody is twisting an owner's arm to pay anybody anything. If an owner wants to overspend on players and go bankrupt, that's the American way.

And don't insult my intelligence by telling me that the New York Yankees lost nine million dollars last year. That is the biggest joke and farce. Every large corporation shows the government that they're losing money, but don't expect me to believe that a ballclub with a revenue of thirty million dollars has lost money. If you can't figure a way to make a profit on a club with thirty million dollars in gross revenues, then you don't belong in this business. You shouldn't own anything.

As for the All-Star Game, I asked Jay Horwitz, our publicity director, to talk to Dick Williams, the manager of the National League All-Star team, and convince him not to play Dwight. Evidently there has been a lot of media pressure for him to start Dwight, especially since Joaquin Andujar has decided not to play. I told Jay to tell Dick, "Look, you're the manager of the ballclub. I have no business telling you what you can or can't do. But this kid is twenty years old, he threw 133 pitches against Houston, and I would prefer that you don't use him."

Knowing Jay, I'm sure all he said was, "Davey said don't pitch Doc." And I know that will probably piss Dick off.

Dick didn't play Doc, but when Jay got back from the game, he had a message. "Dick says you owe him one."

The best news of all during the break is that Frank was finally able to acquire a quality veteran right-handed batter, Tom Paciorek, from the White Sox. I haven't seen Paciorek play, but I know by looking at his profile he's a solid hitter. Paciorek's maybe a little older than I would like him, but he can fill the role better than a John Christensen. Now I can send John down to Tidewater, where he can play, and I can call him up in September. It'll help John more to be playing than to be here sitting, because I wouldn't be able to play Johnny very much going down the stretch. If we're facing a veteran left-hander, and the bases are loaded, I would want a veteran to hit. When we opened talks with the White Sox for Paciorek, they asked for our number one draft picks, like Sean Abner and Stan Jefferson, and when we wouldn't do that, they asked for a couple of our young minor leaguers, including Dave Cochrane. I really like Dave, but I felt we could afford to let him go. His problem is that he doesn't have a position. But he's a strong switch hitter with a lot of bat potential. In the American League he can DH.

We probably overpaid for Paciorek. He is thirty-eight years old. But if he can help win us a pennant, it will be worth it.

With Paciorek on the team, I'm sure all the guys, Keith, Carter, Ray, are saying to themselves, "We're better. We should win easier." And on this team especially, it makes a huge difference.

40

THE SECOND HALF BEGINS

TOM PACIOREK ARRIVED at the ballpark before our game with Atlanta, and I had a little meeting with him. I said, "We tried to get you two months ago when Strawberry was out. I would have been able to use you more. Now you'll be a utility player, but you'll be my number one right-handed pinch hitter, and I'll try to play you enough to keep sharp."

"Dave, I'm happy to have this opportunity," he said.

After our meeting I went upstairs to talk to Frank Cashen, who said he wanted to discuss Gary Carter's knee. What he really wanted to talk about was Dwight Gooden. He said, "I was displeased that you pitched Dwight against Atlanta after only three days' rest."

I said, "Frank, I did it to keep him from pitching in the All-Star Game, which would have been tougher on him." I told Frank that Joe McIlvaine had agreed, and so had Mel Stottlemyre, and so had Doc. I couldn't believe Frank was getting on me for doing it.

He said, "If I had known you were going to do that, I would have stopped it."

What Frank was *really* concerned about was something else.

"Dwight is going to pitch too many innings this year," he said. "My God, he's only twenty years old, and he's going to end up pitching 280 innings."

I said, "I know that. He pitched 211 two years ago. He pitched about 218 last year, and now, because I pitch him every fifth day, he's going to pitch almost 300." Which is a lot.

I said, "Frank, I understand what you're saying. But the only way I can figure out to prevent it is if he gets knocked out early; but he doesn't."

Frank said, "Think of something."

I said, "There are two things we could do. One, you could order me to send him home September 1. Or two, you could give me a signed letter from you and McIlvaine telling me to take him out in the sixth inning of every game. If you'll do that, I'll walk out to the mound with the paper, and show Doc that this is when I'm supposed to take him out."

Frank said, "You always think of something. Think of something here."

I said, "If you feel that strongly about it, you think of something."

But the only thing I can do is keep in really close contact with our trainer, and if Doc has any unusual discomfort between starts, I'll put him back a day.

I don't think it's so terrible that Dwight may pitch 280 innings. He had two 200-inning seasons at ages eighteen and nineteen, and this year he's bigger and stronger. He can handle it.

Of course, I would prefer Doc only throw 250, 260 innings. But you have to take into account that Dwight doesn't throw as many pitches in a game as most power pitchers. He's unusual. Nolan Ryan will throw 150 pitches in a ballgame. Dwight seldom gets over 140. Most of the time it'll be between 100 and 130. So the strain is less.

To keep Dwight under 280 innings this year will be a problem. As I told Frank, "All I can do is monitor how his arm feels, and if he has a problem, skip him one day." But that's what I do anyway.

41
STRIKE TALK

OUR NEW COMMISSIONER, Peter Ueberroth, came in and talked to the ballclub. He said, "I'm optimistic there won't be a strike because we have great people on both sides of the table. If we don't get together, it's not a strike; rather it's a failure for all concerned."

Ueberroth told the players that he doesn't believe in the salary cap. He said, "I think it is wrong." The players liked that. He told the players that everyone had to work this out because a strike would be the worst thing that could happen.

After the meeting I talked to him in private. He said, "Dave, the thing that worries me is that I'm not convinced that all the ownership is stable. They are not all sound, baseball-oriented, reasonable individuals who can work out a collective bargaining agreement by August 7."

That scares him. He's afraid that before the owners can work out an agreement, they will get hacked off and say, "The hell with the players. Let's just shut down the operation and go home." I can see his point. Among the owners are oil magnates, entertainment people, and there's Marge and Schottsie the St.

Bernard in Cincinnati. They are so diversified. A couple of them are crazy, some are conservative, others liberal. I can see Steinbrenner saying, "We'll *tell* them what we'll give them." That kind of attitude. For the owners to get together it is going to be tough.

To be honest, the whole problem stems from the owners' inability to control their own egos. If somebody else wants a player another owner wants, he'll outbid him. They can't control themselves, and many of them are only looking out for their own self-interest.

I'm between a rock and a hard place, because I'm supposed to be part of management, but if the players come out with a compromise, it's going to benefit me.

42

STORMING ATLANTA

OUR TEAM IS FUNNY. We can beat the toughest pitcher in the league, and then a guy with lesser credentials comes in and makes us look like little leaguers. The Braves' Zane Smith beat us in a tough one, 1–0. From what the hitters told me, Smith had a lot better stuff than he had the last time he pitched against us in Atlanta.

It was a tough loss. In eight innings Rick Aguilera gave up one run, threw outstandingly, and should have won the game. But we only got four hits and no runs.

Paciorek played right field. I didn't want him to sit around for a week and not get in a game. He grounded into a double play in the first inning and grounded to the shortstop, and then in the ninth hit a little flair over the head of the first baseman's head, so he's hitting .333. He'll be able to sit on the bench a little easier now.

My biggest concern, bigger even than the game itself, was the state of Gary Carter's knee. After being out four days, he caught, and it looks as though the initial report will be favorable. We'll have to see if the knee swells up overnight, or if he can't get it loose, but I'm encouraged.

When I went in to check on him, Gary was lying on the training table. He said to me, "Davey, I can't let Doc down. Doc needs me!" Doc is pitching tomorrow, and I know Gary wants to be in there.

The next day we went out and beat the Braves 16–4. I had some fun. Although I would rather win 8–4 and save those other eight runs for the days we don't score any, it helps a ballclub that's been hitting below its average to have a feast.

In all we got eighteen hits. Darryl drove in seven runs with a grand slam and a three-run homer. He also had a triple. Everybody played great. Lenny got three hits. Howard Johnson got three hits and fielded like Brooks Robinson—maybe even better, if that's possible. We had five home runs. Two by Darryl, and one each by Danny Heep, Howard, and Clint. It was just a delightful day for a big league manager.

Dwight Gooden pitched and I took him out of the game in the sixth inning with a twelve-run lead. He had given up one run, a home run, and only two hits. In the fifth inning, with a ten-run lead, I called the press box and asked Jay Horwitz to ask Frank Cashen when he wanted me to hook Dwight Gooden. I said, "Call Frank and ask him when he wants me to take Dwight out." Jay waited for me to indicate that I was joking. But I hung up. So he went over to Frank and asked him. Frank cracked up.

Frank was in high spirits after the game. He liked that I had taken Dwight out after six and got Carter out after five. Clint Hurdle, Gary's replacement, hit a home run.

It was a four o'clock start because we were on NBC with Joe Garagiola and Vin Scully, and so it was six-fifteen in the evening when Clint hit his home run. After he returned to the dugout, he pointed to the clock. "It's only fitting. In batting practice I'm a great hitter from six-ten to six-forty. I can *always* hit during batting practice." We were all laughing and loose on the bench.

It's always nice, and everybody's happy, when you win big. We had 36,000 happy fans, and tomorrow our attendance will go to a million four hundred thousand, and I don't think we've had half our home dates. Ownership and Frank are happy, and as long as they're happy, I'm happy.

This ol' cracker boy is very happy. Tonight everybody's feeling very good about themselves. After the game I went into the clubhouse, and there was Gary Carter, all smiles. It tells me he's feeling good about his leg. Before he left the clubhouse he said good-bye to me twice. The second time he had his little boy with him. The kid's as big as a house. I said to Gary, "What is he, a year old?" He said, "No, he's only eight months." I said, "Man, he's going to be a hoss."

I'm not real good at taking compliments, or criticism, for that matter. During the ballgame, Ray Knight said, "Dave, I played for a lot of managers, and you know, you're the best. You make very few mistakes on the field, and when you do make one, you admit it right away." He was pumping me with these compliments, and I know Ray well enough that it's not because he wants to get into the lineup, but because he really means it. He said, "And Gary feels the same way."

It's almost too much of a responsibility to live up to. I've made mistakes, and I'm going to make more. It's funny how uncomfortable I get when somebody tells me I'm doing a good job, especially when the decisions I make affect his livelihood. But it's nice to know that your players like you, and that they think you're doing a professional job.

The next day we scored fifteen runs and beat the Braves. It was a big day for us. When I got to the park, Eddie Lynch was very dizzy and had to check into the hospital. It looks like he's going to miss the next four or five days. They say he's completely dehydrated, and that they need to build up the fluids in his system. He's lost twelve pounds.

When I found out Eddie couldn't pitch, I had to find a starter. Jesse Orosco came in and said he'd be glad to give me five good ones. I said no. But it was tempting, when you think about it.

I decided to start Terry Leach. Terry had been released twice by Atlanta. I know Terry's an intense competitor and that he would get up for them. Also, Terry's right-handed, and the Braves have a predominantly right-hand hitting ballclub. He

211

pitched six stellar innings for a pitcher whose last major league start had been in October 1982. After the game Terry said, "I'm in a two-year, four-month rotation."

Our big hero of the day was George Foster. He got three hits and drove in five runs. In his last 23 games George has driven in 27 runs. Every year George gets his hits and drives in his runs. I don't know why the fans are always picking on him. He may not be flashy, but he gets the job done. Tom Gorman gave up four runs in one inning and made it close again, and then we scored another four runs behind him. Everybody's swinging the bat, and that's what it takes to win a pennant. Keith got three hits, is 30 for 75, and raised his average thirty points to .286. We won it 15–10, all in all a great day for the Mets. We're sixteen games over .500 right now and tied for first.

We finished the series with Atlanta, winning ten games out of twelve from Ted Turner's self-proclaimed America's Team. The Braves, who were supposed to be pennant contenders, are now in fifth place, twelve games out, and manager Eddie Haas has to be feeling the heat.

Eddie is like most managers who feel they have to manage by the book and not do anything outrageous, only making standard moves. Eddie is good, but he is not very likely to pinch-hit for Chambliss or do something that might seem strange to people. Eddie's predictable.

Most managers are that way. The young ones like John Felske of Philadelphia, Buck Rogers of Montreal, Bob Lillis at Houston, even Chuck Tanner at Pittsburgh tend to manage conservatively. Shell-shocked managers are also that way. You can be shell-shocked after managing only a month. Several managers have already been hammered pretty good by the press, the fans, and the bosses upstairs. By managing conservatively, you never open yourself up to being second-guessed. But you also don't always play as aggressively as you should.

Of course, sometimes a manager has to play it close to the vest, particularly if he doesn't have the talent. With real talent, you tend to say to yourself, I got something good going. With bad talent, you say to yourself, I'm just holding on.

Compare Whitey Herzog's Cardinal pitching staff to Eddie

Haas's. Whitey has four starters, Andujar, Kepshire, Cox, and Tudor, who do a credible job and are backed by an offense that averages six runs a game. Whitey's dealing from a very strong position. And when his starter gets in trouble, he can come in with a Dayley for an inning, and come back with a Lahti and then a Campbell. Whitey just left-rights you to death. He's a great manager, but he has the horses to do it with.

Eddie Haas, on the other hand, doesn't have very good starting pitching, and his offense isn't generating the kind of hits that they were hoping it would. So Eddie's between a rock and a hard spot.

Somebody at Atlanta needs to make a decision. "Let's quit trying to hang in there with the Barkers and wild man Pascual Perez and go with our young arms like McMurtry. Let's do things that may be unusual, but for the long haul best for the ballclub."

Their pitching is their biggest problem. And they haven't addressed it. The general manager and the manager have to relate. A general manager has his own mind too, and if he doesn't like the direction that the manager is taking, he can push him a little. What happens in a lot of cases is that they start out with a lot of dialogue. The general manager suggests which players he wants out on the field, and the manager puts them there. Then if the team doesn't do well, the general manager suddenly backs off, and it's no longer a joint venture. He leaves the manager floating with the ship. The manager will one day say to the general manager, "Don't you think this is right?" and the general manager will say, "I don't know." It's no longer, "We're in this together, kemo sabe." The general manager in effect says to his manager, "What you mean 'we,' white man? It's you. And you're going." The last stage of such a relationship is for the general manager to slit the manager's throat and send him on home, telling him, "We need a new direction."

43

BEARER OF BAD NEWS

WE WENT into our three-game series with Cincinnati a half game out of first. We had beaten them eight games out of nine, and I was expecting that we would shortly be in first place.

Maybe we were tired from scoring all those runs and running all those bases against the Braves. Maybe we were a little flat. Maybe the opposing pitchers pitched a hell of a ballgame and hit a lot of corners. Maybe it was a combination of all those things. In three games we scored exactly three runs and got swept.

A large part of the credit for the resurgence of the Reds has to go to Pete Rose. It's very difficult to manage and play, to be out on the field thinking ahead and making substitutions. Generally, if you manage I don't think you should play. Pete's making it work, but that's because he's Pete Rose. I don't think anybody else could handle it. And maybe even Pete would be in trouble if he didn't have George Scherger to handle the details.

Before the second game I heard a lot of commotion coming out of the trainer's room. I went to investigate. Ray Knight was in there. Ray's leg has been bothering him so he hasn't been able to go out and play, and he has a lot of energy to burn. Brent Gaff, a pitcher who has been out all season, was on the training table, and Ray started messing around with him. Like a little kid, Ray started trying to pick him up off the table.

Now Ray has a bad hip point, and he had no business fooling around like this. Ronnie Darling, who's another guy with a lot of energy, came in and started after Ray. The two of them started wrassling, and Ray threw Darling down.

When I found out that Ray had aggravated his leg, I fined them both two hundred fifty bucks. I told a few of the players, "There's too much of that going on, and the next time there's horseplay, and somebody gets hurt, it's going to be a thousand per man." There's no excuse for it.

As for the game itself, we played terribly. I started Kelvin Chapman at second. He didn't play very well, and the fans were unmerciful. They were booing him, yelling for Wally.

What makes the New York fans different is that they expect nothing less than perfection. New York fans are the best-informed fans in the world. Everybody's got four or five papers to read, and they are always yelling for a substitute when a player is going through an extended period of ineffectiveness. It wouldn't be New York if they weren't yelling for somebody's neck.

We lost the Cincinnati finale playing stupid baseball. Little things can beat you in a ballgame, and we did our share of little things this afternoon. In the first inning Darryl threw home and overthrew the cutoff man. The batter went to second, and there was no play at the plate.

Darryl also got thrown out trying to steal third. That's a no-no. He was on second base with one out and a three-two count on Clint Hurdle. We had a hold sign on, telling Darryl he wasn't allowed to steal. But he went anyway and was thrown out by a mile. I want Darryl to be aggressive, but I don't want him to be ignorantly aggressive. With Darryl out, nobody was on, and then, even though Hurdle walked and HoJo got a base hit, we didn't get the run. And we lost by one run.

Rafael also made a dumb play when he got thrown out at home

on a base hit by the pitcher. He tried to score from second, didn't get a good jump, and he made a bad turn at third.

The next day in the paper Raffy said, "I thought he was bunting." No excuse. He took too wide a turn.

It's the little mistakes that beat you.

Those are the games that infuriate me. In the dugout the players could see I was hot. I don't have to jump up and down and yell at the guys, "You dumb SOB." My way of voicing displeasure is to tell the guy immediately, "It's a horseshit play, you can't do that." They can sense my displeasure. I don't have to make a scene or make an obscene gesture for them to know that they messed up. Sometimes a look is enough.

Darryl came into my office after the game and had a hundred-dollar bill out for me. I said, "Darryl, when you aggressively run through a hold sign, thinking that you can make it, I'm not taking your money. You just keep playing hard like that and don't worry about it. You knew you were wrong." I gave the money back, but I thought it was a great gesture from a young man who's really grown up. I really appreciated it. Darryl's going to dominate the league one of these days. He can certainly carry us to a pennant.

After Darryl came to see me, I had a meeting with Frank Cashen. Eddie Lynch is still sick, and my best chance against Houston is to call up Bill Latham from Tidewater to replace him. To do that, I'm going to have to make one of the toughest decisions I've ever made as a manager: I'm going to have to send Kelvin Chapman down.

I didn't tell him right away. First, I called Kelvin in and said, "I'm going to start Wally the next time a left-hander starts."

He didn't take it very well. I didn't expect him to like it, but he hasn't been hitting well, and he knows it. He's hitting too many balls in the air.

The next day I told Kelvin the rest of the bad news. I said, "It's a combination of things. Unfortunately, Ray Knight is hurt, and I need someone to back up Howard. I need to give Raffy a rest at short. I need more flexibility on the left side." I told him I was going to reactivate Ron Gardenhire, because he could play third and short as well as second.

"I'm going to have to send you down," I said. "This is the toughest decision I've had to make since I started managing. You're my kind of player, but it's something I have to do. Go down and get plenty of playing time and be ready if I need you."

"It'll be tough," he said. Kelvin's eyes were a little misty, and I grabbed his hand and shook it.

At my press meeting later I made a special point to praise Kelvin. "He hasn't hit for average, but he's been instrumental in a lot of the victories. It was a very difficult decision."

Unfortunately, I don't have any choice. As I told Kelvin, I must bring up Gardenhire. I need a backup for Howard and Raffy, and Gardy is that guy. Kelvin can only play second base. Sometimes you have to do things you really don't want to do, but I have to make the move that gives us the biggest edge. I know Kelvin wants to play in the major leagues very badly. He certainly has played well for me.

I don't like it. I really don't like it. But it's in the best interest of the team. That's why it's so tough to manage in the big leagues, baby.

44

STAYING OUT
OF TROUBLE

FROM MY STATION in the home-team dugout I watched the Astros' Glenn Davis hit a shot off Dwight Gooden that went out in center field over Lenny Dykstra's head. As Lenny raced toward the wall, I was praying he would catch it, and as he got closer and closer to the wall, I said to myself, If he hits the wall, I hope he doesn't drop it. I wasn't concerned that Lenny would hurt himself. If a player goes hard, the chances of his getting hurt are slim, very marginal, even if he runs into the wall hard, because at Shea it gives. Players usually hurt themselves when they play tentatively to keep from getting hurt.

Lenny got to the wall just about the same time as the ball. Lenny hit it full force, and he collapsed in a heap. When Lenny went down and didn't move, then I began to worry.

When I got out there, Lenny was lying flat on his back, but he kept insisting he was all right. Our trainer wanted him to stay down, and every time Lenny tried to get up, the trainer pushed him back. If it had been me and the trainer kept pushing me back, I'd have popped him one.

Lenny lay there a while, and when he finally was allowed to

get up, he said he was all right. He looked a little shaken. But then again, Lenny always looks a little shaken, so how can you tell?

Later Lenny hit a drive to right and went diving into second base. One player said, "I guess there's nothing wrong with him." Another said, "I wouldn't go that far."

The other home run hit off Doc was by the Astro catcher, Bailey, who should have been called out on strikes the pitch before. Umpire John McSherry raised his right hand and screamed something, and then said, "No, ball." That aggravated everybody, me included. I was ready to choke him, because it upset Doc completely. He just laid the next one in there, and Bailey hit it out.

Doc is usually very calm, but he was upset then. He was swearing at McSherry, accusing him of blowing the pitch and costing him a run. And he had every right to. McSherry then started jawing back at Doc, and I was ready to go out there too. I was screaming at him, "You owe us. You gave them that one." I was really hot. Somehow I managed to stay in the dugout and keep myself from getting thrown out.

After he got the third out and came back to the dugout, I told him, "This umpire's got you riled. For God sake, don't let him upset you enough to lose this game."

We won on a Gary Carter three-run home run, after Keith was intentionally walked. It was a big hit for Gary, because he's been slumping of late. After he hit it, he went bananas. I've never seen such enthusiasm.

Gary hadn't hit a home run in about a month. He's been struggling at the plate, and his knee's been bothering him. When you struggle, you wonder to yourself whether you're ever going to get another big hit to drive in some runs. And when they walk a guy to get to you, that's the ultimate slap in the face. Gary reminds me a lot of Frank Robinson. He has a chip on his shoulder and dares the pitcher to knock it off. I was yelling at him, "Make him pay. Don't let 'em do it to you, Gary."

And he hit it out.

After the ball went over the fence and he started for first, I was worried about his knee because he was pounding around the bases so hard. He hit first base funny, he was so charged up, and he was punching the air. When he crossed the plate he high-fived Keith and almost broke Keith's hand. When he went to give me a high five, I subconsciously pulled my hand back so he didn't get a good lick on it.

After he came into the dugout, the fans cheered for him to come out and take a curtain call, and when he went out, he gave his helmet a quick wave over his head, and it slipped out of his hand and sailed out nine miles onto the field. It was a little embarrassing because it's the one he wears to catch, and he needed it, so he had to ask the batboy to go out there and retrieve it for him. That's Gary. He gets excited. Certain people take it a little more matter-of-factly, like Jack Clark. Jack's attitude is, "That's what I'm supposed to do. What's the big deal?" For me, I prefer the electric emotion rather than the ho-hum.

45

FOR BETTER AND FOR WORSE

WE PLAYED HOUSTON in a Saturday doubleheader and won the first game 16–4! In the Mets' whole history, before this year the team scored fifteen runs in a game five times. In July of this year alone we've done it four times.

After the game I was told that all sixteen of our runs were scored as unearned. All I could do was shake my head. Red Foley, the official scorer at Shea Stadium, goes out of his way *not* to help us. Foster hit a bullet to the third baseman, who didn't even lay leather on it. Dykstra hit a slow roller in the infield and it came up and hit the guy in the chest—took a bad hop. They should have been scored as hits. Foley scored them as errors.

If there's a doubt, for crying out loud, give our guy a base hit. Red thinks that he's a purist. He knows how I feel. When I question him, he gets offended.

Ray Knight is able to play again. I found this out while I was sitting in my office talking to Frank Cashen. The door opened, and Ray barged in. He was wearing a rain slicker and said, "Look, Dave, my leg is all right," and he went running from one side of

221

my office across the carpet into the shower room and back out, showing how he can move laterally, bouncing around. I thought he was going to slide headfirst underneath my john.

I told Ray, "Okay, okay, you'll play tomorrow. I don't care how your leg is. You're driving me crazy wanting to get in there, showing me how healthy you are."

I got him in there, and he hit a three-run homer and a double, driving in four runs against the Astros.

We lost the next night to the Astros in large part because of Ron Darling's lack of control. He hasn't had rhythm or command in his last three or four outings. He's been a hundred percent better this year than last, but until he can pitch with control more frequently, he'll never be the pitcher he's capable of being. In four innings he threw 103 pitches! That's what you should throw in a nine-inning ballgame. I don't know. It's a mystery to me and to Mel. We'll just have to wait and see. His next start will be against the Cubs in Wrigley, and he better have it there.

I get so tired of telling him, "Throw it down the middle and hit a corner." He's still trying to nip here, nip there. He may say he's aiming for the middle, but I don't know if he really is. I don't think he knows where the ball is going. He sure doesn't have the control in the strike zone he should for someone as talented as he is.

I brought Doug Sisk in to mop up, and though he gave up some hits and we lost, I see improvement.

Doug and I don't have talks. Dougie doesn't want to hear idle conversation. It's simply an issue of, "Put some zeroes on the scoreboard. You know what you need to do. Go do it." Doug doesn't need to be patted on the back. Some pitchers do. But I know that when things are down with me, the last thing I want is pity or sympathy. It just makes me feel miserable. When I'm miserable, let me enjoy being miserable. Don't try to sympathize with me when I'm irritable and miserable. Let me get through it. I'll survive.

After the game I saw Darryl and his wife in the parking lot. He was carrying his baby boy. I said, "This is the next superstar." He said, "Yeah." I said, "Don't you be feeding at the bottle at all

hours of the night and let your bat blow out." I looked at his wife.
I told him, "Let your wife do that." That's what happened to me
when we had a little baby.

I don't want the ballplayer getting up at three in the morning to
do it. I told him, "Kick the wife out of bed." I was serious. Let my
guys get their rest. She can sleep during the game.

Actually, Darryl has been playing great, even with a sore
thumb. Tonight he hit two home runs. Before the game he came
up to me and said out of the blue: "Look, I'm not going to let the
pain bother me. I'm going to block it out. I'm going to stay in
there and grit it out, whether my thumb is hurting or not." I said,
"That's fine with me." He certainly is swinging the bat well right
now, but I don't want to aggravate his thumb, so any time there's
a nasty left-hander, I may take him out.

I had called Bill Latham up to pitch the second game of Saturday's doubleheader against the Astros, and on Sunday I told
Frank Cashen that as soon as he was finished pitching, I wanted
him to send Latham back to Tidewater so we could bring up Ron
Gardenhire. Rafael Santana's shoulder and elbow both bother
him. He has ice on it both places after every game. He doesn't
want to come out, but I would like to be able to rest him for a
couple of days, and play Gardenhire.

I called at eleven-thirty AM, and no one in Frank's office could
tell me if Gardy would be available for the game. I called again at
two-thirty, and there was still no word. I said to myself, Once
again, they are going to wait and wait and wait until I scream.

By game time it was clear Gardy wasn't coming, and so I again
had to play Santana. Just before the game, I talked to Frank.
"Listen, just get Gardy here, please. I need the flexibility of having another infielder. I don't care how he's hitting. If he can run
to first base and field his position, get him here."

Frank and I haven't had to make any major decisions lately.
About a month ago, when we were desperate for a right-handed
batter, Frank talked to the Seattle Mariners about a couple of
their veterans, Steve Henderson and Al Cowens. These players
are not only older veterans, but at the end of the season they will
also be free agents, and I would bet Seattle ends up losing them
entirely. The Mariners told Frank they wouldn't even discuss it.
Once we got Paciorek, we were no longer interested. And now

Seattle is calling to find out if we're still interested in Cowens and Henderson. It's too late for Seattle. The horses are out of the barn. The gate has been left open.

It shows you the ineptitude of some club officials. To me, clubs fire the managers a lot of the time, but the one who should be axed is the general manager—for failing to act when he should act, or for putting too much value on a player and then having to eat his contract. If the truth were known, I'm sure there are far more GMs who have mugged it than managers.

46

"DO SOMETHING!"

BEFORE THE GAME I had invited the owner of a big car dealership to come to my office to talk business. He had lent me a BMW to drive during the season, and he was coming in to give me the owner's manual and the insurance papers for my car. If we win the pennant, I can buy the car at cost.

He also came down to see Darryl, who is also driving one of his cars, and I told him, "I can't let you into the clubhouse, but you can sit in my office and wait for him." I went into the trainer's room, because I didn't want to sit and make small talk.

Frank, meanwhile, came down to see me, and spotted the car dealer and his friend sitting in my office. "I don't want those guys in the clubhouse," he said, jumping all over me. I said, "They're not in the clubhouse. They're in my office." He said, "That's not ..." I said, "People can go into my office. It's my business there. It has nothing to do with the clubhouse." He said, "We'll see about that." I said, "Then you see about it." It was pretty ugly.

I was worried enough about Rick Aguilera's arm without having to argue with Frank. Rick had hurt his forearm his previous start, and as a precaution I had rested Terry Leach so that he could pitch if Aguilera couldn't make it. Montreal is a predominantly right-handed hitting ballclub, we're 1–5 against them, and here's where we need to start playing well if we're going to be a bona fide threat. We're two games under .500 in our own division, and we can't allow that to continue.

At five o'clock Aguilera came over to tell me he was going to be all right. The young man is very mature and very much aware of what he can do and what he can't do. Rick went seven-and-a-third innings, pitched three-hit ball, and I hooked him because I didn't want to take a chance pushing him further. I'm going to give him eight days before his next start to be on the safe side of any arm problems.

I brought in Jesse, who's been really successful lately. I told him a couple days ago, "Jesse, hang in there because I'm going to overwork you. You're going to have 18 saves from here to the rest of the year." And I mean big-time saves. I also brought him in because it enabled me to make the Expos' two switch hitters, Tim Raines and U. L. Washington, bat righty, giving us a better chance for the double play.

Jesse got them both on pop-ups, making me look pretty good. The next inning Jesse got an out, a base hit, and an out, gave up a two-run homer to Tim Wallach, and got the last out. We won 3–2.

During the game Keith came over and said, "Aggie is going to be our number two pitcher." I said, "Yeah, I know, Keith." I probably talk to Keith more than anybody else on the ballclub. Before he goes up to hit, he'll say, "I'm going to look for an inside fastball this time." Or if I put the hit-and-run on, and he gets a base hit, he'll come over afterward and say, "Tough pitch to hit. That ball was a foot inside. But you saw the Mex do it, didn't you?" I'll say, "You're the greatest, Keith, you're the greatest."

We have these conversations all the time. He'd get two hits to left field, and he'd say, "I'm looking in. I'm looking in. If I get it, I'm going big fly." And more times than not, he'll get his pitch, and he'll hit it hard. He may not hit it out, but he'll hit it hard to right field.

Tonight Keith got up in the first against Bryn Smith and ripped him for a double. Later he said to me, "It's the hardest I've ever

seen Smith throw." I said to myself, Keith, is that the reason you just hit a shot two inches inside the foul line? He continued, "He was throwing harder than I've ever seen him. That's why I took that first fastball right down the pipe. I wanted to see one before I swung at it."

During his slump he'd say, "I'm back, Dave, I'm all the way back." And then he'd go up to the plate and strike out. That's Keith.

Once in a while, he'll make a boneheaded play, get picked off or be stealing on his own or something, and I'll tell him, "You had vapor lock." He'll shake his head and say, "Big-time vapor lock."

Another time he hit a ball down the right field line and the runner scored from first, but Keith didn't run to second. I said, "Keith, you have to be on second base on that play." He said, "That's right. Take my money. Take my money." I said, "No, I'm just telling you, next time you're not on there when you should be, I'm going to fine you two hundred fifty dollars." And so then he'll get up and stretch a single into a double, and come back and say, "How am I doing? How am I doing, Skip? How am I doing?"

Keith has been so outstanding recently. During July, he was on base fifty percent of the time, and he was hitting .400. His sixteen game-winning ribbies speak for themselves.

Gary started again, and it looks like he may make it through to the end of the year. His knee is about eighty percent. He's riding the bike a lot and doing the Nautilus, the Cybex, doing everything he can to strengthen the knee, and he's going to nurse it through the rest of the year.

About half an hour after the game, Gary was sitting watching TV. His legs were still taped up, and he had the brace on. I asked him if he was all right. He said, "I'm fine. Dr. K tomorrow. I'll be all right. I'll be ready." He wants to catch Dwight. He's like a little kid with a new toy every time he puts on a uniform. You like them that way. You have to have a lot of kid in you to survive in this game, otherwise you go bananas.

The sportswriters have been fighting with the TV and radio people. After the game last night the guys with the microphones came in and asked me dumb questions, like, "Why did you leave

Darling in there for six runs?" I said, "Because I wanted to. My bullpen was short and Darling is inconsistent and I wanted to let him pitch out of it . . ." You try to explain, but you really want to choke them. And because they ask too many questions, the regular writers, like Joe Durso of the *Times* and Mike McAlary of the *Post*, get upset, and want more time for themselves to ask the same dumb questions. "Why did you leave Darling in there for six runs?" I can't stand it.

Afterward I said to Jay Horwitz, "I want you to do something." He said, "I don't know. This is a bad situation. Durso is upset about . . ." I said, "Jay, just handle it. Don't tell me about it. I live it." Jay said, "Well, what if we put one mike down there and . . ." I said, "Damn it, Jay, I don't want to hear about what you're going to do. Just do it."

I went out into the clubhouse, and this bozo came up to me and said, "How about Gooden?" I said, "What do you mean, how about Gooden?" He said, "Would you have hooked Gooden if he had been pitching and not Aguilera?" I said, "Listen, you idiot, Gooden doesn't need any help in the seventh inning. Besides that, he has a record of finishing his games." The guy turned out to be a fan who had crashed the clubhouse. After asking me this dumb question, he stuck out his hand to shake mine. I looked up at him like, "You got to be kidding me."

When I finally arrived home after the game, I started thinking, trying to put things into perspective. I said to myself, I'm getting a good salary, I get about $100,000 a year, but my stomach gets eaten up after a ballgame, because I really grind to win. I have to throw antacids down to put the fire out in my stomach. And if the organization won't protect me from aggravation within the club, I might as well start grooming someone else who they can drive crazy. Because this job will drive me bats.

47
TWO DOCS

THE AGGRAVATION really has me down. I'm feeling so much tension, my heart seems to be beating so hard, I think I'm dying. I try to eliminate the pressure, but it's never-ending in this town.

People don't understand why Yogi doesn't want to manage another team this year. I know! I'm probably the only one who really does. If I got fired, I would need at least a year to rest. A half a year managing in New York is worth two anywhere else.

I came to the ballpark all agitated, went into the training room, and had the trainer give me Tagamet, which I take four times a day for my stomach. Then I got a B_{12} shot in the arm to see if he could pep up my energy level, but it doesn't seem to help much. My blood pressure felt like it was going off the Richter scale, but the trainer said it was fine. So I realized it was in my mind. I must be going crazy.

Last night, before I went home, who should walk into my office but our traveling psychologist, Dr. Sol Miller. He said, "How ya doing, Davey?"

I was feeling paranoid. I said to myself, He thinks he needs to psychoanalyze me. I told him, "I can't talk to you today." Dr.

Miller's favorite saying is, "If you don't like the picture you're seeing, change the channel." I was changing the channel by getting rid of him!

Dr. Miller came back this morning, and I was more willing to talk. I told him, "I'm feeling really tense. I need to relax. Please let me relax. Get my aggravation down. I know you have techniques for relaxing a hitter. What can you do for a manager?"

I first met Dr. Miller when I was managing in Jackson. He had done some work with the Mississippi State teams, showing them how to relax, ease tension, and concentrate.

He would tell a pitcher, "To keep from overthrowing, think of yourself as a guy with a twenty-foot bullwhip. Get the whip going, let it out, and pop it right at the end." He would say, "A pitcher should think of himself as a big, sleek cat." I saw that his techniques had value. In fact, I was so impressed, I wrote an article on him.

On my recommendation the Mets hired him to do part-time work. I figured we had guys like Howard Johnson, Doug Sisk, Foster, Strawberry, guys who could use a sympathetic ear to ease them over the humps. I never said to the players, "We have a resident shrink. If you have any problems, lie down and talk to him." But he shows up periodically, and he's helped them.

Dr. Miller said, "The first thing you need to do is learn how to breathe. Breathing consistency is power. Whether we know it or not, we forget to breathe anytime there's a stressful situation."

He said, "I now want to show you the forms of tension that restrict breathing. Tighten your fists and turn them in toward your body. Notice how it restricts your breathing. Press against your side. You don't breathe as well. Another form of tension: lie down and raise your shoulders a half an inch. You don't breathe as well."

He said, "The antidote is to breathe. You can do it while you're driving the car, but it's better to do it during a quiet time when you just concentrate on breathing regularly—in like the ocean, and out as it crashes."

We did a short session, maybe ten minutes, and when it was over I felt better. He said, "During a ballgame, situations build such that you don't even want to take a breath. You're afraid you might miss something."

I don't want to make a big deal out of Sol Miller, but anything a person can do to relax in a tense situation has to help.

As for the game itself, the other Doc, Dwight Gooden, pitched a five-hit shutout, and that helped me relax as much as Dr. Miller. Dwight Gooden had a normal day, struck out ten, threw 120 pitches. He was topping out at 96 miles an hour. The slowest fastball he threw all night was 90 miles an hour!

When people ask me to describe Dwight Gooden, I try to downplay him. I say, "Let's not go into superlatives. We've used them up." They say, "Is he the best pitcher you've ever seen?" I tell them, "I don't want to get into that," and I try to change the subject. He has enough pressure on him without having to hear that he's as good as Sandy Koufax or Bob Feller or Christy Mathewson.

The truth is, he's the best pitcher I've ever seen! No one else has the command and the stuff to overpower and dominate a team like Dwight Gooden. He's so good it's scary. When he gets in a jam, I know he's going to make the pitch to get us out. He's a tremendous competitor. I can't say enough about him.

In the fourth inning Montreal starter Bill Gullickson threw a pea at Gary Carter's head. The media made a big deal about the feud between Gary and his old team. My feeling is that it's being overblown. The Expos have a professional respect for Gary Carter, as does everybody in baseball. Gullickson has always been up and in high. His message to Gary was, "Don't crowd the plate." But since it was up around the head, it was grounds for retaliation.

After we went onto the field, I waited to see what Doc would do. Gullickson was lucky he hadn't actually hit Carter, because if he had, Doc would not have hesitated. And he wouldn't have waited for the pitcher. He would have hit the next guy up.

As it was, Doc struck out the first two batters. He wanted to face Gullickson with the bases empty. Then Doc let fly, and Gullickson went diving into the dirt. Doc's message was clear, "Don't be messing with any of our players, and especially my catcher." Doc got a warning from the umpire, but he went on to strike Gullickson out on three straight pitches.

Before the game George Foster had asked if I would go down to the batting cage with him. We took Tony Ferrara, our batting practice pitcher, and I watched George swing.

I said, "Try pivoting hard off that back leg." We were only down there five minutes, when George said he was feeling better. "I feel real quick. I feel good. That must be it." The important thing was that he was convinced in his own mind that he had found the solution to his problem. I left him, saying, "You have it now. You don't need me anymore."

Against the Expos, he drove in our only two runs. They walked Darryl to get to him, and he drove in that run, and later in the ballgame he hit a low-and-away breaking ball to drive in the second run, and we won 2–0. I was happy for George. Any way you look at it, it was a nice night for the skipper.

48
TALK

BEFORE THE GAME, Donald Fehr of the Players Association asked me if he could address the players. Fehr said that he didn't have much hope of avoiding a strike, that the owners were taking an awfully hard position.

The players had voted to strike if there's no agreement by August 6. They were unsure whether setting a strike date was the same thing as voting to strike. Keith said, "Maybe we should revote."

I spoke up. "Gentlemen, you have already voted on a strike date. If you have a revote now, that will be a sign of weakness."

That killed the revote. I said it because I feel that if both sides remain strong, there is more likelihood for an agreement. If I wanted to be strictly management, I could have said, "Yeah, go ahead and vote. I don't think you should strike anyway." And there would have been chaos in the Players Association. But I have more invested in my player's pension than I do in my job security. They can fire me tomorrow.

Eddie Lynch started against the Expos, and I could see that he was looking pretty ill. Eddie sometimes is hard to read. Sometimes he drags his big feet around out there, and if you look at him, he looks exhausted, but he still has plenty left. In this particular case, he was coming back from a virus, and it was a hot, hot day. Before he went out for the fifth inning, I knew he had about had it, and I told him, "Give me one more inning." He made it through and won his eighth.

Roger McDowell pitched four excellent, welcome-back innings in relief. After the game Roger said, "Somebody's been wearing my uniform for the past two weeks. That wasn't me."

After Gary Carter caught Gooden last night, I was intending to give him the day off, but he handed me a note saying, "Skipper, I would love to play today. Please let me play." When I read the note, I chuckled and decided to let him. Gary hit a home run, and we completed the three-game sweep of the Expos.

He was so happy. Anytime a player hits a home run against a team that traded him, it's a real boost to his ego. He has beaten his old buddies, the guys he lived with for ten years and has had a lot of sentimental feeling for. And it's not always easy. A lot of players fall flat on their faces when they go up against their old teams.

Gary had gotten a lot of bad press in Montreal since they traded him. This is common anytime a club trades a superstar. When he was an Expo, management extolled him. After they traded him, management would never say, "We're sorry to see him go." I said, "Good riddance." When the Cardinal management traded Keith, it said, "He cared more about crossword puzzles than he did about playing." It's a management survival technique, and it's also for the benefit of the remaining players.

Of course, it sounds ridiculous for the Expos to be knocking Gary. "So what if he led the league in rbi's and hit more home runs than anyone and hit .300 and was the MVP? He wasn't good for the club."

Nevertheless, Gary has taken the criticism personally, and will come back to haunt the Expos because it's going to make Gary play all the better against his old teammates.

With tonight's game, we finished the month of July with 21 wins. We're two games out, and we're back on stride after two-and-a-half months of poor batting. Everybody has started to contribute and has been playing well, and it's about time.

49

BEFORE THE STRIKE

SID FERNANDEZ opened our four-game series with the Cubs in Chicago and was all over the place. I got so mad I took him out after four innings, even though he had only given up one run. He was fighting himself, reacting childishly to bad pitches by making faces or stomping around the mound. It upset the whole team. If you're playing behind a guy who's fighting himself, it's like an accident waiting to happen.

A pitcher who is fighting himself is waiting to get beat. I want a guy out there who has composure. If someone throws a punch to your midsection, don't double up and lay on the ground. Try to act as if it doesn't hurt.

When I hooked Sid, I went to Terry Leach, and boom, immediately Terry gave up a home run to Gary Matthews that ultimately beat us 2–1. I was standing at the end of the dugout, fuming anyway, and now thirty seconds after Matthews hit the home run, I noticed Mel Stottlemyre talking on the telephone. Jay Horwitz was calling down to the dugout, asking whether there was anything physically wrong with Sid Fernandez.

All the other second-guessers in the press box were telling Jay,

"See if something's wrong with Sid." Trying to create some kind of bull. Mel handed me the phone. I said, "Nothing is wrong with him. It was time for me to make a change. He had thrown 93 pitches. End of story." Then I started yelling at Jay. "If you want to call down when I make the change, and ask 'Is he okay?', fine. But don't call *after* the new pitcher gives up a home run. That's really brutal."

Jay said, "I was wrong. They pressured me into doing it. But I was wrong. I shouldn't have called."

I was hot. If he had been down with me, I would have choked him to death. Just laid him on the ground and choked him till he quit moving.

After the ballgame was over, Sid evidently wanted to talk to me but was wary. Clint Hurdle told him, "Go ahead. Dave isn't going to be mad at you." Sid said, "I'm not too sure." Clint said, "Go on in there."

When Sid came into my office, his first question was, "Why did you take me out? Was it the number of pitches?"

"Sid, there are three reasons. Number one, and probably the most important, you weren't showing any poise. When you fight yourself like that, it makes everyone behind you nervous. Number two, you didn't have any command. You walked the number eight hitter on four fastballs that weren't within a yard of home plate, and next you walked the pitcher to load the bases. My goodness. You were just waiting to get beat. And number three, you had thrown 93 pitches in four innings and normally you throw 115 pitches in a nine-inning game. If you had poise I'd have let you go further. But you were fighting yourself. I can't have that."

Sid said, "My dad always told me to get mad out there when I wasn't doing well."

I said, "That's fine. Get mad inside. But don't ever let them see that you're mad."

He understood. "Thanks. I was afraid to come in here, afraid you might be real mad at me."

I said, "Listen, you have a great future. What are you, twenty-three?"

He said, "I'm twenty-two."

"You're going to be around a long time," I said, "so just don't let it get to you." So it was a good conversation. I'm sure from here on out he'll be fine.

The next day, two of my other reclamation projects, Ron Darling and Howard Johnson, won the day. Ron started out wild. I was sick of his always trying to hit the corners and missing, of his walking eight batters in a game. After the team came in at the end of the second inning, I called Gary Carter aside. I said, "Gary, I want you to call more breaking balls than fastballs, and more important, I want you to hold your target right in the middle of home plate. If Darling gets ahead on the count oh-and-two, then you can move to the corners. But once you get to two-and-two, move back in the middle. And that's the plan for the rest of the year."

When I took Darling out in the eighth, he had only given up two runs, but after he gave up a walk, a single, and another walk, I brought in Jesse, who allowed two more runs on a suicide squeeze that he threw away at first.

We were losing by a run with two outs in the ninth and were up against the Cubs' best reliever, Lee Smith.

It wasn't looking good, but I hadn't given up. When you've been in this game as long as I have, as a player and then manager, you know strange things can happen. All it takes is a bloop and a blast. In Wrigley Field anything can happen, and I don't care if it's Lee Smith or Godzilla out there, though at times I'm not too sure there's any difference.

Wally Backman beat out an infield single in the hole, and Keith ripped one down into the right field corner to score Wally. Tie game. And then we beat them in the tenth.

HoJo, the hero, started the game on the bench.

I didn't start him because the day before he was swinging so badly and fighting himself, he wasn't even close to the ball. I said, "Howard, jeez, are you thinking about tomatoes, or what? You're not thinking about making contact or timing the ball. I don't know what you're thinking about."

When I posted the lineup, and Howard saw he wasn't playing, I told him, "Howard, you're struggling, so just take it easy, relax, think about getting your stroke and timing back, and you'll be back in there." He said, "I know I've been pressing. I don't mean to press, but I do."

Ray Knight played, and late in the game he pulled a leg muscle running out an infield hit, and so I took him out and pinch-ran Howard. When we come to bat in the tenth George Frazier was on the mound for the Cubs. Howard, batting lefty, not only had to face Frazier, but was also opposed by a gale wind blowing in from right field. I said to myself, He's going to have to nail that ball to get it out of here. Howard swung and knocked the dog out of it, deep into the right field bleachers. Most people don't realize that Howard has that kind of power. The problem is that he doesn't put that swing together very often. Back in the dugout he got a lot of high fives, I'll tell you that.

After the game, Ray came over and said, "Dave, you ought to start me every game and then put HoJo in," because every time I start Ray against a right-hander and then bring in HoJo, soon thereafter HoJo hits a home run to prove he belongs.

This game shows the difference between our team last year and this year. Last year we would lose close games because we hadn't yet learned to win. This year we do not expect to lose. We feel we're improved. Not just with the addition of Gary, but with the development of our young pitchers and the strengthening of our bench. They probably even think that because I'm in my second year, I'm a smarter manager. I always am when I have better players.

The next day Dwight won 4–1, but he gave me a scare. In the eighth inning, after batting, he was coming in, and coach Bill Robinson asked him, "How do you feel?" and Doc said, "My ankle is stiffening up." I asked, "Bill, why is his ankle stiffening up?" Apparently he had twisted it running out a double earlier in the game. It was the same ankle he had injured during the winter playing basketball. I immediately called time and went out to the mound to make sure it wasn't bad, and Doc assured me he was okay to pitch. With a 4–1 lead, if Dwight said he was okay, I had to go with him. Unless I saw him favoring it and changing his motion when he wound up and threw, he was going to pitch.

We're now a half game back with one game to go before the strike date. The writers asked me if I was intending to talk to the team. I told them no. "We try to play every game as if it's the most important."

The point is, if they're going out and giving you the best effort they've got, how can you tell them to give more?

We swept the Cubs behind a gutty performance by Eddie Lynch and three home runs by Darryl Strawberry. Philadelphia ended up beating the Cardinals, and we moved into first place, just before the strike deadline.

It's a bittersweet feeling, because it appears the gap between the owners and the Players Association is so great that we're not going to continue playing.

I take no great pleasure in being in first place at the strike date. If we don't play the rest of the year, there isn't going to be a playoff and World Series anyway. And who's going to remember a club that was in first August 6 in a strike-delayed season? I don't even want a two-day strike, because, unlike us, the Cardinals are a tired ballclub, and I want to wear them out.

We're waiting to hear. Commissioner Ueberroth has set up a meeting between management and the players, but it's the eleventh hour.

50

THE STRIKE

BEFORE THE PLAYERS actually went out on strike, Frank Cashen and I discussed whether we should do the paperwork to send Bruce Berenyi and Brent Gaff down to Tidewater, so they could play in the minors. They aren't ready to pitch anywhere yet, so we decided against it. Frank is the opposite of George Steinbrenner, who called up Mike Armstrong to the Yankees from the minors for the express purpose of not having to pay him during a strike.

We had flown to Montreal just in case. The strike deadline was midnight, and the next morning I was in Keith Hernandez's hotel room waiting to hear how the negotiations were coming. By three in the afternoon it was clear there wasn't going to be a game that night. I took a flight back to New York.

The next day I decided to fly to Orlando to take care of some real estate business. I figured that even if the strike were settled, we wouldn't be flying back to Montreal just for one day. I also figured that if it weren't settled by the time I got on the flight, which was 12:50 P.M., chances were we couldn't go back to Montreal the next day.

Ten minutes before I was to step on the plane, an official from Delta invited me to have a cocktail. As I walked into the Crown Room, the guard there said, "Davey, did you hear? It's settled!" I said, "What?" He said, "They just agreed on the deal."

My bags had already been checked into the plane. The flight was about to leave for Orlando. I said, "Let me call the ballpark." Vern Hoscheit was sitting at my desk, where he knew I could get him. He said, "No calls yet."

"Why don't you put me on hold and check?" I said. He put me on hold and called Jean Cohn, Frank's secretary, and she said, "They have a tentative agreement." Vern came back on the line. "Get your ass back here. It's settled."

Oh man. I considered going to Orlando, but I said to myself, "If it's settled, we ought to work out. I'm not taking any chances." My luggage consisted of a Mets bag and my golf clubs. They weren't that hard to locate.

I went back to Shea Stadium and stayed there the rest of the afternoon, talked to a bunch of writers, and that night my coaching staff and I flew up to Montreal with some of the players to be ready for the game the next day. We could have stayed in New York overnight, but I'm leery about waiting until the last minute and having to rush. I didn't want to take the chance of not getting there in time.

When the strike ended, there was a feeling of euphoric relief, a kind of a "Phheww, now we can go play baseball, and not have to worry about it for four years." Everybody felt that way.

51

KEITH AND DOUG

DURING THE GAME Keith was real wound up. He was chatting nonstop. The Expos' Joe Hesketh was pitching, and Keith was pumping himself up, saying, "This guy likes to pitch in, he likes to throw the hard stuff in, so I'm going to look in." Keith ended up hitting the ball over the first base bag and down the right field line for two runs. Afterward he said, "Man, Hesketh made a stupid pitch. He hung me the curveball. Anybody could have hit that."

Keith and I were standing together in the dugout when Gary hit a David Palmer change-up out of the park. Keith said, "He hung it. That was a duckfish, right where Gary Carter likes it." After Gary came in, Keith said, "Gary, you had that little hesitation, and then you popped. That's you. That's you, big guy."

He was talking all game long. After another of his at bats Keith said, "He made a great pitch down and in, and I inside-outed it."

In the game, which we won 14–7, Keith had four singles and a double. I don't think anybody in baseball has been swinging the way he has the last month. His on-base percentage is over .500. He's hit right at .400 for a month and driven in a lot of runs. He was down around .250. We all knew he should be hitting .300. What we didn't know was that he'd reach it by hitting .400 for a month.

The one thing our club still could use is a dominant left-handed middle reliever, someone who would come in and make the opposing manager switch his lineup.

Short of getting another reliever, the one thing that could make a difference would be the reemergence of Doug Sisk.

Dougie has been feeling that everyone is against him. A couple of days ago he was all over Vern Hoscheit. He told Vern, "You're another one of those SOBs. You don't think I can pitch." Vern said, "Doug, I think you can pitch. It's you who doesn't think he can pitch." They argued, and Doug stopped talking to Vern.

Before today's game against the Cubs I walked out to our bullpen to watch Bruce Berenyi throw. When I was done, I noticed Doug in the outfield playing catch with Jesse. I walked over and said, "Doug, how are you feeling, big guy?"

He said, "Fine, but I'm not getting anybody out." And he proceeded to throw the ball wild past Jesse.

"How are you feeling about your arm and your stuff in general?" I asked.

He said, "It's kind of embarrassing."

"You'll get it back," I said. "There have been great relievers who have had bad years, and then came back to be great again. You have to keep grinding. I thought your command the last couple outings was much better. You just lack the good bite on your sinker."

"You're right," he said. "They're hitting them back off my shins, knocking me off the mound." Doug'll joke around with you, but you never know what he's really thinking.

"What do you think we can do?" I asked.

He didn't answer the question directly, but he said, "Mel doesn't want to work with me. All he wants to do is work with the stars, the Goodens, Darlings, Aguileras, the McDowells."

I said, "Doug, you know that isn't true. Mel would do anything to help you. We all would."

"Mel won twenty games for three years and threw a good sinker," Doug said. "I'd like to get mine back. He could help me but he doesn't. When he sees me, he turns his head and walks away from me."

I knew that that wasn't true. In fact the opposite was true. Mel had been wanting to work with Doug, but Dougie wouldn't work with him!

I said, "Shoot, he's been trying to get you all year. Let's do it right now."

"I'm not going to pitch today," Doug said.

"Let's go right now," I repeated. Doug looked down at his sneakers and said, "I don't have my right shoes on."

I said, "Listen, Doug . . ."

He said, "I got my tennis shoes on."

I said, "Dougie, run in and get your spikes. I want to watch you throw with Mel."

"I don't know," he said. "I may need to get my arm rubbed on."

"Dougie, meet me in the bullpen."

He said, "Why?"

I said, "I want to see you throw, and Mel is going to watch you. Can you be there in five minutes?"

He said, "I don't know. Uh . . . uh . . . I don't know. We'll see."

I said, "I'll meet you in the bullpen?"

On the way to the bullpen, I said to Danny Heep, "Boy, your buddy is a hard read. I don't understand him." I went by Jesse. "Your buddy is impossible," I said to him.

Jesse said, "It's tough for me to even talk to Doug." I can understand it, because it was tough for me too when I was having arm problems.

When I got to the pen I told Mel, "Doug is coming down to throw. I think." Doug did show, and I started him throwing with Ronn Reynolds.

The week before, I had noticed that Doug was throwing over the top whereas in the past he had been throwing three-quarter. "Would it be stupid for him to throw out here?" I asked Mel, holding my arm out at about two o'clock rather than over my head. He said, "No, that's where he should throw from." So we told Dougie, "Get your arm out. Think about throwing three-quarter."

What he was doing, it turns out, was trying to get extra speed by throwing straight overhand, and it was lousing up his form and his rhythm. After getting his elbow away from his body, we told him, "Okay, go ahead and throw the son of a bitch." Now when he threw his sinker, it was hard and biting. That one little flaw had been messing him up.

Ronn said, "That's nasty. I couldn't hit that." Doug felt good. As he practiced, Mel kept reaffirming that Doug had solved his problem. Doug says it feels like he's throwing sidearm, but he's not. Let's just keep our fingers crossed. I think we have Doug Sisk back.

During the game I let Doug warm up. Clint Hurdle was catching him, and Clint didn't know about what had happened in the bullpen. Afterward, Clint came running over to him and said, "That shit is nasty. You haven't had that all year. Where did that come from?"

52

NINE STRAIGHT

DWIGHT GAVE UP THREE straight hits, boom, boom, boom, good for two Cubs runs in the first inning, and everyone was amazed. Me too, but I wasn't worried. I just said to myself, "Doc is going to bear down." The next inning he struck out the side. He went to the whip, even though he doesn't like to do that until late in the game. This time he decided, "I got to shut them down now." And he did. He went all the way, striking out nine. I suspect one day Doc will get knocked out of a game, but probably not in my lifetime.

George Foster, who has gotten a lot of big hits for us lately, got the big blow, a two-run homer. George is ideally suited to hit sixth on this ballclub. He's not a good on-base percentage guy, like Keith. Strawberry gets on more, and so does Carter, but George is a home run hitter, and he drives in a lot of runs. He's been leading the club in rbi's most of the year.

George is quiet. In his own mind, he's the number one guy, but he doesn't mind other guys getting more credit. He never causes trouble. He's happy-go-lucky. I've never seen George get angry.

Our typical conversation runs, "Hi, Skip." "Hi, George." That's about the extent of it.

After we swept three from the Cubs, the writers baited me to criticize Jimmy Frey. The Cubs are now twelve games out of first and sinking fast, what with so many injuries. The reporters kept asking me, "What about Jimmy?" I kept repeating, "Jimmy has lost three of his starters. I sympathize with him."

"The Cubs don't have any sympathy for you," the writers would answer. "Don't you think a team should be able to win despite its injuries?" All I have to do is say yes once, and the next day the headline would read, JOHNSON RIPS FREY. Walking through a mine field would seem easier than facing these guys.

The next day was Gary Carter Day at Shea Stadium. Gary put us ahead with a two-run home run, they tied it, and he put us up for good with another home run. It was our seventh win in a row. It was the Cubs' eighth loss in a row. The Cardinals lost. That put us a full game up.

After the game Keith said to me, "When Gary gets hot, look out . . ." I said, "Keith, you're right. And I think Gary is going to get hot and be hot the rest of the year. Be nice if everybody's hot." He looked up at the ceiling of the clubhouse and said, "Whew."

For the last month Wally Backman has also been on a hitting tear. Before each game he has me rub his bat for luck. He brings it up to me just before he goes up to home plate. Whenever I do that, he seems to get two or three hits. Sometimes he doesn't remember until the middle of the game, and then only gets one.

Eddie Lynch continues to be a mainstay. He's won six straight ballgames and has upped his record to 10–5. I like Eddie a lot more than he realizes. I admire his talent more than he realizes. And I think we're better friends than he realizes. But I have no problem talking with Eddie. I've gotten joy watching Eddie play up to his potential. Seeing him 10–5, I couldn't be happier for anybody.

The Phillies came to town for four games, and in the opener Sidney pitched for the first time since I yanked him out of that horrible game ten days before in Chicago. He had great poise, as compared to the last start. He walked three, but the walks didn't interfere with how he dominated the lineup. There wasn't a single batter who looked like he was going to give him any trouble. Sid doesn't know how much talent he really has. But he'll get there.

Going into the ninth, Sid had a one-hit shutout. I thought about hooking him, because he had thrown 128 pitches, but he had a one-hitter, had struck out thirteen, and the last two times I brought in Roger, he blew the games. I said to Mel, "I have made so many bad decisions on this kid, you tell me when you want to hook him."

Mel said, "I want to go with him for at least another hitter."

Sid got two quick strikes, then boom, a double past first down the right field line. Later I learned that Sidney went over to Keith and said laughing, "You're a Gold Glover. You're supposed to make that play." Sidney was showing humor in a tough situation. I like that.

The next batter was Mike Schmidt, a slugger, who got on with a perfect bunt. Now they had Glenn Wilson coming up. Sid had thrown 133 pitches. He hadn't pitched in ten days. Wilson can hit it out. They have three right-handed batters coming up, and Mel agreed it was time to get Sid some help.

I went out to the mound, and the fans were booing me for hooking him. When I got out there, I said, "Sidney, do me a favor. Walk in with me." But as I was getting ready to hand the ball to Roger, Sidney left ahead of me and got a standing ovation. I knew when I walked off that mound to go back to the dugout I was going to get booed to death, and sure enough as I made my way back to the dugout, the entire stadium filled with boos. Then the fans started chanting, "We want Sidney," and Sidney came out and tipped his hat on the curtain call.

Roger got behind on Wilson, who then hit a bullet that struck the top of the center field wall and went over. Lenny almost made a great play on it. Our 4–0 lead had been cut to 4–3. After another hit I brought in Jesse.

When I gave him the ball, I said, "Pick me up, Jesse." He ended it, and we got the win, but the next time Sid needs relief, I'll only bring in Roger if we have an eight-run lead.

Games like that take a toll on me. Maybe I waste too much energy, and maybe I take it too personally. When I first managed in the big leagues, Harry Dunlop, the bullpen coach for San Diego, told me, "Dave, just remember, you can't hit for them and you can't pitch for them." But you can sure root for them, and it takes a toll on your stomach. I wish I didn't care as much. I care for these guys. I care for my team. I care for the fans. But it takes a lot out of me.

If you're successful, the fans will like you. If you're not, they won't. And if you interfere with a great performance, they're going to be mad, even if you're making the right decision.

Rick Aguilera beat the Phils 4–2 for our ninth straight win. Aggie ran out of gas after seven innings, and I went to Jesse, who bailed me out for the second game in a row. Jesse's back, that's the main thing. He's gone through a bad time and come out of it. He's just what we need coming down the stretch.

Frank Cashen asked me on the sly, "Would you like me to get you a veteran starting pitcher for the stretch drive?" He mentioned Mike Krukow of the San Francisco Giants. I told him, "I have four young pitchers and Ed Lynch. And Berenyi is coming around."

I told him I could use a left-handed reliever, a true left-hander who can get lefties out, like a Rod Scurry or a Vande Berg from Seattle, guys like that. I also mentioned Britt Burns, who might be on the market. A left-hander who could also spot-start would be ideal.

I told Frank, "The middle-relief corps is where I need help. I don't need another starter."

Ron Darling lost a tough 2–1 game to the Phils' Kevin Gross. Ron had outstanding control compared to his last four or five outings. We should have won it in the ninth.

We had the bases loaded and nobody out with Backman, Hernandez, and Carter coming up. I could have pinch-hit Ray Knight for Wally, but I have to show Wally I have confidence he can drive in the run.

Wally hit the ball hard in the hole, but the third baseman made a good play and got the force at home.

Keith came up, and I was sure he'd get at least one run in, but he grounded into a double play, 4 to 6 to 3, to end the ballgame. Everybody in the ballpark was in a state of shock because Keith has spoiled us, getting runners in at a rate of about sixty percent.

Back in the clubhouse Keith was upset. He came over to me and said, "You know, Skip, this is a funny town. While I'm hitting .500 for a month, with all those rbi's, I don't see many writers. But the minute I don't drive a run in, they're over me like a swarm." He smiled. "But I made them wait twenty minutes to see me."

53
ACHES AND PAINS

I WAS CHATTING with team owner Nelson Doubleday. He had brought some pistachio nuts for the players, and I asked him, "Where are mine?" He said, "You have enough nuts."

It was the only laugh of an otherwise incredibly aggravating day. Before our game I was standing in the dugout, and I noticed that about fifteen fans were hanging over the railing, leaning into the dugout, yelling for players to sign balls and programs. One guy was even taking movies. It was a zoo. We were preparing for a ballgame, and I didn't want the players distracted.

I said to the security guard, "Send these people away." He said, "They're here as part of the first-ball ceremony." I said, "I don't care. They have no business taking pictures and getting autographs. Move them down a ways. Get them away from the mouth of the dugout."

Then the game began and Dwight Gooden didn't have his good stuff. It was the hottest day of the year, and Doc never pitches as well during the day as he does at night. In the daylight it's much easier for the batter to see the rotation of the ball. Anyway, he showed he was human. We got six quick runs, but he could barely hold it.

In the fourth inning I said, "Give me one more inning." He did, and it was his best, but I still took him out. It was the first time he's been knocked out of a ballgame all year.

In the second inning Ron Gardenhire, who was starting for Santana, hurt himself running out a ground ball. He pulled the inside of his groin muscle, a new and different injury. I feel for Gardy, who's had all sorts of leg problems this year, but I immediately called Jay Horwitz and said, "Tell Frank to get Larry Bowa." The Cubs had just released him, and we have to have a backup shortstop down the stretch. I have Argenis Salazar in the minors, but I don't want him up here sitting on the bench.

Then Gary Carter left with a stiff neck. He couldn't turn his head to his left. Gary keeps telling me, "Dave, I'm going on a Nautilus program. I'm going to come in looking like Ozark Ike. I'm not going to have these little injuries driving me crazy." And then something like this happens. He said, "This is ridiculous. I feel terrible about it." He couldn't turn his neck. He couldn't play.

After a sloppy game, which we won 10–7, my aggravation continued. We have a rule that nobody can come into the clubhouse for thirty minutes after the game. But my office is different. I had invited in a couple of businessmen, but the security guard chased them out and I couldn't do my business. So first I can't get the fans away from the dugout, and now I can't let my own friends into my office.

I drove all the way home in a fury. I was talking to myself: Is this the way it's going to be around here? Because if it is, I want out.

The next morning I got Frank on the phone. I was hot. I said, "I've got two complaints. Number one, the fans around the dugout are interfering with the players and me. It's like home video week. I want them out of there. And I don't want to have to say it twice."

253

He said, "I guess it is getting out of hand."

I said, "Handle it. And number two, the security guard chased some people I was meeting out of my office. I take it those were your orders."

Frank said, "Yeah, there are too many people in the clubhouse."

I said, "If a guy's down there meeting me, he can stay there as far as I'm concerned."

Frank said, "I don't want *anybody* down there."

I said, "It's the only time I can see those guys."

Frank said, "I don't like it."

I said, "Is that the way it's going to be?"

He said, "Yeah, that's the way it's going to be."

I said, "Okay then," and slammed the phone down.

About an hour and a half later I returned to my office at Shea. The phone rang. It was Frank. He said, "Are you calmed down?"

I snarled, "Yeah, I'm calmed down."

He said, "I want to talk to you." He came down and was really trying to smooth it over in his diplomatic way.

"I'm not trying to keep these guys from you," Frank said. "But they bug me."

I said, "Some of these guys may bug me too, but I have to make a few deals on my own to make up for the money you're not paying me."

He said, "I'm not trying to stop you."

"Then don't try to control my life. If I decide to do something, I'm going to do it. If I decide not to do it, I won't do it. When it doesn't concern the baseball operation, don't interfere. If I can't have a few little privileges, you can have this job. I don't want it."

When we boarded the plane for Pittsburgh, I had calmed down, and Frank again said, "How about another starter?"

I still couldn't figure out why he was pushing another starter on me. I told him, "Frank, I don't need another starter."

He said, "Tom Seaver is available, and we can get him for a Terry Blocker or a John Christensen, one of our minor league players." Ahhh, so that's what he's been angling at. He had let Tom get away once, and now he had a chance to get him back. It would have been a real PR coup. Tommy's a legend, and I could use him for the stretch run this year, but when I was told he had another year on his contract, I immediately was turned off to the idea, because he would push one of my four young starters, Aguilera or Fernandez, out of the rotation next year, and that would be unacceptable to me.

I know that people will say, "Johnson made that decision because he didn't want Seaver around to take his job." I assure you if it were best for Seaver to come here and take my job, I would recommend that. But as long as I'm in on the decision making, I'm going to make sure nothing gets in the way of our building a dominant club for years to come.

54
THE PITTS

THE LOWLY PIRATES BEAT US two out of three. A lot of people will attribute that to Al Harazin, our business manager, going with us. I keep telling Frank, "I don't want him to come on the road." Frank is grooming Al to handle some of his duties, the road trips I guess, but the players have noticed that whenever Harazin comes with us on the road, we do not play well. Even before we got to the stadium, at least six guys came to me and said, "Can we send Al home? We'll chip in and buy his ticket." They are convinced he is bad luck, but when I tell Frank, he won't listen. He is planning to send Harazin with us to the West Coast, and the guys are paranoid about it. I don't know why someone from the general manager's office has to be on the trip, unless they have him counting the gate receipts. I thought they only did that in Venezuela.

In Pittsburgh the media said we looked flat. When you're in a pennant race, the press's definition of flat is someone pitching a hell of a ballgame against you. And that's what happened, though part of our problem playing in Pittsburgh is that we suffer a letdown because so few fans come to Three Rivers Stadium.

The Pirates are threatening to move out of town, and the fans are staying away in droves. It's like playing a spring training game.

I do know that the Pirates are a better team than their record. I've never been associated with a team that's done quite that badly. They are 34 games out and I don't see how that's possible with their talent.

I'm surprised there isn't a rule that says, "If a manager is twenty-five games out, he's fired." Or perhaps, they ought to fire the general manager. I'd rather have that rule.

While we were in Pittsburgh, there was a drug investigation that named a bunch of players who in the past had bought cocaine. Keith Hernandez was named, but I know he's clean now. In fact, I'm not concerned about any of my players. I think that everybody on my ballclub knows enough about cocaine now to stay away from it.

Frank Cashen is scared of players with a drug habit. He got burnt with Ellis Valentine. Ellis was a bad egg. I don't know if that had to do with drugs, but the way he acted on the field and in the clubhouse was not exemplary. When I told Frank I wanted Rod Scurry of the Pirates to bolster my relief corps, Frank was skeptical. Scurry is an admitted cocaine user, and I'm sure that's why Frank was hesitant about getting him.

It's not always easy to tell when a player is on cocaine. What I look for is whether a player is acting moody. Anytime you take drugs, there are going to be highs and lows, and you can sense that in a player.

I don't know what I would do if I discovered one of my players on drugs. Probably choke him. As I was choking him, I would probably be saying, "Why? Why? Why? Why?"

And after I finished choking him, I'd scream how he's hurting himself and the team. If he wants to spend his money on something, give it to the poor. Don't use it to kill yourself.

55

THREE SHUTOUTS IN FOUR GAMES

WE WENT INTO MONTREAL to play one game, facing their ace, Bryn Smith, and Ron Darling, who had a toothache, had been up all night. Even with an abscessed tooth, he pitched an absolutely great seven innings. So did Smith. Both looked like they were unhittable, but we scored a run on a Backman double. Roger pitched two perfect innings, and we won the ballgame, 1–0. It was Ronnie's first win in a month.

There was a joyous celebration on the mound and a feeling of electricity in the clubhouse after the game. I could sense what the players were feeling; We have to beat Montreal. We have to beat St. Louis. These are the games we have to have to win. And we are going to win the pennant.

The game was proof to me that Ron Darling is no first-half pitcher. He's pitched two good games back-to-back. My idea of keeping the catcher's mitt in the middle of the plate seems to be helping. Ron's been throwing the ball better, plus his rhythm has been much better. He hasn't tried to overthrow as much.

After the game we flew home for a homestand against the West Coast teams. Dwight Gooden opened against the San Francisco Giants. After Dwight got knocked out by the Phils last week, a reporter asked me what I thought about his poor performance. I said, "I feel sorry for the Giants," because Dwight has had a history of having a bad game and coming back to prove, "I can't have two in a row." He certainly did. He pitched a shutout.

By the end of the game I was worried I would have to hook him. He had thrown a lot of pitches. Eddie Lynch, who was keeping track, knew exactly how many, but I decided not to ask. If I knew, I might feel morally obligated to take him out since Frank Cashen is always saying, "He's throwing too many pitches. He's throwing too many innings." In the end I asked Mel Stottlemyre, "What in the heck should I do?" Mel said, "Would you have 48,000 people mad at you or one general manager?" I said, "Good point, Mel. I appreciate your putting it in perspective for me." I left Doc in to finish the game.

Doc was almost unhittable. One of these days he's going to throw a no-hitter. There's no doubt in my mind. Wait till he fills out a little bit and gets a little stronger! As it was, he struck out sixteen. The K's were lined up along the upper deck for twenty feet.

The fans were so psyched up by Dwight's strikeouts that one time a batter hit a pop-up, and when Keith caught it, they booed him. They wanted him to drop it so Doc could get another strike-out! Of course, Keith would never drop a ball just so Doc could get a strikeout. He wouldn't have enough money to pay that fine.

In the next game Eddie Lynch allowed one run for eight innings. Darryl hit a home run to tie, and when Howard Johnson pinch-hit a home run for Eddie in the bottom of the eighth, a long blast over the left-center field wall, about 420 feet away, I was looking like a genius.

All we had to do was get through the ninth. My choice was between Jesse and McDowell. Driessen, who hits Jesse pretty well and who already had homered, was coming up. Also, the Giants had three righties up after him. I decided to go with Roger.

He got Driessen out. So far, so good. Chris Brown came up.

Roger jammed him, and he dribbled a thirty-eight-hopper through the infield. The next batter was their catcher, Bob Brenly, and before I even had a chance to get my Rolaids, Roger threw a slider that Brenly parked over the left field wall. We lost the ballgame, 3–2.

I don't like to second-guess Gary, but I hated the pitch selection. Gary and Roger should have known that on a two-two count, you can't throw your second best pitch. A slider only works if it's thrown in a good spot. This one hung because Roger was trying so hard to throw a strike, and puff, presto, there went our one-run lead.

Gary knew he mugged it. When he came in, he was mumbling, "Damn slider."

Terry Leach made up for that game by shutting out the Giants the next night, 7–0. Originally Sid was scheduled to pitch.

During batting practice I was watching the Giants hit. They are a predominantly right-handed hitting team, and I said to Mel, "You know, if I had my druthers, I would have bumped Sidney for one more day and pitched Leach." Leach is a righty, whereas Sid is a lefty.

I went into the clubhouse around seven. The game was to start in thirty-five minutes, when the trainer came over and said, "Nothing to be alarmed about, Dave, but Sidney's had dizzy spells. The doctor examined him and there's nothing wrong with him, but I just wanted you to know." I said, "Hold on a minute." I called Mel and went running into the training room to talk to Dr. Parkes and Sid. Sidney was lying on the training room floor doing his stretches. "What's the problem here?" I asked the doctor. He said, "Could be dehydration. I had him take a Dramamine. It might have been that." That scared me, giving him a drug like that and sending him out to pitch, but Dr. Parkes kept saying, "He'll be fine. He'll be fine."

"He's going to pitch tomorrow," I said. "I'll get another pitcher for tonight."

That conversation took about ten minutes. When I came back out to the clubhouse, Terry Leach was sitting in his shorts doing the crossword puzzle in the middle of the room. I said, "Terry, I hate to tell you this, but you're pitching tonight." He jumped up all excited and said, "Oh yeah?" I said, "Yeah, in twenty minutes." He yelled, "All right!" and he walked over to his locker and got his uniform on. I'm sure he didn't have time to have his arm rubbed or stretched. But I know Terry, and you can't surprise him.

Nine innings of scoreless ball later, he walked off the mound with a three-hit shutout.

I first saw Terry Leach play when I was at Jackson in Double A. They didn't like him in Triple A, and they sent him to me. I started him, and he won the first six games, so they called him up to Tidewater. The next year, when I was roving instructor, he was pitching in Tidewater, and then when I went there he pitched for me. At that time he was a spot man and long reliever. One thing I knew about Terry was that he always wanted to pitch.

I remember one time on the mound in Charleston I came out to get him, and he said, "Dave, don't take me out. I'll get these guys. I'll get them." I said, "You really feel that strongly about it, Terry?" He said, "Yeah, leave me in here. Please leave me in." Before I got back to the dugout he gave up two more hits. And I had to come and take him out. The same thing happened again in Columbus, but that time when I left him in he did a good job.

He just wants the ball. He doesn't want to give it up when he's on the hill, and if he's not on the hill, he can't wait to get there. Fact is, if you tell him to get warm, he may call down and tell you he's ready after three pitches, he wants to be in the game so bad.

He was released twice last year by the Atlanta Braves. I don't know why they didn't like him. He had a reputation for not being able to get left-handers out, but he's shown me that he can. He's spotting the ball, moving it around much better. Terry throws underhanded. His ball really sinks, and his breaking ball moves up—a little different wrinkle from most pitchers. A guy like Terry you can't give up on. I'd never release a guy who wants the ball so badly.

56
DOUBLE DIP

ON THE RARE DAYS when we're scheduled to play a doubleheader, my key decision is often whom to pitch first. We were playing the Padres two on August 23, and the choice was between Sid Fernandez and Rick Aguilera.

In Sidney's favor to start in the first game: Sid matches up stronger against the Padres. Also, I know that Dick Williams prefers to play his regulars, Kennedy, Gwynn, and Nettles, in the first game, and left-handers are more effective against them.

In Aguilera's favor: Williams was starting Thurmond, a left-hander, in the first game, and Jackson, a righty, in the second. I felt I had to start Gary Carter in the first game, because I only wanted him playing one game and I'd prefer he hit against the lefty. And I wanted Aguilera pitching to Carter, because the last time Gary didn't catch Aguilera, I felt it hurt us. Also, I feel that Aggie will hit better against a left-hander. Aggie's a good hitter.

I opted to pitch Aguilera in the first game and Sidney in the second. We ended up losing them both.

Right in the first inning home plate umpire Bruce Froemming made a couple of questionable ball-and-strike calls, and Aggie got upset. After one pitch that Froemming called a ball, Aggie stared in toward home plate. A pitcher often does that because he wants to know whether it was called for being high or being inside or whatever. A professional umpire will say, "I called it for high."

The belligerent umpire will just call it a ball and not give an explanation. Bruce Froemming is like that.

When Bruce saw Aggie staring, he yelled, "The damn ball was inside." To me that was totally unacceptable and uncalled-for.

I waited until the inning was over, and I went out to Bruce. I didn't want him intimidating Aguilera. "Bruce, there's no call for that," I said. "There are other ways to handle it."

"He did this, he did that . . ." Bruce was mumbling.

I said, "Bruce, I was watching Aguilera, and he didn't say one word to you. All Aggie did was look."

"He looked at me," said Bruce, as if that were a crime. "And furthermore, you come out again, and you're gone." Belligerent. Baiting me. I was out there to calm him down. And now he had gotten me so hot I wanted to choke him. He was looking at me with his snarly, mean-ass look.

I said, "Let me tell you something, that was the most horseshit thing I've ever seen." I was yelling at him, and some of the moisture in my mouth accidentally got on him.

"You spit on me," he shouted.

"I did not spit on you."

"Yes, you did."

"If I did, I'm sorry, I apologize."

"Wait till Chub Feeney hears about this."

"You really got to be horseshit. You've got to be the worst I ever saw," I yelled, and started walking off.

He yelled, "Shut up. Shut up."

I said, "You have to be the ultimate worst."

He screamed, "Say one more word . . ."

"You're horseshit," I said.

So I got thrown out before we even got to hit, and I spent the rest of the game watching it on TV in the clubhouse. And all Tim McCarver and Ralph Kiner talked about was how much Gary Carter's bad knee affected his swing. Every time Gary got up, they said, "He's just hitting with the top of his body. He no longer pushes off with his legs. He's lost a lot of power."

These guys overplay everything. I guess that's the nature of being an announcer. Gary has always hit with his upper body. Even when his knee was good, he didn't use his legs all that much.

If you're an announcer, you can embellish any situation that comes up in a ballgame and make it sound like you're an expert by explaining what you would do and what you wouldn't do. Announcers can never make a mistake, which is irritating, but I know I can't let it get to me. Their job is to make themselves look good and to interest the people. One way of doing that is to say things no one can refute, because no one has information to refute it.

Timmy's a firm believer in what he calls "first-guessing." I heard him ranting and raving the other day about my not pinch-hitting for Bowa late in a game. I was down three runs, and I had two men on, and Bowa was up. Santana was already out of the game. If I had pinch-hit for Bowa and tied the game, I wouldn't have had anyone to play shortstop in the bottom of the inning. Did Timmy want me to play Rusty at short? Or should I have played Rusty at third and the third baseman at short? There was no way I was going to pinch-hit for Bowa in that situation.

Sometimes Timmy and Ralph talk themselves in a gar hole and they can't get out of it. If I was on the other side of the mike second-guessing them second-guessing me, I would have to say, "You guys have to be the dumbest people I've ever heard in my life."

We're going to have good days and bad days like today. Hopefully we won't have too many bad days in a row. Even after losing a doubleheader I try to be an optimist and say, "Sometimes those things can help." It's a reminder that we still have forty-one ballgames to go. We've played so well and for so long, and so have the Cardinals, who are one game up on us. We need to hang in there. I can't expect this ballclub to continue winning three out of four for the last six weeks. I'd be happy if we just played .500 ball, and then went on a tear for the last three weeks of the season. If we can do that, we will win the pennant.

57

"AS KEITH GOES"

WE FINISHED OUR homestand losing twice to the Dodgers and set off on a ten-game road trip to the West Coast, starting in San Francisco. We're three games behind the Cardinals, and I'm wary of the Giants. They have played us very tough this year. In addition to having to battle the players, any visiting team must also contend with the terrible conditions of Candlestick Park. Built too close to the water, it's windy and cold, even in the summer. A terrible place to play. We lost our first game with the Giants when Chili Davis batted against Terry Leach in the tenth inning and hit one nine miles. We won the second game when Giant outfielder Dan Gladden dropped a fly ball that the wind took as he was chasing it.

Howard then drove in the winning run with a double.

We should have won the next game, but didn't on some bad luck. With one out and runners on second and third, and Dwight scheduled to bat in the eighth, I sent Clint Hurdle up to pinch-hit, and after he fouled off a couple balls, he lined a ball just inside the first base line. Their first baseman, Driessen, stepped on first for the second out, threw home, and Heep was tagged out at the plate to end the inning. We never caught up.

Keith Hernandez had gone oh-for-four in the game, and afterward I mentioned to reporters that Keith's two-for-twenty-one slump was hurting us badly. "As Keith goes, we go," I said.

We're just not scoring runs. That's our big problem. We've been averaging below three runs again for the last two weeks. We need to kick it, to get the offense going. The saving grace was that the Cardinals lost, a rarity, so we were only two games back. The way the Cardinals are playing, we can't afford to fall back any farther. Even though Jack Clark busted up his ribs, the Cardinals haven't folded as I had hoped they would. Cesar Cedeno has filled in well in his place, and we haven't been able to gain on them.

In our last game against San Francisco, Keith Hernandez proved me to be a prophet. I rested Keith, because he was hitting about .100 against Giant starter Dave LaPoint. He said, "I really appreciate what you said about me yesterday—if I hit, the team wins. It fired me up. Later in the game, if you need me, just call on me. I like the pressure to be on me." I promised him I would.

I started Ronn Reynolds behind the dish, Carter at first, Paciorek in right, and Lenny in center. The game shaped up to be a disaster. Nothing went right for us, and worse, the Cardinals were winning. I was having visions of last year's early-September fade.

Losing by two runs in the eighth, I had two men on base and my sluggers, Carter, Foster, and Strawberry, coming up against their top right-handed reliever, Scott Garrelts. Carter struck out. Foster struck out. Darryl struck out. We were three outs away from disaster. The Cardinals had defeated the Astros.

After the Giants were retired, we faced Garrelts in the ninth. HoJo led off, and he doubled. I sent Rusty up to hit against Garrelts, and he doubled and now we were only down 3–2, with a runner on second. I sent Lary Bowa out to pinch-run for Rusty.

I pinch-hit Mookie Wilson, who hadn't played in two months. Mookie got up and hit a quail shot over third that the shortstop almost caught, a hit that should have tied the game. I was picturing in my mind Bowa rounding third and scoring. I was envisioning a tie game and ultimately a victory.

But Bowa rounded third too hard and wide, stopped halfway down the line, and was tagged out coming back to third. Larry should have read the play better, but Buddy didn't give him much help either. Buddy kind of hung him out to dry.

Now there were two outs, and Mookie was on second. We still needed one run to tie.

I needed a pinch hitter. Keith had asked me to send him up in a crucial situation. This was the time. I said, "Okay, Keith, it's you."

Giants manager Jim Davenport brought his ace left-hander, Mark Davis, into the game to pitch to Keith. Davis is tough on left-handers. He has struck out more batters than any other relief pitcher in the National League. If you didn't know Keith, you'd think he was way overmatched.

Davis ran the count to two-two and then threw him a curveball. Keith guessed curve, and he hit a prodigious shot into the empty upper deck in right field.

That home run was as important as any hit this year. It lifted the heck out of us. We had been in a dogfight for three days, and were looking at losing three out of four, which would have been devastating, and all of a sudden, bingo, Keith hit a home run, and we ended up winning. In the clubhouse everybody was on a high, shouting, "Let's go to San Diego. Now we'll kick some butt." All because Keith Hernandez asked me to send him up so he could hit a home run with two outs in the ninth.

We moved on to San Diego, where in our first game Keith had five hits, including another home run, a bullet shot that sailed into the right field seats.

As I told the reporters, when Keith hits, we win.

58
GARY'S TURN

THE NEXT DAY Gary hit three home runs the first three times up. After two long home runs off Dravecky, reliever Luis DeLeon hung him a breaking ball, and he hit that out too. Afterward all the fans in the left field stands jumped over the railing to stand where his homers had fallen and waited for another one.

The next day Gary hit two more home runs, five in two days. He now has 25 dingers.

Gary's problem is impatience. He always wants to make it happen. It's a great attribute, but sometimes it works against him. When he's feeling pressured to supply the offense, he'll go after high pitches and balls he shouldn't even swing at.

But now he's in a groove, feeling strong and comfortable, and acting as if the ball were as big as a basketball. When you get in that groove and you're as strong as Gary is, you're going to hit home runs.

Rick Aguilera pitched a really nice game. If I had had him all year long, he would have won fifteen games. He just needs to learn how hitters are going to react to his stuff. It takes experience to know whether or not you can get a batter out with your fastball if you keep it in on him or whether you can't and have to throw it away from him. The only way to find out is to learn by your mistakes.

Keith didn't play because he had to fly to Pittsburgh to testify in the federal drug case against a clubhouse guy who was supplying cocaine to some players. Keith took the stand under federal immunity and told a horrible story of how drug dependence in 1980 and 1981 almost drove him crazy. Keith said he stopped all cocaine use in June of 1983 when a Cardinal teammate, Lonnie Smith, was so doped up he couldn't play. "Cocaine is the devil on earth," Keith told the grand jury.

I was hoping that Keith would be able to fly back to LA from Pittsburgh in time for our opening game against the Dodgers. It was Gooden against Valenzuela, matching two of the best, who battled 0–0 before I took Dwight out in the ninth. We couldn't score off Valenzuela in the eleven innings he pitched.

Keith arrived about the sixth inning looking haggard. The ordeal had worn him out. I wanted to get him right back in the lineup so he could turn the page on what happened, and I sent him into the game in the ninth. He immediately robbed a batter of a hit in the hole that no other first baseman could have gotten to.

Nobody said much about the trial. Nobody wanted to make a big deal out of it. We were just glad to have him back.

My feeling is that Keith has been clean since he's been with the Mets, and that's all I care about. He's admitted paying a big price getting involved with the stuff. I just hope his experience will be a lesson to a lot of other people, not just my players, but anybody else who thinks about using drugs.

Keith was extremely upset over having to testify in Pittsburgh and the negative publicity that followed. One evening after his return he was singing the blues, saying that the New York fans would jump all over him. Once again, Rusty put things in perspective for him.

Rusty told him, "Keith, you did it, and you're going to have to live with it. Nobody made you do it. You did it, and now you have to stand up and take your medicine like a man."

Keith didn't want to hear that, and he got mad, but of course, Rusty was right, and Keith will have to ignore any booing and harassment by the fans and continue to play the game as well as he always has.

59
BRAWLING

IN A HOME GAME in late August, Eddie Lynch was pitching against Los Angeles, and two of the Dodger players, shortstop Mariano Duncan and outfielder Pedro Guerrero, started ragging him. Eddie was throwing change-ups, moving the ball around on them, and keeping them off balance. They weren't hitting the ball well, and they were frustrated. You could hear them, running down the first base line as they were grounding out, taunting Eddie about how softly he was throwing.

Duncan's a cocky kid. He has a lot of talent, but he thinks he's better than he is. At the time I said to myself, I'm not going to tell Eddie what to do. If he wants to listen to that chatter, that's his business. If he wants to drill him, that's his business too. If he had asked me, "Do you think it's all right to zip him under the chin?" I would have said, "You bet."

I remember one time I yelled at Larry Jaster, and he threw three pitches right at my coconut, sending me sprawling in the dirt.

When we got out to LA to play the Dodgers again, Eddie pitched, and again Duncan and Guerrero baited him. The first time Duncan was up, he grounded out to the shortstop, and he yelled, "Go warm up so you can throw the ball hard." The third time up, Eddie struck Duncan out, and as Duncan was on his way back to the bench, Eddie shouted at him, "Yeaaaaaah, take that!"

Duncan looked back over his shoulder and yelled, "Fuck you."

Eddie smiled and with his right hand made a circular motion inviting Duncan to come out to the mound. Duncan ran straight for Eddie, and then everybody ran onto the field.

Ray Knight got Duncan in a bear hug and pulled him away from Eddie. His knuckles were all bruised from rubbing them up against the side of Duncan's head. Joey Amalfitano and Manny Mota pulled Eddie away. I was there to make sure no one roughed Eddie up.

I got a little hacked off when I saw Pedro Guerrero running around the pile of bodies trying to jump up and sucker punch one of our guys. Boy, it's a good thing I didn't see him actually punch somebody. That would have been my breaking point. I'd have gone after him.

Right after the brawl, Eddie gave up a home run. When I took him out after six innings he said he had a burning sensation in his leg. While he was in the pile he wrenched his back.

60
FIRST PLACE

WE RETURNED TO Shea Stadium to play a three-game series with the St. Louis Cardinals, with whom we were tied for first place. The Cards have lost three in a row, Clark is still out, and maybe now we can put some distance between us.

I feel pretty good about things. I've learned to handle the games a little better. Maybe it's because we're playing better, but the games don't tear me up as much. I'm trying not to let the gut-wrenching things that happen affect me so much. I'm building up a wall of resistance against letting them do me in. My health is much better, and in the last week to ten days I've felt a lot happier. I can't analyze it. All I know is that I'm not letting it tear me up inside mentally and emotionally to wrack me. Maybe it's because the players are doing the right things, and I have confidence any one loss won't do us in. I do know we're playing awfully well.

Even though our series against the Cardinals is crucial, I don't want to let on that I think the games are any more important than any others. As manager, I program my players to consider every game a big game. Otherwise, all you do is put more pressure on the guys. "Hey, he didn't do this to me before. Why's he doing it to me now?"

Keith was very concerned about how the New York fans would react at his first home game since the trial. I knew that the only thing that was going to ease his mind was getting into the game and playing. I told him, "If they're going to boo you, they're going to boo you."

But when Keith got up to bat for the first time, the fans gave him an incredible standing ovation. I'm sure it sent chills through him. It sent chills through me. Afterward Keith said, "I was deeply moved. I almost cried. I've never been that touched by a crowd my entire career."

The fans were telling Keith that they understood he had been through a bad period in his life and that it was something in his past. They were telling him, "Let's get back to winning games for us."

I decided to start Mookie Wilson in center. As far back as a month ago, my plan was to have Mookie ready for the Cardinal series. Before his arm operation, Mookie was hitting .300 against all four of their starting pitchers, and I felt that because he's been with the Mets as long as anyone on the team, he should be a part of this series.

Mookie rewarded me with a leadoff base hit. Then with Keith up and a three-and-two count, I put on the hit-and-run. Keith got a base hit to left center. Coleman slipped on the wet turf as he was fielding the ball, and Mookie scored from first. He was flying. So I was looking pretty good right off the git.

With a runner on, Cardinal manager Whitey Herzog ordered his pitcher, Cox, to walk Darryl and pitch to George Foster, questionable strategy. Foster waited Cox out, four times stepping out of the box and then in. Cox also was delaying, watching planes, God knows what. Finally Cox drilled George in the leg out of sheer meanness. The benches cleared, but this time nobody was hurt. The umpires issued Cox a warning. The bases were loaded.

Howard Johnson was the batter. On a two-one pitch HoJo hit a fastball off the scoreboard in right. HoJo never hit a longer or more important home run in his career!

Larry Bowa is always teasing Howard. Before a game if Bowa sees that the opposition is throwing a right-hander against us, he will yell down the bench, "It's a good day to be you, Howard." Larry complains that Howard isn't as sociable on the days he starts as on other days. Bowa says, "Howard, you're playing today, so I guess you won't be sitting with me and the rest of the scrubs."

Howard has become an integral part of this team. I am watching this young man mature right in front of my eyes. It pleases me, not just because my original estimation of his talent has turned out to be correct, but also because he is such a fine individual.

Howard's loosening up, growing up, learning more about himself. He's still a young player. He's in his second year in the big leagues, and he's proved to everyone he can play under pressure.

I have a very young ballclub, not just in age, but in experience. But they're growing together, and that's the enjoyable part of it. That's why I say the best is yet to come.

Winning this game means a lot to us. The Cardinals had beaten us seven out of the last eight. We hadn't played well against them. We needed to show them that we could beat them, instead of waiting for someone else to do it for us.

The Cardinals aren't as good a team with Jack Clark out, but his replacements, Cedeno and Jorgensen, have done a good job. If I could choose who would be out, I would prefer Coleman or McGee.

The next day John Tudor beat us 1–0. Dwight pitched nine scoreless innings, and then Cesar Cedeno hit a home run off of Jesse in the tenth.

I bet I got forty fan letters calling me an idiot for taking Doc out of the game. They all said, "You dumb idiot. We would have never lost that game if you would have let Doc pitch ten or eleven innings." If fifty of them write me, that means five thousand of them, maybe fifty thousand of them, are thinking the same thing. Five million, who knows!

But I have to do what I think is right, and I'm not going to tire out Doc and bury him. If the rest of the pitching staff can't get us the win, then we don't deserve it.

I have critics who are pushing me to go to a four-man rotation. Not this year. You go to a four-man rotation with veteran pitchers. It places too much stress on a young pitcher, and I have too many young pitchers.

After Cedeno's home run put us back even in the pennant race, it made the rubber game even more important. We came out smoking. We scored four in the first, two in the second, and had a six-run lead when they started pecking away.

Eddie Lynch started and didn't look sharp at all. He got five innings in, but it was tenuous. Eddie's ERA over his last seven games is 5.77. Everyone can see Lynch isn't the pitcher he was, but I have no idea why. He doesn't have his usual pop, and he's making mistakes.

I made up my mind to bypass him in Pittsburgh. I haven't told the press this. Let them find out when I do it. I thought I'd go with Terry Leach. He's been successful in three of his spot starts. If Lynch still isn't ready to pitch by the time we play the Cardinals at the end of the year, I'll have to throw a rookie out there. And if he gets knocked out in the first or second inning, I'll have my head on a chopping block. You thought Billy is getting ripped in the papers? Watch what they do to me.

We were ahead by only one run in the ninth. Jesse was pitching. Against the Dodgers Jesse allowed a home run to Mike Marshall. Yesterday it was to Cedeno. Now in the ninth Willie McGee, a slap-singles hitter, got up, and Jesse threw him a pitch up by his eyes. McGee smashed one way over the center field wall to tie the game.

I was in shock. I couldn't believe what I was seeing, but I did know that the ball wasn't going to come back. It wasn't a mirage, but a home run by McGee off Jesse is not supposed to happen.

I'm still in Jesse's corner though. I have to be. Last year he gave up seven home runs and had 31 saves. This year he's given up seven already, so my logic says that he's not going to give up any more. I have to have confidence in Jesse.

No one will remember that the inning before McGee's home run Jesse had come in with runners on first and third and managed to get out of it. Nobody writes about that. It's "What have you done for me lately?" That's why short-relief pitchers get as much abuse as managers.

As manager you can have the highest winning percentage, but

if you lose a game in which they don't think you've made the right moves, it's "Get him out of here. Fire him. He hasn't done anything for us lately." You say, "But our winning percentage is .700." Their answer: "That doesn't mean a thing. You screwed this one up."

In the ninth Mookie got an infield hit, and Wally sacrificed him to second. Keith came up, took an outside pitch and hit it to left field, driving Mookie home. It was fitting, and Keith loved it. That was his twenty-second game winning hit, tying the major league record for a season. I knew Whitey'd leave his lefty in to pitch to Keith, and I liked my chances. Keith knows that after I bunt a runner over to second, it isn't enough for him to get that runner to third. I want the run.

In the clubhouse after the game Keith was feeling very good about himself. "I took him inside out, Skip. Did you see the Mex do it?" I was feeling very good about him. And myself.

It was a very big win. We didn't hold a six-run lead, and they came back and tied it. For us to win it says to the Cardinals, "We're not through yet. There's no quit in this dog."

I'm really proud of this team. The Cardinals are leading the league in hitting, and they're outscoring the opposition by 160 runs. They've scored 60 more runs than we have. Vince Coleman, their leadoff batter, gets on base almost every time, and he steals a lot of bases. The second-hole hitter, Willie McGee, is hitting .370. Their third hitter, Tommy Herr, has been outstanding, and so have Clark, Pendleton, and Van Slyke. For us, only one player, Dwight Gooden, is having a great year. But who's in first place? We are. We deserve it too.

We have character. We come back from devastating defeats to win. We always win when we have to. I'm happy for my players. I don't try to measure my part in it, because to me, I still believe in the old adage, "The players win, and the manager loses." That's why so many managers are fired.

Today Jim Davenport bit the dust. The Giants fired him. There will be a few more heads rolling through this winter. Before long, I'm going to have the longest tenure in the league, two years. Whitey, Lasorda, and I will be the only ones left.

61

"YOU GOT TO BE A DOG"

AFTER PLAYING the Western Division—leading Dodgers three games that either went into extra innings or were decided by one run, and then playing the Cardinals three more nail biters, we went to Montreal, where we suffered an emotional letdown. Playing in Olympic Stadium was part of the reason. It's a huge monstrosity. You're way away from the fans. It has a cold atmosphere.

The schedule called for us to play a Friday doubleheader, and we lost the first one. We got four hits and one run. We threatened a couple of times, but that was all. Then we came back and won the nightcap.

I pitched my bulldog, Terry Leach. I was taking a gamble with him, but the batters in the Expo lineup who can hurt you—Wallach, Dawson, and Law—are predominantly right-handed, so he seemed a good choice. Terry's a gutty little sucker, and he pitched a beautiful game.

I started Larry Bowa at shortstop in the second game to keep him sharp, and Larry got the big hit, a two-run double. Larry has been a great addition to our team. He has great work habits and keeps the guys loose. Larry and I talk about signs and where guys should be played. He told me, "You know, Dave, last year, when I was with the Cubs, we stole all your signs because your catcher, Fitzgerald, used the same ones all the time. The runner on second would flash them to the hitter." Larry also gave me the old Cubs signs in case they don't change them. Larry said, "The Cubs are mad at me for telling all their secrets. I told them, 'I'm a Met. I'm no longer a Cub. You guys released me. I'll do anything I can to help those guys win.'"

The next day Howard cost us the game. He made an error and a couple of mental mistakes. On a slowly hit chopper he threw to first when he should have held the ball, and it cost us three bases. Twice he was late covering third on a throw from the catcher. One throw went by his glove, and he missed the other because he fell away from the ball as he was trying to catch it.

I said, "Howard, that just can't happen. You have to anticipate those things. You're not mentally in the game."

The next day during infield practice, I picked up a ball and said, "Okay, Howard, we're going to have a little drill. There he goes, he's stealing." I threw him a ball, and he caught it while he was running to cover the bag. I said, "See, you can catch it." I threw him another. I was about sixty feet from the bag. I said, "Okay, end of drill."

The idea was to keep it light, but make it clear that it was his fault, so that the catchers, Gary Carter and Ronn Reynolds, don't start bickering. In both cases the Expos' official scorer gave the catcher the error, even though it was Howard's fault.

I asked Gary, "What did you do to the Expo official scorer?"

He said, "Nothing."

"What's he got against you?" I asked.

"Beats me."

In the Expo finale the next day Darryl begged out at the last minute. He went to the trainer and told him he was hurting. When the trainer came and told me, I scratched him from the lineup.

I was irritated by the way Darryl handled it. If a player's hurting, he should come to me, not the trainer.

I've been a player for many, many years, and I didn't walk around with my eyes closed. I said to myself, He wanted out because he didn't get enough sleep. I suspect Darryl stayed up all night watching TV or maybe he drank too many beers. And he used his thumb as an excuse.

In the papers all I said was, "He should have taken a couple of aspirins and played." I even hedged that a little by saying, "Some guys don't have a high pain tolerance. Boog Powell had a low pain tolerance, but Frank Robinson would play if you cut off one finger. Maybe Darryl doesn't have a high pain tolerance."

I substituted Danny Heep for Darryl, and Danny won the game with a three-run homer. On the bench Larry Bowa said, "Guess who the MVP of this game is?" Another player said, "Heep?" Larry said, "No. Strawberry, for letting Heep play."

After the game Heep expressed his anger with Darryl for making him play with no warning. Danny always wants to play, but he doesn't want to find out he's playing halfway through batting practice.

Every day I make a trip to the trainer's room, and every day Gary Carter is in there getting his ankles or legs taped, or he's in there riding the Exercycle. And he always has a cheerful grin on his face. A lot of the conversations that Gary and I have are a grin and a grin back. I say, "You got to be a dog," and he grins and screws his face up and keeps pedaling. He knows from my expression how much I appreciate what he's done for us. He puts his heart and soul in it. He wants to win real bad.

There was a time when Montreal was ahead of us in the standings, and that was killing him. He'd say to me, "This can't be." Since we have put some distance between us and Montreal, he has stopped worrying about justifying our four-for-one trade to get him. In any case I'd say we got the better of that deal, and now Gary can concentrate all his efforts on beating the Cardinals.

Gary is a special player, a Frank Robinson type. He plays hurt. His total energy is in competing and being better than the other guy. It's very refreshing to see a player making a total commitment, reveling in it, and enjoying it.

The only way Gary could have possibly alienated his Expos teammates was to be so dedicated that he angered those players with more talent and less commitment because he was overshadowing them. That would point a finger directly at those who were criticizing him.

62
STANDING STILL

I BROKE one of my own rules today. Normally, when a player begs out of the lineup like Darryl did, I wait for him to come looking for me to say, "I'm ready to play."

But I'm in a pennant race, and I know Darryl is feeling guilty and won't face me, so I went looking for him.

I found him sitting on the trainer's table with a pile of fan mail about three hours before the game. I went over to him and stood there without saying anything.

He said quietly, "I'm okay. I'm in there."

I said, "You sure?"

He said, "Yeah." I put him in the lineup. I'm hopeful I won't have to have another conversation like that for the rest of the year.

The last time Dwight pitched against Philadelphia, he gave up four runs in five innings, and I had to hook him. Determined to pay the Phillies back, today he pitched a two-hit shutout. Only one ball was hit hard against him all afternoon, a double by Mike Schmidt. The other hit came in the ninth.

We had a nine-run lead for him, and about the sixth inning, he knew the only way I would let him finish the game was if he cut down on his pitches. One inning he retired the side on three straight pitches.

He even got two hits and drove in two runs. After the game that's all he wanted to talk about. He said, "I'm available for right-handed pinch-hitting duty. I'm the guy you should use." He was serious. And I just might do that in spring training next year.

Doc told me, "I'm going to switch-hit next year. I have even more power left-handed."

I said, "Doc, you're taking the chance that the opposing pitcher might hit you on the throwing arm." Then I thought about it and said, "But come to think of it, I don't think anybody is going to throw at you, do you?"

He laughed. "I know they're not."

Robin Roberts used to switch-hit. If Doc wants to switch-hit, I'm going to let him. I fear for the life of any pitcher who hits him. Doc would incapacitate him.

The Yankees got Rod Scurry, the pitcher I wanted. I'm amazed at that, as I was at the Cardinals getting Cesar Cedeno and at the Yankees buying Joe Niekro, who would have been an ideal player for us to get too. We need another starting pitcher for the pennant drive, and one who would be a free agent at the end of the year would have been ideal.

As for Scurry, maybe the Pirates wouldn't deal with us, but they were certainly willing to sell him to the Yankees. It seems to me that when the other clubs need a player, they get them.

Frank knows my wishes and our needs. I'm reluctant to ask him questions, because he's my boss. But Whitey Herzog got Cedeno after having lunch with Cincinnati pitching coach Jim Kaat. Am I supposed to be more involved? I sure would like to be. It's a question I need a better grip on. Can I go and have lunch with guys and make phone calls and help arrange deals like that? I don't know. Maybe I need to clear these things up with Frank. It's going to have to be discussed.

There are a lot of potential deals I never hear about. Last year we could have traded Doug Sisk for Britt Burns. I didn't find out until the deal fell through. I need to know those things. I need to know more about what's offered, what's available. I need to be kept informed, because it's my future.

63

SISK BOOM BAH

WHEN WE WERE UP in Montreal, I had put Doug Sisk into one of the games, expecting a stellar performance. He had had eight outstanding appearances in a row, but Doug came in and proceeded to give up a hit and three walks in one inning. Before the game the trainer told me he was getting treatments for his elbow, and when I saw that Doug was forcing the ball, I suspected his arm was hurting him.

After the game, which we lost sloppily to the Expos, I grabbed my toothbrush and headed for the lavatory, and who did I see already in there but Doug Sisk with a towel around his middle. I said, "What are you doing here?" He said, "I came in here in the seventh inning to ice my arm." I said, "Dougie, under no circumstances are you supposed to be showered and shaved by the time the game is over. That is a no-no, baby. It just can't happen."

I asked Vern to find out who had allowed him to leave the bullpen early. Vern said, "Doug's arm was killing him so badly that he couldn't have pitched if you'd have wanted him to."

I was hoping it was just a little inflammation, but when we got back home, our doctors x-rayed him and told me Doug needs an operation. He has a big bone chip in his elbow and needs the same procedure McDowell had. Without cutting any muscle, they take the chips out and smooth out the elbow.

Dr. Parkes said he would operate as soon as the swelling went down. Without Doug, our prospects of winning are not as bright.

Frank came down to see me when I got to Shea. He said, "I have some bad news for you and some good news for you." I said, "Give me the bad news first." He told me about Doug's arm. I said, "Jeez, the good news better be good." He said, "I have six dozen jumbo steamed crabs to eat after the game." I said, "That's great. But I'd rather have Sisk."

Turns out the crabs weren't even jumbos, but only mediums. I said to Frank, "I'm damn glad you're a better judge of baseball talent than you are of crabs."

64

DOWN THE STRETCH

THIS TIME OF YEAR, having gone through 145 games, I become worn down. The end of the story is in sight. Montreal is out of the picture, and so there are only two places to be settled—who's going to be first, and who's going to be second. Since we're not playing the Cardinals until October, we're suffering a little emotionally. We have to keep playing ball as well as we've played all year, because the Cardinals aren't showing any sign of a letup.

In fact, they've been unbelievable. They manhandled Pittsburgh, scoring ten runs a game. They're very hot right now. They have to play six more games with Montreal. Montreal has always been tough on them. But who knows? They've just been winning games, and winning them handily, 9–3, 10–4. That's one reason they've scored 160 runs more than the opposition. The other is their relief pitching, which has been outstanding. We just have to match them win for win, and then come in and beat their socks off in October.

The players know what's at stake. I don't have to go around

and say, "Hey, guys, you want a World Series Championship ring? Let's win this one." We're grinding. We know what we have to do.

I'm tired. I can give my players a day off every once in a while, but I never get one. I've found tricks to survive the pressure of the everyday grind, and one of them is to take a short nap in my office before the game. I try to get eight hours sleep at night, and when I come to the ballpark around three o'clock, I get the other team's lineup and go over my choices. I ask myself, How many runs are we going to need to beat their starter? Has my pitcher been pitching well lately? The answers to those questions determine my strategy. I then watch batting practice, talk to reporters, and do a few television interviews before the game starts.

Bobby Valentine came by last night. I really miss him. The way the Texas Rangers are playing, I think he misses us too. I asked him, "Still like it?"

He said, "Dave, a funny thing. After a three-run outburst that knocks out my starting pitcher, I find myself taking those little antacid pills."

I said, "About the eighth inning, you start throwing them down, huh?"

He said, "Yeah, the trainer brings them right down and says, 'Take these.'"

I said, "Welcome to the club."

It's scary to me to see what is happening to Billy Martin. All year long Billy has been touted as the man responsible for turning the Yankees around. When he and I were rated equally as managers, I felt honored to be in his class. And then he has three or four losses, and the press starts calling for his head.

I knew what Billy was doing when he left Brian Fisher in the game only to see him give up a bunch of runs. He was showing confidence in Fisher, and it backfired. How many times has Billy been successful, only to have it go unnoticed in the press, which always seems to be out for his blood?

What's happening to Billy makes me realize that whether

you've had two or three real good years, or whether you've had five great years or five-and-a-half great months, in this town if you make a mistake—and it may only be a mistake in the minds of the press—they can bury you in ten minutes and run you right out of Dodge City.

65

AGGIE AND SID

DESPITE THE COLLAPSE of our bullpen, we've managed to keep up with the Cardinals thanks to our two newest young pitchers, Rick Aguilera and Sid Fernandez. Rick and Sid were both outstanding as we swept the Cubs two games while the Cards were splitting with the Phillies. We are one game back with ten to play before traveling to St. Louis.

For us to stay in contention, I need Rick and Sid to get some wins. Since he came up in June, Rick has been inconsistent. He would throw a good game, and then he would try to pitch too fine, worrying about hitting the corners, and throw high in the strike zone. I told Rick, "Concentrate on keeping the ball down. Stop worrying about the in and the out." Against the Cubs he kept the ball down and pitched effectively.

Sidney's improvement goes back to the game in Chicago when I yelled at him for losing his composure. Now he's stone-faced, and I don't worry as much when he goes three-and-two on a batter. He still doesn't have the control I'd like to see him have. He walks a few too many people, and gets three balls on too many batters, but he is maintaining his poise. Against the Cubs he struck out eleven and only gave up one hit.

All Rick and Sid really need is experience. The more you pitch, the more you know umpires, parks, mounds, hitters. You are able to handle travel better, become more comfortable with your teammates, develop a closer relationship with your catcher.

I haven't gotten as many wins out of Rick and Sid as I'd have liked, but that hasn't been their fault. From here to the end of the season, I have to go with these guys. I'm committed to them. They have good arms and good futures.

I wouldn't substitute for them because I wouldn't want to impede their maturation. I wouldn't want them to think I don't have confidence in them in this crucial time. Besides, the chance that a change would result in improvement is slim.

There's another good reason why I'm going to stick with them going into the stretch run: I want fighting for a pennant to become normal for them. In the most crucial game, I want them to be able to say to themselves, "I want the ball. I want to be the one who brings us the pennant." I'm training them to be perennial pennant contenders.

66
DOUBLE TROUBLE

AFTER SPLITTING the first two games with the Pirates at Shea, I decided to start Terry Leach in the rubber match. Eddie Lynch is still unable to pitch, but whenever I start Terry, I know that even though I'll get five good innings, I'll have a problem getting to the eighth and Roger McDowell. Terry just can't go that far.

As expected Terry did fine through five. At the end of the inning, I said to myself, Should I risk letting him go a sixth? With Doug Sisk no longer available, my options weren't great. I figured that if he could give me one more inning, then I would go directly to McDowell, and we'd have a good chance to win.

With the Pirates leading only 2–1, Terry started off the sixth by walking the leadoff batter and then giving up a hit to Sid Bream. I still wasn't really worried, because Mike Brown and Tony Pena, right-handed hitters, hadn't been giving Terry much trouble. Pirate manager Chuck Tanner had Brown bunt the runners over, and then I elected to walk Tony Pena to load the bases and try for the double play.

I still wasn't thinking about making a change, though I had two of my Tidewater recruits, Wes Gardner and Randy Niemann, warming up in case Tanner decided to pinch-hit.

Terry should have handled the next two batters, Jim Morrison and Sammy Khalifa, easily. Instead, Terry jammed Morrison, who hit a little Texas blooper scoring a run. Khalifa then hit the ground ball I wanted, but it went through the infield, and now we were down by three more runs, and we never caught up.

The Montreal–St. Louis game was as upsetting as our own. After our loss, I went into my office, closed the door, and watched their game on the TV.

The Expos were leading by a run with two outs in the ninth, and it looked like they were a lock to win. The Cardinals had a base runner. I was expecting the Expos to bring in their ace reliever, Jeff Reardon, to close them down, but Reardon was hurt and couldn't pitch. When I heard that, I said to myself, Does that mean he will miss the entire St. Louis series and then recover in time for their three games against us?

Montreal brought in a left-hander named O'Connor to face Tommy Herr, who all year had hit only five home runs. Herr connected, and I said to myself, A fly ball to left.

Unfortunately, it wasn't. The ball carried over the fence into the crowd and instead was a two-run home run. Instead of remaining two games out, now we're three.

I left Shea and returned to the Long Island house that I share with four of my coaches. We decided to have a barbecue, and I cooked some steaks. We were sitting there eating, having a glass of wine with dinner, and all of a sudden, Vern looked at me and said, "Davey, how can Pittsburgh beat us?"

67
GRINDING

WE EMBARKED on the last road trip of the season on September 23, a ten-game swing to Philadelphia, Chicago, Pittsburgh, and finally St. Louis. I fully expect that the season will come down to those last three games. At least I hope so.

During the last six weeks, just about every game has been a pressure game. Early on in the season, we didn't inflict the mortal blows on some teams we should have. The fact is, the Cardinals got better licks in on us than we did on them. Now we've got to be stronger here at the end to catch them. And we're going to need some help from the other teams.

I feel like a fighter in the tenth round. I've used up all my reserve. I'm still functioning, but I can't throw the hard right to take somebody out. I just hope I can stay on my feet longer than the other guy.

I'm not sleeping very well. I'm sleeping shorter. I don't wake up rested. The games last a little longer in my mind. The decisions seem a little tougher.

I really admire the managers who have had the job for years—

guys like Lasorda, Tanner, Herzog, and Gene Mauch. I can see why Mauch's hair is white.

Last year was even worse than this year for me. And last year the team wasn't in the pennant race the last two weeks. It's the grind of the 162 games. Day after day. It's not just the games. It's the press and the travel.

I'm edgier, snap more easily. I read that Billy Martin got into an ugly brawl with one of his players, Ed Whitson. I guess the pressure finally got to Billy. I'm lucky. At least I don't have the owner on my back, calling me up in the middle of the night, giving me suggestions.

Still, I can't see fighting in a public place the way Billy did. I can see going at it out of view, and settling your differences. But never in public.

When I played with the Atlanta Braves in 1973, I got into a fight with my manager, Eddie Mathews.

Early in the season, Eddie would periodically rest me, but late in the summer he started playing me every day, even though I begged him to give me a day off.

He would say, "Okay, I'll give you a day off tomorrow." And that night I'd hit a home run, and the next day I'd be in the lineup again. This happened three times.

The third time I asked him we were in New York. I said, "Eddie, the first game in Philly, please give me off." He said, "Okay, no matter what happens, I'll let you have off in Philly." I hit two home runs that night. We went into Philly, and I was still in the lineup! In that game I hit four balls to the warning track, and I was angry. Really furious. I just wanted one lousy day off, and the SOB wouldn't give it to me.

I came back to my room after the game. I was lying on my bed, and there was a banging at the door. It was Mike Lum, my roommate. He had forgotten his key. When I finally opened the door, he pushed me, fooling around. But I wasn't in the mood to be taking any foolishness, and I left-hooked him. We scuffled, and the other players came in and broke it up.

They locked me in Phil Niekro's room, right next to my own. I said to myself, The hell with this. I'm not going to be caged in like an animal, and I went out to the balcony and jumped to the ground. I found a pay phone and called the hotel manager. I asked him, "Would you switch me to another room and charge it to American Express. I've had a little problem with my room-mate, nothing serious, but it would be better if I had another room." The hotel manager said, "Take room so-and-so. I'll send the bellman up with the key." I was waiting by my new room, when Eddie Mathews showed up. Instead of bringing me the key, the hotel manager called Eddie.

"You're just mad because I hit you sixth in the lineup instead of fifth," Eddie said. I couldn't believe he had the nerve to tell me that.

"No, Eddie, it has nothing to do with that," I said. I'm just upset that you haven't given me a day off yet."

He said, "That's not the problem, and you know it." Now he was calling me a liar.

We went back into my room. Eddie said, "Get it off your chest. Go ahead. Hit me."

I said, "Eddie, you're the manager. I'm not going to hit you."

He said, "Come on, forget that. Man to man. Let's get it off our chests. Hit me."

I said, "You mean just man to man?"

He said, "Yeah, let's settle this right now."

We were standing in the middle of the room, and I reached out with my left fist and hit him very lightly on the chest. His eyes went back, he drew back his fist, and when he did, I coldcocked him as hard as you can hit somebody. I mean I hit him with everything I could hit him with. He went flying over the bed, and I dove on top of him, and the next thing I knew the whole team was in the room pulling us apart. Mathews was screaming, "I'll kill ya. I'll kill ya. Let me loose. Let me loose."

Of course, we both finally calmed down, and when it was over, Eddie invited Lum and me back to his room, where we drank a whole bottle of Crown Royal and everything was forgotten. Eddie had a big old puffed lip, Mike had a black eye, and I had a few abrasions. But from that day on, Eddie and I had a great rela-tionship. I never asked for a day off the rest of the season, and he never gave me one.

More important, the press never got wind of the fight, so they couldn't blow it up out of proportion and make a federal case out of it, as they did with Billy.

68
DRUG TESTING

ON SEPTEMBER 23 AND 24 we took our two games from the Phillies. The Cards took their two games from the Pirates.

I arrived at Veterans Stadium around three before our first game and spoke with Commissioner Peter Ueberroth and several general managers and owners about the drug problem. The commissioner said he intended to institute volunteer drug testing on the major league level despite criticism from the Players Association.

When I originally heard about drug testing, I was vehemently opposed to it, but after learning of the seriousness of the problem, I began to agree with Ueberroth that we have to take the offensive.

I called a meeting of all the players to explain the commissioner's position. I told them, "If a guy is off drugs for over two weeks, he will test clean. Random urinalysis helped the military drop drug usage from forty percent to less than ten percent. It's a deterrent. I think we need it. Otherwise, there will be more

295

grand-jury hearings and more congressional subcommittees investigating baseball players."

A lot of players disagreed. One said, "It's not a hundred-percent accurate." Larry Bowa said that he was worried that if a guy took a Darvon, it would show up. Other guys argued it would be a hassle. Darling asked, "Who's doing the testing? Should I have my own doctor test me at the same time, in case they get the records mixed up?"

Some players said they thought the commissioner was grandstanding, that this was nothing new. In the end, everybody agreed that baseball needs to do something. As to the specifics of the program, we agreed to discuss that at a later date. And that was the end of it.

We voted to agree with the commissioner, but insisted on learning the details of the program before we agree to volunteer testing.

I never would have believed I would be supporting such a position.

69

A HEARTBREAKER

WE MOVED ON TO CHICAGO to play two games at Wrigley Field against the decimated but still dangerous Cubs.

Gary Carter hit a grand slam in the sixth to give us a 4–1 lead. The Cubs scored three runs in their next two at bats and the game was all tied up in the ninth when I brought Jesse in to pitch.

He started the inning by striking out Dave Owen and Thad Bosley. He was looking sharp, and I was feeling pretty smug. He walked Davey Lopes, but I was expecting out number three when Jesse suddenly picked Lopes off at first. Keith, however, couldn't get the ball out of his glove and Raffy was a little late getting to the bag, so Lopes was safe at second.

Bob Dernier was the next batter. Jesse went to two-and-oh, and I went out to the mound to talk to him.

To me Dernier wasn't a threat. He had exactly 21 rbi's in 430 at bats, and anybody else they sent up was going to have a higher percentage of ribbies than that.

I said to Jesse, "I want Dernier. Don't give him a cripple pitch. Go right after him. Even though you're behind on this guy, I want you to make him hit it."

Jesse quickly got the count back to two-and-two and then threw two balls. The last pitch could have been called strike three. Gary said it should have been strike three. It was called ball four. Lopes stole third on the pitch.

I was going with Jesse all the way. Cubs manager Jim Frey sent Chris Speier up to hit for the pitcher. Frey didn't have a lot of choices because he'd used most of his bench. Speier was his best bet. He's a good rbi man, but he has real trouble hitting a breaking pitch, and Jesse's slider had been wicked.

Jesse worked Speier to two-and-two. Gary then called for a fastball. Speier pulled the ball fair into the left field corner, and Lopes came in to score, giving the Cubs a win that means zip to them and a loss that means a great deal to us.

After the game Keith was furious with Gary and Jesse. He kept saying, "We should have won. We should have won. But Gary called for a fastball when everyone in the league knows Speier can't hit a fucking curveball."

Gary said the pitch was supposed to be thrown inside but that Jesse got it too far out over the plate.

I couldn't help thinking that somebody better start knocking off the Cardinals. They've won twelve out of thirteen and have a four-game lead.

The next day Dwight shut out the Cubs 3–0, but the Cardinals won again. Four games back and nine to go.

70

FOUR-AND-A-HALF OUT

BEFORE OUR OPENER against the Pirates on September 27, my biggest question mark was the physical condition of starter Eddie Lynch. He hasn't been right since his scuffle with Mariano Duncan, and I really don't know whether he's fit to pitch or not.

I said to him, "Eddie, are you okay?" He said, "Yeah." I said, "You wouldn't tell me if you weren't, would you?" He just grinned.

Before he went out to the mound, I had the nagging suspicion that Lynch *was* hurting, but I didn't have a clear-cut choice as to who would be better. I could have started Terry Leach, but the first part of the Pirate lineup is all left-handers or switch hitters, not good for him, and my other choice, Bill Latham, didn't get the Pirate left-handers out back in New York. If Eddie told me he was healthy, he had to pitch.

We got a two-run lead, and then Eddie quickly gave up two runs. In the bottom of the second, I could see he'd dropped down, slinging the ball, pushing it. There was certainly something wrong with him.

Eddie thinks it's great to be macho and brave, but the pennant race is not the time to do that. He should be honest and say, "I'm hurting." I don't like to hear "I'm okay," when a player's not okay. If I had known Eddie wasn't right, I could have had my bullpen up and ready.

We were leading by two when I took him out of the ballgame in the third inning. The left-handers at the top of the order were up, and so I brought in Tommy Gorman. This year Tommy had pitched 11⅔ innings against the Pirates and only given up one run.

Tommy proceeded to throw nothing up there. Three batters out of four got hits.

To face the right-handed part of the lineup I brought in Wes Gardner, another guy who'd pitched well the last few times out. Wes wasn't able to throw a strike.

Maybe he didn't get loose in the bullpen before he came in. Maybe it was the pressure. In his other appearances Wes didn't have to protect a lead. This time he was pitching for the pennant.

Wes walked Mike Brown, loading the bases. HoJo then booted a double-play ball. We still might have been all right, but Wes walked Khalifa to tie the game. I still had enough confidence in Wes to allow him to pitch to their pinch hitter, Lee Mazzilli.

Mazzilli, a switch hitter, hits for a higher average from the right side than the left side, but most of the time he's been hitting left-handed this year, so I figured Wes had the advantage. But Mazzilli singled to left, driving in the winning run.

The carnage wasn't over yet. I brought in another of my Tidewater shock troops, left-hander Randy Niemann. Randy began the season with the White Sox, and he's pitched very well for Tidewater. He came in to face left-handed Joe Orsulak, and got him to top a grounder between the mound and first that Randy went after. Unfortunately, he couldn't make the play. Pena scored from third and Khalifa hustled home from second. We never caught up.

When the game ended, I grimaced, shrugged my shoulders, and walked back to the clubhouse. Thinking back over my pitching choices, I decided in the same situation I would make the same decisions all over again. Anyway, I'm not somebody who kicks batting helmets and breaks bats. It would be easier on my insides if I just tore up the place. But I can't see it. It's like a guy who hits a bad golf shot and breaks his golf club. The club did its job. The guy wielding it didn't. What good does it do to destroy equipment?

As upset as I was with Tommy Gorman's performance, I reminded myself not to be unduly harsh.

I never want to be known as a manager who buries players. If you put a guy in a doghouse after just one bad outing, he may never get out of it. And, practically speaking, you may be forced to go back to that same guy.

Sure I was disappointed at the loss. Now we're four-and-a-half games behind the Cardinals with only eight to go. I'm more disappointed for my players. I've played on a championship team. I know how great it is.

It's all for nothing if we don't win. Nobody is going to remember the second-place ballclub. If you come in second, in memory you're no different than a club that finishes fifth. Close, but no go. Close only counts in horseshoes and hand grenades.

71

FROM THE
BRINK

BEFORE THE SECOND PIRATE GAME I told the players that if we won the next two games and the Expos could beat the Cards two out of three, we'd only be three games out going into St. Louis, putting our destiny in our own hands.

Rick Aguilera started and went eight. We were leading by two runs when he came out. The Pirates rallied in the ninth, only I wasn't able to watch the action because umpire Joe West threw me out in the fourth inning for arguing a dumb-ass call and calling him a "bullshitter." What pissed me off is that West enjoyed throwing me out, especially because the game was on national TV. With him you can never make a point without his taking it personally.

As a result I had to listen to the rest of the game on the radio, because Three Rivers Stadium doesn't have a TV in the visitors' clubhouse. I was sitting in my office when McDowell came in to pitch the ninth.

Immediately Jim Morrison doubled down the left field line,

Khalifa walked, and Mazzilli pinch-hit and walked to load the bases.

We had one out. The tying run was on second. I was going crazy. I got up and started pacing.

We brought in Jesse. Pirate manager Chuck Tanner countered by sending up Sixto Lezcano to pinch-hit. Jesse struck him out. Two outs. I was chewing on my cuticles. Jesse worked Reynolds to two-and-two, and then he threw him a hard slider and struck him out swinging to end the game. At the end of the game I noticed that my fingers were flowing blood.

The next day we started four games behind the Cardinals after they split a doubleheader with the Expos. Our final game against the Pirates should have been a laugher, but instead it turned out to be another stomach churner.

Sidney had a two-run lead when I took him out at the end of seven after he gave up a home run and a long fly ball to the warning track. I went to Roger McDowell, figuring he would mop them up. The Cardinals had lost to the Expos. All Roger needed was six outs, and we were back in the pennant chase.

Roger gave up two singles, a double, and a long fly. The game was now tied with a Pirate runner on third and one out. Afterward I had to remind myself that Roger is just twenty-four years old and in a pennant race for the first time. Roger is still learning the hitters. He's still inexperienced. When he doesn't do the job, everyone jumps on him. But I cannot lose sight of the fact that he is only twenty-four.

It's a little too late to be concerned about Roger. Or about anyone else, for that matter.

Jesse came in to try to keep the runner on third from scoring, and he got the second out, but Tony Pena, the Pirate catcher and a star player, got a base hit, and now they were ahead 7–6.

Going into the top of the ninth, our last at bat, I felt as though someone had stuck a knife into me. I realized that if we lost this game our pennant hopes were over. It's such a helpless feeling. What could I do standing there in the dugout? The Pirates had fought back against my best relievers. They're a bunch of young kids trying to win jobs for next year. They're hustling and trying to impress their fans. You have to admire them for it.

Coming up in the ninth I had Howard Johnson, Rafael Santana, and Tom Paciorek. Chuck Tanner brought in the hard-throwing Cecilio Guante to hold the lead. Tanner was doing everything he could do to win the ballgame and show the fans that next year the Pirates will be a force to be reckoned with.

I stood in the dugout and waited to see what would happen. I thought to myself, What can I do to win this ballgame? I grimaced. There was nothing I could do. It was up to the players.

The batter was Howard Johnson, who the past couple of weeks has begun to show some consistency and power.

Guante started Howard out with a hard slider. Howard swung, and I was almost delirious as I watched the ball disappear over the right-center field wall for a home run. It was final proof that my patience with Howard had paid off and a testament that rather than being a player who chokes in the clutch, he thrives on it.

We still had to retire the Pirates in the ninth. I was rooting for Jesse to go easy on my digestive tract. But he walked the leadoff batter, and Tanner had him sacrificed to second. R. J. Reynolds, a future Pirate All-Star, was up. I had a choice. I could either walk him intentionally and pitch to the dangerous Johnny Ray, or I could let Reynolds hit.

I decided to let Jesse pitch to Reynolds, who flew out harmlessly to right.

There were two outs, and the winning run was still on second. I ordered Jesse to walk Ray intentionally.

The batter was Mike Brown, another of the young players the Pirates have acquired in exchange for their high-priced name players. I went out to the mound.

I said, "Look, Jesse, I don't care if you walk this guy intentionally and pitch to Bream. Because Tanner won't hit for Bream, and you can get him out easy."

Gary said, "Let's try to make tough pitches on Brown." Jesse agreed.

I came back to the dugout. A base hit and our season was over. The first pitch Jesse threw was a slider over. Jesse threw a ball, another strike, and another ball. I was talking to myself: Come on, Jesse, make the right pitch. Punch him out. Jesse threw a strike on the outside corner, strike three. We were out of the inning. We hadn't lost.

But it wasn't over yet. It was still a tie, and this game was looking like it might go another nine innings. I was thinking to myself, I know I can't go much longer with Jesse, but after him, then what?

Wally led off the tenth against Larry McWilliams, a tough left-hander, and, batting right-handed, he tried to bunt for a base hit. Batting right-handed, Wally hasn't been able to get on base any other way. All along I've been trying to tell people that Wally should platoon and only bat left-handed, but no one seems to believe me. There was this rush for me to play Wally every day, and I did, but his average right-handed is nonexistent.

Keith Hernandez was up next.

McWilliams threw two quick strikes to Keith and then threw a ball right under his chin, moving Keith away from the plate. That stuff doesn't work with Keith. McWilliams again threw, and Keith bounced a single into right field.

Gary Carter came up. The butterflies in my stomach were fluttering. On McWilliams's first pitch, a fastball, Gary swung, and he hit a long, long fly ball. I stood in the dugout hugging myself as the ball went over the left field wall. It was his thirteenth home run of September and his thirty-second of the year. We had the lead. We were still in the pennant race.

But it wasn't over yet. Jesse still had to get three more outs.

Sid Bream, another of the Pirates' young acquisitions, was the first batter. The first three pitches Jesse threw were balls. The third pitch was so wild it got past Carter and rolled to the backstop. Damn, Jesse, I said to myself. I don't need this. Jesse then threw two strikes, and Bream fouled off the next two pitches. The two of them were battling furiously. Bream won the duel by singling to center.

The Pirate catcher and captain, Tony Pena, was the next batter. Through all the Pirate troubles, Pena has been an inspiration. He has played hard, showing the young kids the way the game should be played. He is a battler, a clutch player. The first two pitches Jesse threw to Tony were balls.

I called time, and again I went out to the mound. As I was walking from the dugout, I was talking to myself. I said, I have

Terry Leach warming up. Maybe I should bring in the right-hander against Pena.

I got to the mound, and I was waiting for divine guidance. I looked at Jesse and told myself, He's our bread and butter. I have to go with him. If I hook him, it will hurt him psychologically going into St. Louis. He's going to have to nail this one down.

I barked at Jesse, "Is anything bothering you? What the hell is going on here? Let's go."

Jesse said, "It's the mound."

Gary said, "Challenge the hitter. Throw some strikes. Forget about the damn mound."

I said, "Good idea." I went back in.

I was worried about Jesse walking Pena and putting the tying run on base.

Jesse threw, and Pena hit a smash into the shortstop hole. Raffy got over there, backhanded the ball, and, turning quickly, got the ball over to Wally for the force-out. The relay was an eyelash late for the double play. We still had two more outs to go in a game that seemed to be going on for an eternity.

Jim Morrison, the next batter, hit a cannon shot deep to center field. I was watching the ball go up, and I was saying, "Stay in the ballpark," and Len Dykstra in center field ran it down. Now there were two outs.

Sammy Khalifa, the rookie Pirate shortstop, was the batter. Khalifa hit a hard ground ball that was headed up the middle, but Wally stretched and made a beautiful backhanded play to get the force at second for the final out.

With a day off before the Cardinal series, I decided to fly home to Florida and get a quick dose of R and R. I had to get away, even if it was just for one day.

72

METS VS.
ST. LOUIS:

GAME ONE

IF YOU'RE GOING TO TAKE a day off, it's much nicer to spend it at home. With the three games against the Cardinals in St. Louis coming up, I knew I needed to sit in my backyard and look at the lake. I sat in a deck chair and watched the birds come and eat the berries off of my camphor tree. I watched them sun themselves on the dock. I thought I saw a couple cardinals, but perhaps it was just my imagination.

When I returned the next day to St. Louis, I was stepping into the middle of a controversy the likes of which I had never seen.

To me the issue was simple. It was Ron Darling's turn in the rotation to pitch, and he was going to pitch. Cards manager Whitey Herzog was moving his ace, John Tudor, up a game, so he didn't have to pitch against Dwight, but I didn't care. I had no intention of changing my pitchers. Ronnie was going to go in Game One.

The most important reason was that this rotation sets us up for the rest of the season: Darling, Doc, Aguilera coming back on four days' rest, and then Fernandez, Darling, and Doc. My way, Darling and Doc were each pitching with five days' rest. If I switched them, Darling would have had six days of rest and Doc only four.

But most important, if I switch a young pitcher of Darling's stature, I am telling him in effect that I don't think he has what it takes.

The other reason to maintain my rotation is that if we beat Tudor, then we have Doc pitching the next day against less than their best, and psychologically the pendulum would swing in our favor. The pressure would really be on the Cardinals that last game. I don't care what anybody says. My job is to do what's best for the team, not the fans. My decision was the right one—the only one—as far as I was concerned.

Not another soul in all of America seemed to see it that way.

I got telegrams telling me that I was a fool not to start Dwight against Tudor. I received one telegram from a doctor in Brooklyn suggesting I pitch Gooden the last five innings of each of the three games! One fan suggested that if Darling was really going to start, I should fool the Cardinals by letting Doc take batting practice and then have him walk down to the bullpen just before the game, as though he was going to warm up. Very clever.

At Busch Stadium there was an onslaught of writers. They were from Montreal, Toronto, Baltimore, and God knows where else. Dick Schaap arrived for ABC-TV. Brent Musburger and Johnny Bench were doing the game nationally on the radio. A lot of people showed up who had never tried to see me before, and they all wanted to know the same thing: Why was I starting Ron Darling in the first game instead of Doc?

Forty-five minutes before the game I shut the door to my office. It was the only way I could fend off the crush of writers and TV guys to relax and concentrate on the game. After I left my office, the questions began again, so I tried to hide out on the field, but Jack Buck called me over from second base to appear on his radio show. "Dave, let me ask you one question. Why are you starting Darling today instead of . . ."

Whitey Herzog strolled over. I said, "Whitey, is Tudor really pitching?"

He said, "Yeah, he's pitching."

I said, "You'll find out who my pitcher is when he goes out to warm up." He just laughed.

It seemed that we were never going to get around to the game, but finally we did.

Over nine innings Darling allowed four hits and no runs. When you take into account the pressure of the pennant race, Ronnie pitched his best game in the big leagues. Against him, John Tudor allowed us six hits and no runs for ten innings. Tudor was unbelievable. He changed speeds, keeping us off stride.

Ronnie was scheduled to lead off in the tenth, and though I was criticized for it afterward, I felt I had to pinch-hit for him. I don't want a pitcher leading off the tenth inning of a tied game. We didn't score, and I sent in Jesse to pitch the bottom of the tenth.

All game long my chewing tobacco didn't taste very good, and even the sunflower seeds I was chewing tasted bad. The Rolaids helped, and when Jesse opened the inning by walking Cesar Cedeno I began swallowing them by the handful. With one out and Ozzie Smith at bat, Cedeno stole second, a brazen move on Whitey's part.

Tudor was up next, but I knew he wasn't going to hit. Whitey sent Jack Clark to the on-deck circle. Whitey was trying to force me to pitch to Ozzie, and he succeeded. A base hit by Smith, and our season was over.

Jesse's first three pitches to Ozzie were balls. He was giving me heart failure. If he walked Ozzie, we wouldn't have a base open to walk Clark intentionally.

Jesse's next three pitches were a called strike, a foul ball, and a hard slider that K'd Ozzie looking. It was the biggest out of the ballgame.

Whitey was still scrapping. Clark was never announced as the batter for Tudor, and so Whitey didn't have to use him. Instead, Whitey sent up Tito Landrum. The one guy I didn't want coming off the bench was Landrum, who hits Jesse real well. With first base open, I ordered Jesse to walk Landrum intentionally. I'd rather have had Jesse pitch to Vince Coleman.

In a move that stunned the Cardinal crowd, Whitey sent up Jack Clark instead. During batting practice, I watched Clark swing the bat, and he looked okay, but I figured that if he was that healthy, he would have started the game.

If Jesse could get Clark, I was figuring that Whitey had done me a favor. We had the speed demon out of the game, and our chances were good that we'd win the ballgame sooner or later.

Clark pulled two vicious foul balls down the left field line, and then Jesse got him to fly out harmlessly to right. Now both Clark and Coleman were gone, and I was liking our chances.

In the top of the eleventh Whitey brought in his ace left-hander, Ken Dayley, who struck out Keith and then Carter on some wicked pitches.

Darryl stood in. Dayley threw him a curveball. Instead of breaking, it hung. What happened next will be etched in my memory forever.

Darryl hit the ball so far and deep that it hit the digital clock about 440 feet deep in right-center field! It was a moment that anyone who attended that game will remember for years to come. We were ahead by a run. We were smelling victory.

The guys went back out for the bottom of the eleventh sky high. Jesse struck out Willie McGee on three pitches. Tommy Herr hit a shallow fly to center, and I was yelling, "Way to go, Jesse," but in center field Mookie Wilson dropped the ball. I took a bite of my cuticle, and the blood started flowing again as Herr pulled into second.

I looked at the lineup. Two left-handers, Porter and Van Slyke, were up next. I said to myself, Your meat, Jesse.

Whitey sent up right-handed Brian Harper to hit for Porter. I let Jesse pitch to Harper rather than walk him to set up the double play. I was not going to put on the winning run.

Harper grounded out to Wally at second and was thrown out at first. Two outs.

Whitey sent up right-handed batter Ivan DeJesus to hit for Van Slyke. DeJesus hit an easy fly ball out to Mookie. I wasn't worried.

Later in the clubhouse you'd have thought we had just won the World Series.

73

METS VS.
ST. LOUIS:

GAME TWO

YESTERDAY the media were calling me an idiot for starting Ron Darling in the first game. Since we won it, the same people are now calling me a genius, saying that I outsmarted Whitey Herzog. Instead of admitting they were idiots, the press said, "Davey's a genius."

With Dwight on the mound for Game Two, we were in the best of hands. The Doctor had it locked up all the way, until the ninth.

Doc's biggest problem early in the game didn't come from the Cardinals, but rather from Keith Hernandez.

Keith is very intense and very emotional, and beating St. Louis meant more to him than to anyone. Whitey had traded him to us, and Keith wanted to show his old team something.

Ordinarily Keith cheerleads the pitchers from over at first base. Keith knows how to pitch every batter, and during the season he has helped our young pitchers a lot by advising them on selecting pitches.

From the first pitch of the game, Keith began screaming over to Doc how to pitch guys. "First-pitch fastball hitter, yackety-yacketyyack." And he didn't let up.

By the fifth inning Doc was getting mad. Doc is too polite a kid to say something to Keith directly, but he told one of the players, "I wish Keith would shut up. I know what the heck I'm doing out there," and when Mel overheard, he went to talk to Doc. Dwight told him, "Yeah, Keith is talking too much. It's bothering me."

I had Mel tell Keith, "Doc knows how he wants to pitch to these guys. You don't have to remind him." And Keith stopped screaming instructions at him.

We took an early lead in the game and built it to 5–1 going into the bottom of the ninth. I only had to take one antacid pill all game. In the ninth Doc quickly struck out Pendleton, his tenth strikeout, and got Porter to pop out to Keith.

The next batter, Ozzie Smith, walked on four pitches. Curt Ford, a pinch hitter, was up next. Doc walked him too. Vince Coleman singled in a run, and now I was starting to sweat a little.

If it was anybody other than Doc, I would have hooked him. I had Jesse and McDowell up. My training is to get pitchers up just in case. But when Dwight Gooden is pitching, I don't go to my pen.

Willie McGee fouled off three pitches in a row, and we were one strike away from winning this game when Willie hit a bouncer up the middle. I was picturing Backman catching it and flipping it to Santana for the force. But instead Santana ran toward Backman after he caught it, they collided, and Wally went down with a bruised knee. I don't know what happened on that play. I don't know why Raffy was over there.

The bases were loaded. We were still leading by three runs. Tommy Herr was up. Doc was tired. He wasn't popping the ball like he can. I thought to myself, The tying run is on first, and it'll take a double to score him. He has to get Herr out. And if he doesn't get Herr, he has to get Clark. And if he doesn't get Clark out, I'm bringing in Roger McDowell against their righties. I added a thought: And there will be a lot of runners on base.

Herr was up. Doc threw strike one by him. He threw again, and Herr hit a pea on a line—right to Wally. It wasn't high enough to go over his head, and he caught it. Bad knee and all. That's the ballgame. You could hear my sigh of relief.

Later I asked Mel, "Would you have brought Jesse in to face McGee?"

Mel smiled. "You did it just right," he said. That's easy for him to say.

The Doctor brought his record to 24–4, which is amazing. It was certainly vintage Doc. It was our 97th win of the year. The Cardinals have won 98. What happens tomorrow will decide it all. At midnight will it be a pumpkin or a royal coach?

74
THE END

I WAS ASKING a lot from a rookie pitcher. Rick Aguilera has only been in professional baseball a short time, and I was starting him in the most pressure-packed game we've played all year. He was pitching for the pennant in front of fifty thousand unruly Cardinal fans.

But I had no alternatives. None. I was uncertain about Eddie Lynch's physical condition, and I couldn't go to Terry Leach, not against a team with so many left-handed batters. My hands were tied. My pitching was short. It had to be Aggie.

It wasn't Aguilera's fault we lost. We just had a lot of little wounds inflicted upon us during the game, so that by the time it was over we had bled to death. Dreams die hard.

We could have knocked Danny Cox out in the first inning. We got four hits but only scored one run. The Cards took a 4–2 lead, and we valiantly fought back, only to come up short. In the seventh we had runners on second and third with two outs, and Gary popped out. In the eighth we had a runner on against left-hander Ricky Horton and Ron Gardenhire up. Gardy was in for

Wally Backman, who had been hit for by Paciorek during the rally in the seventh. Ron struck out looking. He told me later, "The ball looked like a Titleist 3."

After the game several TV reporters criticized me for not pinch-hitting Rusty Staub for Wally. But whenever I've sent Rusty up to hit against left-handers, he hasn't. Batting Staub would have been a sentimental move, but not a percentage move.

Those reporters made me so mad. A bunch of sentimentalist nonsense. I wish I were more like Whitey Herzog. I would have told each of them, "You're an idiot. What do you know about baseball?"

We threatened again in the ninth inning when with two outs Keith got his fifth hit of the ballgame. All game long Keith had taken an unbelievable beating from the St. Louis fans.

Every time he came up to bat, the crowd would chant, "Coke is it," and every time Keith came through with a base hit.

Keith told me later, "Dave, if I can hit .300 with all the things I've been through this year, don't worry about me. I'll hit .300 until I die."

After Keith singled in the ninth, Gary was the batter. He was our last hope. One more out and the pennant race was over. Lahti threw a fastball, and Gary hit a lazy fly ball to right field that Van Slyke caught to end the game. Gary was worn out. He had caught every game down the stretch, and he was feeling it. Our season had come to an end in St. Louis. Sure, we had three more to play at home against the Expos, but the pennant race was over. The Cardinals are champs. So are my Mets.

We had beaten their best two pitchers in the first two games, staying with the Cardinals toe-to-toe. In the finale we fell short. No excuses. No alibis. You have to give the Cardinals credit. They played better. Not much better, but better. I am not feeling much emotion, except disappointment for my players, for the fans, for Frank Cashen, and for Nelson Doubleday and Fred Wilpon.

I remember in 1969, when the Orioles were beaten by the Mets. Everyone on our team at the time made a silent vow: Hey, okay, so we got beat. Let's come back next year and go all the way wire-to-wire. And that's what happened. We won the division, beating Minnesota in the playoffs 3–0, and then in the World Series we beat Cincinnati four out of five games. And that's what I want to see happen to us next year.

As I told the players the day before the season ended, "I want you to make up your minds we're going to win it next year, that nothing is going to stop us, that we're going to win it next year."

After the meeting, I went back to my office to be alone for a while. I swore to myself: Next year, by God, nothing is going to stop us.

AFTERWORD

DURING THE FIRST DAY of spring training in 1986, Davey gathered his players and said to them, "I don't want to just win the division this year. I want to dominate it."

His pride had been stung because for two years in a row his Mets had won at least ninety games, and yet both years he finished a bridesmaid. Davey didn't want to develop a reputation like that of Angels manager Gene Mauch, a "boy genius" without a pennant. To Davey Johnson, there is only one place to finish: first. Anything less is unacceptable.

Such a philosophy seems unrealistic. Victory cannot be willed. But if you spend enough time with Davey, you come to believe him when he declares his intention to win. It's the impressive combination of strength of character, computer-like mind, ability to lead, and indomitability that makes you believe. In time you come to expect that Johnson will somehow finish first, if merely by force of will.

And so it happened, after Davey told his players that he intended them to dominate in 1986, that the Mets won 108 games, finishing the season twenty-one-and-a-half games in first place. Following his lead, the Mets swaggered to a division championship, drawing enmity and scorn around the league for their arrogance, demonstrative high fives, and cocky demeanor, all manifestations of the New Yorker persona and also of the Texan personality of the Mets manager.

At the end of the year Davey knew who had done the best job of managing, and he even had the nerve to say, "I think the Manager of the Year should come from a winning club, even though I think I had a better year than Jim Frey in 1984 and was pretty darn close to Whitey Herzog last year." Of course, Davey deserved Manager of the Year, not only for 1986 but for leading his Mets to a one-hundred-games-over-.500

record during his three years at the helm. He figured he wouldn't get it though, for the same reason Gary Carter—who once, when joyously waving his batting helmet during a curtain call, whizzed the helmet out toward the mound—wasn't picked for MVP, even though he deserved it. They are not humble men. Their style grates, and they are punished for it.

At the same time, this bubbly, emotionally honest exuberance made the Mets perhaps the most popular team of all time, as three million fans flocked to Shea Stadium to watch them night after night, and as all but the most dyed-in-the-wool Yankees fans jumped on the Mets bandwagon in a summerlong celebration of the game of baseball not seen since the glory days of Ebbets Field. Every game was a party, in part because the fans were expecting to witness victory, and in part because they were privileged to be entertained by a team with elegant pitching, a versatile offense, and solid defense. With the magnetic Gary Carter and superbly gifted Keith Hernandez leading the way, "Let's Go, Mets" became the Shea anthem as the Mets brand of magic captivated all New York.

Orchestrating was Davey Johnson, standing quietly in the far corner of the dugout, studying the lineup cards, pushing the buttons. It was rare when his moves didn't pay off, and even then the thinking behind them was always sound. During the season Johnson took advantage of his entire twenty-four-man roster and kept everyone sharp. Even in August, when the team had a twenty-game lead, the Mets drove in their relentless style toward the division championship. There would be no letdown with this team. Davey would not allow it. And if a fight was called for, the Mets would come out swinging. It was a Davey Johnson team in every respect.

As everyone certainly knows by now, the Mets won it all, even after things looked bleak. After they split the first two games with Houston, the Mets were behind 5–4 in the ninth inning of the third game. Wally Backman was on second. The batter was Len Dykstra, who began the game on the bench but who was in the lineup because Davey anticipated that Astro manager Hal Lanier would take out left-handed starter Bob Knepper and replace him with a right-handed reliever. Lanier did bring in a right-hander, Dave Smith, to pitch the ninth. Dykstra homered, and the Mets had a reprieve.

Mike Scott won Game 4 to tie the series, and there fol-

lowed two of the most exciting, memorable games in Mets
history. Dwight Gooden and Nolan Ryan pitched to a 1–1
tie going into the tenth inning. It became a battle of bullpens.
The Mets pen was stronger. In the bottom of the twelfth
Backman singled to start the Shea home folks chanting.
Astro reliever Charlie Kerfeld spun to pick Backman off first,
but he threw it past first, and Wally swirled into second. Hal
Lanier ordered Keith Hernandez walked intentionally, choos-
ing instead to pitch to Gary Carter, in a 1-for-21 slump.
Wrong move. Carter lined a bullet into center, Backman
crossed the plate, and the Mets took a 3–2 lead in games.

Houston began Game 6 by scoring three runs, an ominous
turn of events. Losing meant having to face unhittable Mike
Scott in Game 7. But the Mets tied it up in the top of the
ninth inning. They took the lead in the fourteenth. The
Astros tied it up. The Mets took the lead in the sixteenth.
Houston came back but fell a run short, as Jesse Orosco
struck out Kevin Bass to snuff out the Astros, keeping Scott
on the shelf until 1987 and winning the Mets' third National
League pennant. By game's end Davey had used every player
on his roster except for his backup catcher.

Lenny Dykstra clearly deserved the League Championship
Series MVP. Mike Scott won the award.

The Mets went on to win the World Series, after they were
but one strike away from losing it.

Every move Davey made was put under the spotlight of
scrutiny, questioned, analyzed, criticized, and praised. The
move that drew the most comment was his continuing to
play Kevin Mitchell and Tim Teufel against left-handed pitching rather than Dykstra and Backman—this despite Teufel
making an error that cost the Mets the opening game. And
yet after reading *Bats* you would have known Davey would
keep them in there, because for Davey every player has a
role, and regardless of whether it is a game against the
Pirates in April or a World Series game, Davey expects that
player to fulfill his role. Teufel was acquired from the Twins
to play against left-handers. That was his job. Davey was not
about to change things just because it was the World Series.

Davey also made news when he canceled batting practice
on the off day before Game 3 and gave his players the day

off. The Mets had lost the first two games, the press was on them like wolves, and Davey figured a day away from it all would improve their chances. His Mets responded by winning the next two games, but in Game 5 Bruce Hurst won for the second time to put the Mets one game away from elimination.

The miracle for the Mets came in Game 6. In front of their adoring legions at Shea, the Mets appeared to be dead. They were losing by two runs in the tenth, and the first two Mets batters were retired easily.

The Mets, and their fans, were one out away from losing the World Series. It appeared the Red Sox would win for the first time since 1918, when Babe Ruth led them to victory.

On the mound for the Sox was former Met Calvin Schiraldi, this year a phenom, last year a failure. Schiraldi in relief had won four games and saved nine coming down the stretch for the Sox and had pitched them into the World Series. If ever the Mets' cause seemed hopeless, this was it.

Gary Carter was the batter. Gary singled. There were a few "thanks-for-the-memories" cheers. Kevin Mitchell was next. Kevin singled. Gary went to second. The crowd noise grew. Ray Knight, the man Davey had saved from oblivion, came up. Knight singled. Carter scored. Mitchell went to third. Excitement seemed to bubble up from the stands.

Mookie Wilson was the batter. Red Sox manager John McNamara called time, signaled his bullpen, and brought in pitcher Bob Stanley, the stopper in the pen before Schiraldi.

The Mets still trailed by a run. Stanley wound up, and he fired a fastball that spun Mookie out of the way. As Mookie jackknifed, Red Sox catcher Rich Gedman registered surprise, then turned and bolted toward the backstop as the ball flew past him. Before Gedman could retrieve it, Mitchell scored the tying run standing up, and Knight pulled into second. The game was tied, the Mets had recovered, and now the fans, no longer fearful, began to shower the team with an outpouring of love and cheering not heard since Lucky Lindy crossed the Atlantic.

Mookie stepped back into the box. Stanley threw, and Wilson hit a bouncer down the first base line toward Billy Buckner, the gimpy first sacker. With Knight running toward third and the speedy Mookie racing toward first, Buckner lifted his eyes, and his glove, for a split second. The ball went under it, Knight scored, and much like the Mickey Owen dropped third strike or the Lavagetto hit to break up Bevens's no-hitter, Game 6 of the 1986 World Series went into the history books as one of the most memorable ever. For Mets fans, it was a religious experience. It was a miracle.

There was still one more evening of baseball to savor. The Mets had one more comeback left in them.

It was supposed to be Ron Darling against Oil Can Boyd, and the Mets were looking forward to facing the volatile Boyd, who figured to be jittery at the start of the most important game of his young life. Rain poured down on Shea Stadium, however, and with a one-day hiatus, Red Sox manager John McNamara switched to left-hander Bruce Hurst, the winner of Games 1 and 5. Hurst had seemed as unbeatable as Mike Scott had for the Astros, but after winning Game 6, the Mets radiated confidence they would win the next day, no matter who pitched.

Hurst, again pitching brilliantly, led 3–0 going into the sixth inning. He was pitching a one-hitter, and at this point the Sox were only twelve outs away from winning it all.

After retiring Mets shortstop Rafael Santana, Hurst faced the newest and oldest Met, Lee Mazzilli, batting for Sid Fernandez, who had relieved Darling. Maz singled. Mookie then singled. Teufel, playing second base, walked to load the bases for Hernandez.

This is as good a spot as any to say a few words about Keith Hernandez. He may be troubled, he may be insecure, he may be surly to some reporters. He may have taken drugs in 1982, and he may have had a rocky marriage. Forget all that. Keith Hernandez is one of the great players of our time. He fields like a dancer, he seems to get a base hit every time he gets up in a crucial situation, and he is an on-the-field leader in the mold of an Eddie Stanky or a Leo Durocher, two other former Cardinals. Talk about Most Valuable. I'll take this guy.

Back to the game. The bases were loaded. The Mets trailed by three in the sixth inning of the seventh game of the 1986 World Series. Hurst threw out over the plate, and Hernandez lined a shot over the infield between outfielders Jim Rice and Dave Henderson. Two Mets scored, and when Gary Carter singled, the score was tied.

At this point there wasn't one fan among the 56,000 in

321

attendance or the 56 million watching on TV who didn't know that the Mets would win the day.

In the seventh Calvin Schiraldi returned to pitch for the Red Sox. Ray Knight, emerging as the White Knight, led off with a homer, and there were tears as Knight bounced around the bases, pumping his fists in the air, crazy out of his mind with joy, filled with the thrill of giving his team the lead. Santana drove in another run, inside-outing a ball down the first base line past gimpy Buckner. McNamara brought in Joe Sambito, another former Met, to pitch to Hernandez with the bases loaded, and Hernandez drove in the third run of the inning with a sacrifice fly. The Mets led 6–3.

The Red Sox fought back. They scored two runs against Roger McDowell and threatened to score more, but Jesse Orosco came in and snuffed them out with some brilliant pitching.

Darryl Strawberry, the whipping boy for the fans all year, drew deafening applause in the bottom of the eighth with one of his booming sky jobs, which landed on the other side of the right field wall for a 7–5 Mets lead. Jesse drove in an eighth run on a well-executed bastard play. Instead of bunting with runners on base, Jesse pulled the bat back and bounced a single up the middle. It's called the bastard play because when it's performed properly, the opposition usually vents its frustration by calling out, "You bastard."

It was left to Jesse to finish off the Red Sox, and finish them off he did. When he struck out Marty Barrett to end the game, the Mets players made a pile of bodies out on the mound that would have done the Great Wallendas proud, as the fans cheered on ecstatically. In front of a national audience, Mets players bearhugged one another unashamedly, displaying emotion and feeling for each other not often seen, even on championship teams. The champagne flowed as the New York metropolitan area celebrated. The next day 2.2 million fans lined Broadway to cheer their heroes.

Davey Johnson had fulfilled the promise he had made on the last page of *Bats*.

Said Davey after winning the Series, "It doesn't get any better than this. We deserve it. We had the best record in baseball. We deserve to be World Champions."

That's Davey. Honest to the end.

Peter Golenbock